FALCON BRIGADE

FALCON BRIGADE

COMBAT AND COMMAND IN SOMALIA AND HAITI

Lawrence E. Casper

LYNNE
RIENNER
PUBLISHERS

BOULDER
LONDON

Published in the United States of America in 2001 by
Lynne Rienner Publishers, Inc.
1800 30th Street, Boulder, Colorado 80301
www.rienner.com

and in the United Kingdom by
Lynne Rienner Publishers, Inc.
3 Henrietta Street, Covent Garden, London WC2E 8LU

Photographs courtesy of the Department of Defense.

Library of Congress Cataloging-in-Publication Data
Casper, Lawrence E., 1948–
    Falcon brigade : combat and command in Somalia and Haiti /
by Lawrence E. Casper.
    Includes bibliographical references and index.
    ISBN 1-55587-945-4 (alk. paper)
    1. Casper, Lawrence E., 1948– 2. Operation Restore Hope, 1992–1993—
Personal narratives. 3. United Nations—Armed Forces—Somalia. 4. Somalia—
History—1991– . 5. Haiti—History—American intervention, 1994–1995—
Personal narratives. 6. United Nations—Armed Forces—Haiti. 7. United States,
Army, Mountain Division, 10th. I. Title.
DT407.C374   2000
967.7305'3—dc21   00-044171

British Cataloguing in Publication Data
A Cataloguing in Publication record for this book
is available from the British Library.

Printed and bound in the United States of America

    5 4 3 2 1

*For those service members who died in the
performance of their duties and those who sacrifice
each day to maintain our nation's strength*

CONTENTS

List of Illustrations   ix
Acknowledgments   xi

Introduction   1

Part I
Experiences in Somalia,
September 1993–March 1994   5

1   U.S. Involvement in a Faraway Land   9
2   The Beginning   15
3   Worst Case Scenario   21
4   Task Force Ranger   31
5   Failed Attempt   43
6   The Plan   51
7   The Rescue   59
8   "Mogadishu Mile"   83
9   Aftermath   89
10 The Cavalry Arrives   99
11 Preparing to Fight   111
12 The Withdrawal   125
13 Outcome   139

Part 2
Preparation and Conduct of Military Operations
in Haiti, September 1994–March 1995   143

14 Fort Drum, New York, April 1994   145
15 The Alert   151

16 Haiti   155
17 The Plans   161
18 Preparation   167
19 The Go-Ahead   181
20 Setting Sail   193
21 The Countdown   199
22 The Assault, 19 September 1994   205
23 The Occupation   217
24 Aristide's Return   233
25 Winding Down   237
26 Mission Complete   247
27 Observations   249

Appendix: Killed in Action/Nonbattle Death Summaries   259
List of Acronyms and Abbreviations   265
Bibliography   269
Index   271
About the Book   277

ILLUSTRATIONS

Maps

Somalia	7
Mogadishu	60
Haiti	156

Figures

1.1	UNOSOM II and USFORSOM Command Relationships	12
4.1	Task Force Ranger Chain of Command	36
10.1	U.S. Command Relationships, Somalia	104
11.1	Falcon Brigade D-Day Timeline	118
19.1	Aircraft Configuration on Board USS *Eisenhower*	184
25.1	U.S. Command Relationships in Haiti	238

Photographs

The Embassy compound	23
The University of Mogadishu, home of the 2-14th Infantry and UN Logistics Support Command	27
Task Force 160 Little Birds parked on the ramp at the Mogadishu airport	34
The Mogadishu airport	47
New Port	55
Somali militiamen near the Juba River in southern Somalia	77
Pakastani stadium	84

The author and his battalion commanders   101
The Pasta Factory—Aideed's weapons storage area   121
The author and CSM Dwight Brown pose with clan elders
    north of Mogadishu   141
An OH-58D Kiowa Warrior firing a Hellfire missile   148
An AH-1F Cobra on board USS *Roosevelt*   173
The terrain board in a converted gymnasium used for planning
    and back briefs during Operation Uphold Democracy   177
Black Hawks on USS *Eisenhower*'s deck   188
USS *Eisenhower* somewhere in the Atlantic Ocean   196
Infantry boarding UH-60s on the flight deck   206
A UH-60 Black Hawk preparing to sling-load a humvee from
    USS *Eisenhower*'s fantail   211
The 10th Aviation Brigade Task Force Command Group   222
10th Mountain soldiers in downtown Port-au-Prince   223
The east end of Port-au-Prince International Airport   227
Downtown Port-au-Prince   230
A sniper in a UH-60 Black Hawk   240

ACKNOWLEDGMENTS

I wish to express my gratitude to the many individuals whose contributions made this book possible. First and foremost were the soldiers who unselfishly shared their personal experiences with me and did so with honesty and candor. Thanks go to the soldiers whose written accounts of their experiences, feelings, and thoughts were used to tell not only their own stories, but those of their comrades in arms. Of particular note is the contribution of CPT Christopher Hornbarger, whose accurate accounting and in-depth interviews of the aviators who flew over Mogadishu on 3 and 4 October 1993 vividly capture the activity above the city. Without Chris's written account, I would not have been able to convey the army aviation's contribution nor the personalities who occupied the cockpits that night. To COL Russell Forshag, COL John Bendyk, LTC (Ret) Raoul Archambault, and CSM Dwight Brown for certifying my recollection of events. To Capt. (Ret, USN) T. Lamar Willis, COL (Ret) Jim Stephens, COL (Ret) Townsend ("Van") Van Fleet, and Dr. Ben Adams for their superb suggestions and enthusiastic encouragement. Their feedback kept me on course. A special thanks to COL (Ret) J. David Fletcher, who not only served as an indispensable sounding board but also gave unselfishly of his time to assist in the editing.

I want to express my gratitude to my senior leadership, both at Fort Drum and while I was deployed to Somalia and Haiti, for providing me with an environment in which I could lead and be the best commander that I could possibly be. As a brigade, we took the initiative and were encouraged to do so. My fellow brigade commanders and I shared tough and challenging times, but we also shared a camaraderie and friendship experienced by few.

I owe special thanks to my commanders, their command sergeants major, and their staffs, along with my staff for always giving me timely, well-thought-out advice. They made decisionmaking easy. I am indebted to all the soldiers who were assigned to the many teams, detachments, and units that supported the Falcon Brigade. Although I am unable to mention all these organizations, their absence in the text by no means diminishes the vital role they played and the significance of their contribution. These soldiers and the organizations they represented epitomize our army's professionalism and sense of duty and the essence of team play. I owe a debt of gratitude to all of the soldiers, sailors, airmen, and marines who, without hesitation or reservation, rolled up their sleeves and enthusiastically confronted the challenges and got the job done. I can honestly say that the many successes I enjoyed were made possible only because of the unselfish, untiring efforts of the men and women who pulled together and never quit.

I wish to thank Dan Eades, executive editor at Lynne Rienner Publishers, for his patience and understanding. Through our many conversations and his assurances, he turned what at first appeared to be an intimidating publishing process into one that proved responsive and accommodating.

Thanks to my brother, Ron Casper, whose initial encouragement to tell the story started me on this endeavor. And finally, to my loving and devoted wife, Cathy—none of this would have been possible without your tolerance of the long nights, scattered pages of manuscript, and cluttered work area—thank you for your steadfast support, personal sacrifice, and love.

INTRODUCTION

The new world order seems to be long on new and short on order.
—*Les Aspin,* Secretary of Defense (1992–1994)

During my 2-year brigade command tour spanning the early fall of 1993 through October 1995, I was afforded an opportunity few commanders experience. Over a period of 15 months the brigade I commanded, commonly referred to as the Falcon Brigade, not only participated in two major military operations but was the linchpin during critical phases for both. One operation was violent and reactive and conducted with an ill-equipped, undermanned force; the other was permissive and methodical and involved a well-equipped, overwhelming force. Both operations represent the type of missions our army is likely to find itself involved in over the coming years.

The first operation occurred halfway around the world in Somalia, where our nation intervened to prevent the further starvation of a people struck by years of famine and civil strife. The second was in Haiti, a neighboring country whose oppressive leadership robbed the people of their dignity and civil rights. Neither country posed a national security threat to the United States, nor did we have much at stake in either land. Few Americans had ever heard of Somalia, and the only concern most Americans held for Haiti was the large number of illegal immigrants the island nation generated. Yet our political leadership committed military forces to both lands as our citizens struggled with the nation's foreign policy.

I discovered both operations to be personally and professionally rewarding, and each of historical significance. I was privileged to command the U.S. Army's 10th Aviation Brigade, 10th Mountain Division. In Somalia, the brigade headquarters provided the command and control for the United Nations Quick Reaction Force. It marked the first time in military history that an infantry battalion task force came under the direct command of an aviation brigade headquarters during combat operations. The brigade eventually grew to over 3,500 soldiers in six battalions: two infantry battalions, an armored battalion task force, a combat engineer battalion, an aviation battalion task force, and a support battalion.

During Operation Uphold Democracy, the aviation brigade spearheaded the operation by air-assaulting over 2,000 combat troops from the U.S. Navy's fleet carrier, USS *Eisenhower,* onto the shores of Haiti. The air-assault of combat troops from a carrier was a first for the army, and not since 8 November 1942, D-Day for Operation Torch off the coast of Morocco, had army pilots participated in an air operation from a navy carrier with the magnitude of that launched from the *Eisenhower.* It was during Operation Torch that seventy-six U.S. Army Air Forces aviators took to the sky in their Curtiss P-40 Warhawk fighters from the flight deck of the aircraft carrier USS *Chenango* in support of the invasion of Morocco.

This book aims to describe my experiences, and where possible those of the soldiers under my charge. I focus on the first 15 months of my command because that was the period of international involvement for the brigade. The book is essentially written in two parts, Operations in Somalia and Haiti. In the Somalia part, I discuss the rescue of Rangers and Delta Force operators in Mogadishu. The remainder of the book takes the path of a journal, discussing chronologically my experiences and the events leading up to the time the brigade exits Somalia, and the subsequent events 5 months later that led to our involvement in Haiti. Finally, I end with my personal observations.

I begin with Somalia shortly after my arrival in the country and focus on the events, personalities, and circumstances leading up to the battle of 3 and 4 October 1993. During the first third of the book, using eyewitness accounts, firsthand recollections, and previously published sources, I seek to reconstruct the events surrounding the courageous 10th Mountain Division Lightfighters and their comrades who fought and died during the arduous 15-hour fight—the most intense combat by U.S. infantrymen since Vietnam. This was a significant occurrence in my life and for those who shared the experience. There have been a number of published works covering the fighting on 3 October, but most have focused on Task Force Ranger. For the most part Somalia is a forgotten episode of our history, and the Quick Reaction Force soldiers the forgotten participants. In this part of the book I recommend that the reader refer to the map and chronology in Chapter 6. These will aid in navigating a complex maze of events and terrain.

We went to Somalia in December 1992 expecting a deprived people eager to share in our humanitarian effort. What we found was a country ruled by self-serving clan leaders at odds over pieces of barren desert and starving people they sought to control. As the mission made the transition to UN control in May 1993, the United States retained a modest military presence to support the United Nations. As the UN mission matured, the U.S. force in Somalia was asked to do more, and it began to experience what was later called mission creep. There was little concern for U.S. involvement by the Clinton administration, for victory in Somalia had been declared earlier in May when the United States transferred the mission to the United Nations.

The executive branch appeared uninformed about the events unfolding in Somalia throughout the summer and the frequency of U.S. soldiers engaging in gun battles with the Somalis. Senior State Department officials' involvement was marginal, as much of the initiative went by default to the Department of Defense to deal with the problems in the Horn of Africa. In turn, there was the perception that the Defense Department viewed Somalia as a problem for U.S. Central Command and the army because that department habitually deferred its concerns to that command and service.

On the evening of 3 October 1993, it all changed. With six Americans confirmed dead and the body count rising, the president found himself deeply involved in what was happening in Somalia. Suddenly, the Defense Department was not alone; the entire cabinet was energized. The army found that it was not the only branch of the military identifying forces to deploy to East Africa, for all of the services scurried to dispatch troops and equipment to reinforce the 10th Mountain Division soldiers. The events of 3 October not only changed the nature of operations in Somalia, but also caused a reassessment of our foreign policy and how we would conduct future operations. When it was all said and done, our exploits in Somalia were considered a foreign policy failure.

Operation Uphold Democracy was an example of the fallout from Somalia. President Clinton worked hard to win over the nay-sayers and build a coalition in Congress and his own administration for military involvement in Haiti. The National Security Council, Department of State, Department of Defense, and the rest of the cabinet-level agencies were involved in the planning from its inception. The military approached the operation as a joint fight, where flexibility and overwhelming force became the basis of each contingency plan prepared. Although our involvement is far from over and our gains toward restoring genuine democracy have been eroded, I believe history will reflect our intervention in Haiti as a foreign policy success— at least a temporary one.

This is a personal account of my experiences and those of the soldiers from all ranks who did everything that was asked—and more!

PART I

Experiences in Somalia, September 1993–March 1994

War is always and will ever be obscene. . . . While war is obscene, those who charge the machine guns, who bleed, who go down to the aid stations and who are put in body bags are not obscene, their sacrifices have no measure—theirs has a purity where mankind shines and is beyond corruption. I am not blasphemous when I say that in the brutality and evil of war soldiers who have offered themselves up so that their buddies may live, have in them the likeness and image of God. And damn those who debunk courage, valor, fidelity, love of country, love of home, family, hopes and dreams for a better tomorrow. Our soldiers give up much—that others may live, not only in freedom but even luxury. They deserve our great, great gratitude and affection because they are willing to serve. They are some of God's noblest people.
—*General Dick Cavazos,* United States Army

Central Somalia, 3 October 1993

My head was beginning to throb, the first indication that I was probably going to have a headache. I had not experienced one in several months. The rushing of wind through the door gunner's window of the UH-60 Black Hawk helicopter didn't help. We were traveling at 130 knots just a couple of hundred feet above the desert floor, returning to Mogadishu from the small town of Beledweyne near the Ethiopian border in central Somalia.

I had been in the country just over 2 weeks and in command of the U.S. Forces–Somalia Quick Reaction Force, better known as the QRF, for 3 days. As the name implies, the organization was doing a lot of reacting. Although a great deal of planning was occurring at the QRF headquarters, the nature of our mission resulted in soldiers often

5

executing operations with little or no plan. This was not the case for my first two operations.

Late in the afternoon on my first day of command, we had conducted a heliborne attack hurling TOW missiles at a complex in northern Mogadishu called the Pasta Factory.[1] The plant was used to store militia weapons. In calmer times pasta was actually made there. The following morning, we provided the infantry reserve and attack helicopter support to Egyptian, Malaysian, and United Arab Emirate forces as the coalition conducted a rare joint cordon-and-search operation looking for weapon caches. Both operations had resulted in no casualties and were deemed a success, but today would be different. The day's events would have a profound affect on my view of life, and would change our nation's approach to future foreign policy.

I stared out the window at the aircraft's shadow sprinting across the landscape and recalled the days before my posting to Somalia, remembering how I had questioned the decision to change QRF commanders during such a volatile period. I certainly wanted the command, but was it healthy for the organization or would it jeopardize the mission? I was not alone with these thoughts. Later, I discovered many people had harbored reservations about changing commanders during the peak of hostilities. But to my good fortune, the Department of the Army insisted on compliance with its 2-year command tour policy, and my predecessor had served his 2 years. The army based its position on the experience in Vietnam: the practice of changing commanders regardless of circumstances was commonplace, but this is a controversial policy still debated today. Although it creates some dissension at battalion and company level, it poses less of a disruption with brigade command.

Still, this was a rather unorthodox arrangement. By accepting the unit colors, I was not only assuming command of the 1,300-soldier QRF, but I was the commander of the 10th Aviation Brigade, 10th Mountain Division. Two of the brigade's organic battalions remained on the other side of the world at Fort Drum, New York, having had their turn in Somalia months earlier.

Note

1. TOW is an acronym standing for tube-launched, optically tracked, wire-guided missile. The missile, armed with a shaped explosive charge, trails a thin wire that transmits flight instructions back to the missile from the acquisition sight located on the nose of the aircraft.

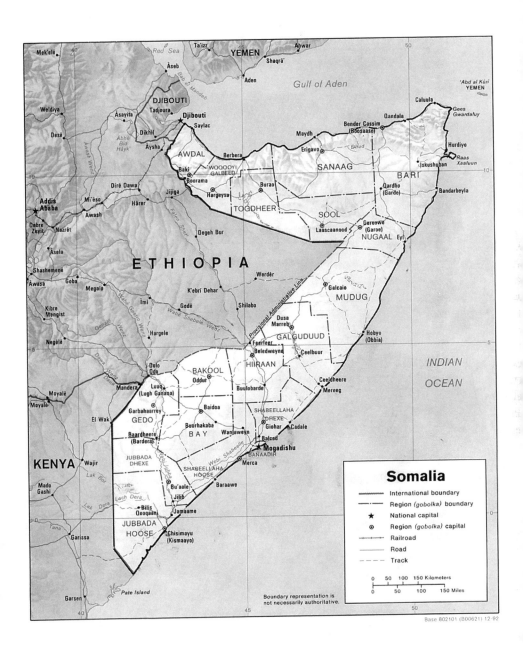

Somalia

—⌇⌇⌇— International boundary
—·—·— Region (gobolka) boundary
★ National capital
⊚ Region (gobolka) capital
+—+—+ Railroad
——— Road
- - - - Track

0   50   100 150 Kilometers
0   50   100 150 Miles

Boundary representation is
not necessarily authoritative.

Base 802101 (B00621) 12-92

7

1

U.S. INVOLVEMENT
IN A FARAWAY LAND

> We wish that the United States would sponsor us since the U.S.
> now has responsibility for the whole World.
> —*Abdulkardir Mohamed Aden,* Vice-president, interim government
> of the United Somali Congress (1993–1994)

In April 1992, the UN Security Council approved resolution 751, establishing the United Nations Operations in Somalia (UNOSOM) with a mission to provide humanitarian aid and facilitate the end of hostilities in Somalia. The initiative involved fifty unarmed UN observers headed by Pakistani Brigadier General Imtiaz Shaheen. Although armed with good intentions, the UN monitors made little difference in the plight of the Somali people.

Throughout the spring and summer of 1992 the world's media graphically captured the starvation and strife resulting from years of famine and clan warfare, occurring in the Horn of Africa. The Somali people were suffering immensely under the warlords. The media pushed the despair and hopelessness of the nine million Somali people into our living rooms. As summer turned to fall, the frequency of the dismal conditions portrayed and the grotesque images on our television screens came to sensitize public and congressional opinion.

According to the International Red Cross, famine had claimed the lives of some 300,000 Somalis. The U.S. Office of Foreign Disaster Assistance reported that in southern Somalia 25 percent of the children under the age of five had succumbed, and another million and a half were in imminent jeopardy. The world was asking how the United States, which had emerged victorious from the Cold War and Operation Desert Storm, could stand by and watch these innocent people suffer under such oppressive conditions.

Our own citizens began to question the nation's passiveness. The congressional Black Caucus—pointing to our recent exploits in Grenada,

9

Panama and Kuwait—led the call for U.S. involvement by asking, "Why not Africa?" Somalis were dying by the hundreds every day, and looting and banditry hampered any outside aid. By November, the political momentum appeared to have sealed our nation's fate in East Africa.

Even a warning from a seasoned regional diplomat could not sway our nation's course. As reported in *Time* magazine, the U.S. ambassador to neighboring Kenya, Smith Hempstone, dispatched a cable to the State Department warning that Somalia was a "tar baby." He prophetically added, "Somalis, as the Italians and British discovered to their discomfiture, are natural-born guerrillas. They will mine the roads. They will lay ambushes. They will launch hit-and-run attacks."

Despite Hempstone's assessment of the Somali people, the media blitz and the special-interest groups promoting this noble cause resulted in the Bush administration's formation of an intervention policy and strategy based on what turned out to be unrealistic expectations of a quick resolution. And on 3 December 1992, the UN Security Council passed resolution 794 authorizing international intervention in Somalia.

The Bush administration was politically seized by the plight of the Somalis, and on 4 December 1992, President Bush ordered the military, led by LTG Robert B. Johnston and his marines from the 1st Marine Expeditionary Force, into Somalia to lead a humanitarian relief effort. A few days later the soldiers of the army's 10th Mountain Division followed.

This was not the Bush administration's first involvement in Somalia's humanitarian crisis. Since mid-August 1992, the U.S. Air Force had been transporting food and supplies from Mombasa, Kenya, into Somalia during Operation Provide Relief. But securing the aid distribution after it arrived in country was becoming a problem. Most food never reached the nongovernmental organizations and UN beneficiaries, and this new step meant for the first time that large numbers of U.S. service members would be on the ground in harm's way. Bush, a lame duck president, assured the American people that the troops would be out by the 20 January inauguration of President-elect Clinton—a promise that could not be kept.

Under the auspices of Operation Restore Hope, Lieutenant General Johnston led a Unified Task Force (UNITAF) onto the shores of Somalia. UNITAF, comprising 37,000 military from twenty nations, quickly fanned out over central and southern Somalia, securing first Mogadishu, then the lines of communications and aid distribution centers throughout the countryside. UNITAF was a large force with a lot of muscle, and was complemented by the effective diplomacy of U.S. Special Envoy Robert Oakley a former ambassador to Somalia. Supported offshore by the carrier battle group USS *Ranger* and later by the USS *Kitty Hawk,* Johnston's forces and Oakley's diplomatic skills joined in a methodical and determined pursuit of the mandate.

But the United Nations needed more time to form a credible UN force to replace UNITAF, and 20 January came and went. By 26 March 1993 Security Council resolution 814 was passed, which broadened the UN mandate. For the first time in UN history, a force would be armed under chapter VII of the UN Charter to restore peace, law, and order, including the disarming of Somali militias and holding those responsible for violence individually accountable. The resolution further established as an objective the rehabilitation of the country's political institutions and economy (nation building).

It was not until mid-March, under the authority of resolution 814, that the United Nations mounted a less potent, but still formidable force, UNOSOM II, which involved at its peak nearly 20,000 peacekeepers from twenty-one nations under the command of Turkish Lt. Gen. Cevik Bir. Bir was joined by the UN special envoy, retired U.S. Navy Adm. Jonathan Howe, and his diplomatic team. The United States provided the deputy commander, MG Thomas M. Montgomery, the logistics apparatus, and the QRF. Bir and Montgomery arrived in Mogadishu in mid-March without a staff and with few troops. The UN command remained that way for the next 2 months. A week prior to UNITAF redeployment UNOSOM II had 400 troops on the ground.

The QRF reported directly to General Montgomery as the commander of U.S. Forces in Somalia (USFORSOM) (Figure 1.1). The initial proposal called for a combat brigade–size QRF able to respond from off shore, then at some point relocating over the horizon while transferring the mission to another donor nation on shore. From the outset floating the QRF did not occur: the convenient deployment of 10th Mountain Division units already located in Somalia assured the division the mission.

Furthermore, because Montgomery had no U.S. staff to speak of for planning QRF operations (he had access to a small cell of U.S. Army officers on the UNOSOM staff), the burden for future operations defaulted to the QRF staff, which was ill equipped for the level of planning necessary.

On 29 April 1993 Marine Gen. Joseph P. Hoar, the U.S. commander in chief of Central Command (USCINCCENT) and Lieutenant General Bir agreed to the terms of reference, which described the

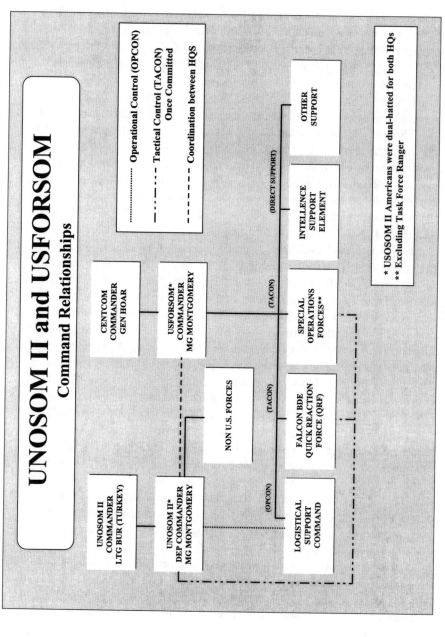

Figure 1.1 UNOSOM II and USFORSOM Command Relationships

staffing, organization, and operations of USFORSOM and their relationship with UNOSOM II. USFORSOM would remain under the overall command of USCINCCENT. Hoar would exercise his authority over the U.S. forces via his representative, Major General Montgomery in his role as commander, USFORSOM.

The agreement went on to stipulate that once the QRF was committed to action, the U.S. commander of the QRF, under some circumstances, could pass tactical control to the UNOSOM commander of the military sector in which the QRF had been employed. Although this was agreed to, it never occurred.

On 4 May 1993 UNOSOM II, consisting of 14,000 peacekeepers, assumed the mission from UNITAF. Simultaneously, the U.S. interagency task force on Somalia that had provided daily overwatch was disbanded. A few days later, President Clinton hosted a media extravaganza in Washington, welcoming home Lieutenant General Johnston and his force. The president applauded our nation's involvement in Somalia and the U.S. military's crucial role in restoring peace and tranquility to the people of this beleaguered land. With the ceremony complete, the president, citizens, and media abruptly closed the chapter on Somalia with a hearty "well done!"

2

THE BEGINNING

What lies behind us and what lies before us are tiny matters
compared to what lies within us.

—*Ralph Waldo Emerson*

Four months had passed since President Clinton's acknowledgment of
General Johnston's accomplishments, and here I was flying in a helicopter gazing down at the Somali desert.

As I stared out the aircraft window, I thought how having two of
my battalions thousands of miles away at Fort Drum brought me little
comfort. Although I felt some ease that they were under the charge of
an able-bodied lieutenant colonel named Jim Kelley. Kelley, a short,
brawny cavalryman, blessed with an irresistible sense of humor and the
enthusiasm of a competitive athlete, was the cavalry squadron commander. There appeared no challenge too great for Jim, but despite his
competence as the brigade rear commander, the extended span of control posed challenges. I had other concerns as well, beginning with the
preparation that I had received before my arrival in country.

I had questioned my training each step of the way after being selected to assume command of this ominous mission. It started with the
routine precommand courses all future aviation battalion and brigade
commanders attend at Fort Rucker, Alabama, and Fort Leavenworth,
Kansas. I was exposed to a myriad of subjects ranging from troop
safety and promotion systems to garrison services provided for the soldier's family. The last week at Fort Leavenworth was devoted to
warfighting, but the focus was entirely on mid- to high-level conflict—
Cold War scenarios involving the massing of large armored and mechanized armies to fight an essentially linear battle. No Somalia, nor a
notional equivalent, was ever mentioned. But more important than getting the latest warfighting doctrine was my desire to find out more

about Somalia. What was going on other than what I was reading in the newspapers? Unfortunately, the course at Leavenworth was not designed for such insights.

My 8-day transition en route to Somalia through the 10th Mountain Division headquarters at Fort Drum was equally disappointing. Although the division staff went out of its way to prepare me for what to expect, it fell short of my expectations. The division operations chief (G3), LTC Tom Miller, and intelligence chief (G2), LTC Chuck Sardo, two quality officers, provided me extensive detailed briefings, as did many other staff officers, but the presentations focused on what had occurred and not on what was expected to occur. This historical fixation may be explained by the fact that the division's forward deployed units had recently experienced combat, and some of the toughest fighting occurred just prior to my arrival at Fort Drum.

Additionally, 10th Mountain Division headquarters was retrieving information the best it could from the other side of the world, but that really wasn't its job. After all, the units in Somalia worked for General Montgomery, who in turn reported to General Hoar. The Mountain Division headquarters was not in the formal chain of command, but was responding to an unwritten obligation as the deployed units' parent headquarters to remain informed and provide support as required.

There may have been a more fundamental problem. Maybe no one in our political or military leadership knew what to expect, nor where the United States was going in Somalia. Regardless, I felt I needed information and assessments on future operations, and it did not happen.

The commanding general, David C. Meade, had been in command of the division for a little more than a month. He was tall and lean, gifted with abilities to solve even the most complex problem and then articulate its solution with irrefutable logic—an impressive quality. I met with Major General Meade on two occasions over the 8-day period. His comments, mostly derived from his recent Somalia visit, were on how things had been going. I was still looking more for specifics on what he expected. Later, upon my arrival in Somalia, Major General Montgomery quickly filled the void.

After my final meeting with General Meade, I traveled to Dover Air Force Base, Delaware, all decked out in my desert camouflage uniform, to board an Air Force C-5 transport for Somalia by way of Cairo. My driver, SGT Paul Rosa, accompanied me. Rosa, a tall impetuous cavalryman and a veteran of the early exploits in Somalia, was 16 years older than the average 21-year-old buck sergeant. His maturity and cautious outlook on life brought me comfort. This was driven home early in our journey. As our C-5 approached the Mogadishu airport, Sergeant Rosa suggested that we put our Kevlar protective vests on before we departed the plane. "It can get pretty rough out there, sir. You never know." I found it hard to believe that the largest airplane in our military's inventory would be landing anywhere that ground personnel needed body armor. Despite my doubts, I did as Rosa suggested.

After the huge transport came to a full stop on the tarmac, the fuselage door opened to a rush of hot air and the smell of burning garbage. Within minutes, we were whisked away on a UH-60 Black Hawk for a quick 3-minute low-level flight to the U.S. Embassy compound—the location of the QRF headquarters. I stepped off the helicopter and was greeted by the outgoing commander, COL Mike Dallas. Moments later, the compound was shaken by the explosive impacts of three 60mm mortar rounds. Sergeant Rosa was right. You never know.

That sobering welcome had occurred a week and a half earlier, for I had arrived in Somalia well before I assumed command from Dallas. During that period of transition there had been plenty of mortar attacks to occupy the QRF's time and send the soldiers scurrying for the safety of their bunkers. But this was day three of my command, and the Black Hawk was up against its operating limits and still could not get me back to Mogadishu fast enough. We had received word earlier that four men in a marine Humvee (the HMMWV: high-mobility, multipurpose wheeled vehicle) had fallen victim to a command-detonated mine late morning in the vicinity of the New Port in Mogadishu. They were a counterintelligence team on their way to work with the populace gathering information. Early reports indicated four injured, but it turned out that a Somali interpreter was killed and three marines injured. A daring rescue by members of a Falcon Brigade Black Hawk crew had already occurred.[1] They landed in the narrow street under intense fire, and as one door gunner returned fire his comrades tugged and pulled at the tangled wreckage, eventually freeing one marine and evacuating all three.

As we flew past the old Soviet airfield at Baledogle, 60 miles from Mogadishu, I thought about what had happened to this country. The abandoned airfield was once the pride of the Soviets in Somalia, and it was a symbol of their Cold War strategy to control the sea routes to the Persian Gulf. But now the former MiG base was reduced to hollow roofless structures overgrown by brush and weeds. Surrounded by desert, its aprons and 10,000-foot runway were weakened by deep cracks and years of neglect. The sprawling complex epitomized what had occurred to this once thriving land, which had fed on itself and imploded.

One end of the apron housed the UN's fleet of Russian-made helicopters—Mi-8s and Mi-26s.[2] The United Nations was paying a Canadian firm $2 million a month for the rotary-wing service—a total of twenty-four helicopters. The all-white UN helicopters had relocated from Mogadishu's international airport to this isolated airfield, because of their concern for direct attacks and mortar attacks from the many clans that occupied enclaves throughout Mogadishu.[3]

One of the more hostile of these clans was the Habr Gidr, a subclan of the Hawiye, and the clan that constituted the Somalia National Alliance (SNA) militia. These militant militiamen were one of several factions competing for power in Somalia, but by far proved to be the most lethal. They were smart, determined, and accustomed to fighting. Because of the SNA, the UN flights into Mogadishu were nearly nonexistent: the UN pilots' contract prevented them from flying into hostile areas. I chuckled to myself as I thought, "Hell, all of Somalia is hostile as far as I can tell."

Somalia was an example of life imitating art, if the 1980s *Mad Max* movies staring Mel Gibson as a futuristic road-warrior qualifies as art. The Somali clans' war machines, called "technicals," were based on Toyota, Nissan, and other pickup trucks equipped with guns of varying calibers mounted on the vehicles' beds. The warlords, all possessing their own kind of technicals, took on the appearance of the movie misfits operating their dissimilar war machines with oversized engines, crumpled fenders, and a collage of weaponry protruding from all sides, as they raced across the desert inflicting chaos and destruction.

The Somalis by nature are a warring people and, as a nation, we had done our best between 1983 and 1988 to arm the Somali military under the iron-fisted rule of Mohammed Siad Barre. A brutal dictator of the Darood clan, Barre had been the recipient during his rule of over $200 million in U.S. military assistance in exchange for U.S. landing rights and other assorted favors.[4] (Only the former Soviet Union, in the early years of Barre's dictatorship, had exceeded the U.S. in the infusion of arms.) With the demise of Barre's regime, thousands of weapons, including rifles, grenades, TOW missiles, howitzers, mortars, air defense weapons, and mines, were now in the hands of the clansmen who were vying for control of the impoverished country.

But despite the threat posed to the average clansmen by the heavily armed militias, many Somalis suffered from a more fundamental, insidious ailment—racism. Even the most revered figure in Somali society, the warrior, was not immune to his culture's racism, which exacerbated the country's volatility. The racist distinction is not predicated on color of skin, but rather on texture of hair and ancestry. Somalis with soft hair and Arab descent call their African brethren *timo jereer,* or "hard hairs." With discrimination left over from a system of slavery that had ended a century earlier, the "soft hairs," through business, political factions, and military might, dominate those who have the hard curls of a sub-Saharan African.

I turned my thoughts back inside the aircraft where I had a helicopter full of soldiers eager to return to the familiar surroundings of Mogadishu.

Notes

1. The aircrew was from Bravo Company, 9th Battalion of the 101st Aviation Regiment, Fort Campbell, Kentucky. The 101st aviators crewed the 10th Mountain UH-60 assault aircraft that were part of the brigade's aviation battalion task force. 10th Mountain aviators during the two previous rotations in Somalia piloted the UH-60 aircraft. To prevent redeployment of the 10th Mountain assault helicopter pilots, the 101st was tasked to provide the crews.

2. The Mi-26 dwarfed any helicopter that it parked near. The largest rotary-wing aircraft in the world, the mammoth heavy-lift helicopter can carry up to 20 tons, either inside the cargo compartment or on an external sling. The size and appearance of its cargo compartment is comparable to that of a C-130 transport.

3. Political affiliation was for the most part by clan. There are six primary clans in Somalia—Hawiye, Darood, Isaaq, Dir, Rahanwayn, and Digil.

4. LTC Daniel P. Bolger, *Savage Peace: Americans at War in the 1990s* (Novato, Calif.: Presidio Press, 1995), p. 270.

3

WORST CASE SCENARIO

There is the danger that we may become so enthralled by machines and weapon systems that we will lose sight of the fact that the man—the individual soldier—is the supreme element in combat.
—*General J. Lawton Collins,* May 1952

My aviation task force (Task Force Raven) commander, LTC Lee Gore, a tall, lanky officer from northern Georgia, was one of two commanders accompanying me on the flight from Beledweyne. The other was LTC Colonel Jack Weiss, a mild-mannered, soft-spoken officer from Wichita, Kansas. Jack commanded the 46th Forward Support Battalion of the 10th Mountain Division. My third battalion commander, LTC Bill David from St. Louis, Missouri, remained at the University of Mogadishu compound with his 2d Battalion, 14th Infantry Regiment (Golden Dragons) task force, the ground component of the QRF. Bill epitomized the infantry officer—a natural leader with a muscular physique who emanates confidence and competence. I was fortunate to have these three fellows leading the battalions that constituted the QRF.

The brigade command sergeant major was also on board the aircraft. A Kentuckian, Dwight Brown was young at 39 for a brigade sergeant major, but not short on experience. He was an armor soldier who had experienced combat in a tank battalion during Desert Storm on the Iraqi desert, and had been deployed to Somalia the first time 9 months earlier as the command sergeant major for the 3d Squadron, 17th Cavalry Regiment. Dwight was a stabilizing influence, possessing an exceptional rapport with the soldiers.

We were all tired. It was around three o'clock in the afternoon and we were approaching the end of a $2^{1}/_{2}$-hour flight after spending the better part of the day with the German troops.[1] Radio traffic was picking up by the time we reached the village of Afgooye. My call sign was

Falcon 06, and a hurried radio transmission requested my time of arrival.

Reaching the outskirts of Mogadishu brought the Black Hawk's altitude even lower as the pilots jockeyed the aircraft through a cleared corridor toward the embassy compound. We were flying within 50 feet of the tops of one roofless building after another. Italian influence was everywhere, a remnant of colonial days. The architecture was predominately Mediterranean, characterized by one- and two-story white-stucco villas separated by high walls topped with broken glass.

As we slowed for our approach into the compound, I sensed things weren't as they should be. Making the approach into Jaybird helipad at the embassy was a little like playing Russian roulette. You never really knew from what direction militia might engage you. You had about 15 seconds in which you felt as naked as a newborn. You were hanging it out.

Five days earlier the helipad and a trailer housing the French exchange (equivalent of the U.S. PX) were hit with 112mm rounds fired from, ironically, a French weapon called an APILAS. This direct-fire system launches a single, rocket-propelled round, but the militias employed it as an indirect-fire weapon. The helipad was constructed of AM-2 matting, a strong aluminum alloy, so it suffered little damage from the APILAS. But the French exchange was not so lucky and was reduced to shambles. Fortunately no one was injured.

As soon as we landed, I walked quickly to the tactical operation center (TOC), located in what was once the embassy's commissary building. It was a blockhouse of a building, but it, like all buildings in Mogadishu, had been stripped by scavengers of everything useful and left with only the brick and mortar of the basic structure. So methodically had the building been dismantled that all the wiring was removed (leaving gashes in the floors, walls, and ceilings). Every piece of metal and wood was gone. Where doors and windows had been, their frames were absent, and the floors were stripped of tile. So thorough were the thieves that the metal strips that protected the edges of cement steps from chipping were taken, leaving only the holes where the attaching studs once were.

I stepped up on the loading dock and entered the back of the operations center. I was immediately greeted by my executive officer, LTC Ellis Golson. Short and lean and a serious man of few words, Ellis could be counted upon to tell it like it is. Just looking at him told me it had been a rough day. I asked him how things were going and he responded, "Well, sir, it has been one heck of a day." He led me over to the base of

The Embassy compound

the operations map where the grid reference graphic (GRG) was spread out on a table in front of the map. The GRG is a grid reference system superimposed on the top of either satellite or other overhead photography, giving an overhead picture of a topographic feature (in this case, Mogadishu) broken down into smaller referenced sections providing greater detail. Ellis stated that the "Task Force" was on the move. The "Task Force" referred to special operations troops known as Task Force Ranger. "They are probably going after Elvis," this being the code name for the elusive Mohammed Farah Aideed, leader of the SNA.

I was astounded by the complete lack of information. We were the reinforcements for every U.S. and UN force in theater and we didn't know what was occurring in our backyard.

The brigade S3 was MAJ John Bendyk (later promoted to lieutenant colonel), a tall, dishwater blonde fellow of Polish decent. John's humor and wide Cheshire cat grin would either make you laugh or piss you off, but regardless of your impression, he was an extremely competent officer—always maintaining a firm grip on the brigade's operations. John was quick to point out the grids on the GRG that had been placed off limits to our aircraft by Task Force (TF) Ranger. Our liaison officer, CPT George LaBlonde, who was collocated with TF Ranger, passed word of the restricted areas to the brigade. The TF was based at an old hangar and a battered building at Mogadishu International Airport. LaBlonde was not totally "read in" on the TF's plan, because of their practice of compartmentalization, but he was provided with a list of grids that essentially depicted the TF's aircraft route of flight and the area where the operation was to occur. There was a second liaison officer from TF Ranger located with Bill David's outfit whose purpose was to facilitate 2-14th Infantry's response if the unit was needed.

As we huddled over the GRG, glancing between it and the large operations map, someone from over my right shoulder yelled that a Black Hawk was down. "What!" I couldn't believe what I was hearing. "How? What do we have up?" "It's a special ops Hawk," someone responded. We quickly plotted the coordinate and saw that it was near the "Black Sea" area and the Olympic Hotel—a known stronghold for the SNA militia and a population center for the Habr Gidr. The Black Sea area was in central Mogadishu and its heart was the Bakara Market where hundreds of tin-roofed shacks in a maze of narrow walkways and alleys created a shopping area where it was said you could purchase any item of contraband. Three blocks east of the market on Hidwadag Street was the Olympic Hotel, a five-story whitewashed-stucco structure. It was known to house SNA militia members and provide a meeting place for their leaders.

During a discussion shortly after my arrival in country with the outgoing QRF commander, I asked what he thought was the worst case scenario we might have to respond too. Without hesitation, he said it would be an aircraft forced down in the Black Sea.

The QRF had discontinued flights over the Black Sea a week earlier, after the loss of one of its Black Hawks to a rocket-propelled grenade (RPG) southeast of the area near Villa Somalia, the old presidential palace. The helicopter, Courage 53, had been traveling on a routine mission at 110 knots and was 100 feet over the city at 2 A.M. It was just after moonset, and it was dark. Without warning the aircraft was violently jolted by the impact of the RPG projectile. The QRF headquarters had had indications days earlier that the SNA militia might be setting ambushes for the helicopters—creating incidents on the ground to lure a helicopter crew to observe the bogus disturbance, then engage the aircraft from multiple sides with RPGs. But the attack on Courage 53 was not premeditated. It was the proverbial "golden bullet," just bad luck.

The Black Hawk streaked across the sky for a quarter of mile as the pilot tried unsuccessfully to gain control and reach a safe haven, Mogadishu's New Port. The RPG had struck the helicopter's underbelly and instantaneously ignited the fuel. Soldiers at the airfield who witnessed the event thought they were watching a shooting star; initially many could not figure out what they were seeing, but it didn't take them long to figure it out. Pilot 1LT Jeffrey Riedel was just turning his Black Hawk, Courage 46, away from the Digfer Triangle area when the sky lit up to his left front. Moments later he monitored the Mayday call from Courage 53 saying that they were hit, on fire, and going down.

As Courage 53 began losing altitude, the pilot, CWO Dale Shrader, quickly looked back to see how bad it was. Two of the crew members were completely consumed by the blaze, which was responding to the 100-knot wind like oxygen to acetylene in a blowtorch. The third crew member was trying desperately to escape the flames and intense heat by crawling up into the cockpit with the pilots. The intensity of the fire caused the flames to reach past the pilots and reflect off the canopy and back into their faces. Shrader later recalled that "the flames were so intense I couldn't see out of the goggles, so I threw 'em off." The helicopter first glanced off the top of a three-story building and then abruptly severed a telephone pole. With its rotor blades shredded, the engines shrieking as they accelerated out of control, and the fuselage completely engulfed in flames, what was left of the aircraft slid a hundred yards down a street and hit an embankment near a concrete-block building.

Three of the five crew members were killed instantly. PFC Matthew K. Anderson, the door gunner, SGT Eugene Williams, the crew chief, and SGT Ferdinand C. Richardson, an intelligence specialist, died in the inferno. (Williams had written his parents a month before lamenting that "for a nation of starving people, they sure did have a lot of tanks and guns.")[2] The pilot and copilot miraculously survived and managed to escape, but not without a heroic struggle to get back to friendly lines.

Facing a pitch-black night illuminated only by the flames of their burning Black Hawk, Shrader and his copilot, CWO Perry Alliman, somehow managed to find each other near the wreckage. Shrader had broken his wrist getting out of the aircraft. He grabbed Alliman, who was badly burned from the fire and unable to see, and pulled him 30 feet from the wreckage. After a gallant attempt to rescue his fellow crew members was thwarted by the ammunition on board the wreckage exploding, Shrader returned to Alliman and they retreated to an alley. The heat generated from the burning wreckage had the intensity of a crematorium furnace; later examination of the debris found pools of melted metal and little recognizable evidence of the soldiers' remains.

Shrader and Alliman sought refuge in a doorway as the Somali militia began to emerge from several directions. One rushed toward the two aviators with a grenade raised above his shoulders. Shrader countered with shots from his 9mm pistol, causing the Somali to flee. As Shrader tried desperately to raise someone on his survival radio, four grenades were lobbed in the alley by Somalis yelling obscenities in broken English. At one point, a Somali ran down the narrow corridor spraying bullets from his AK-47 rifle. Shrader fired the last round from his pistol and the militiaman fell.

Exhausted and becoming delirious, Shrader saw a Somali in his late twenties holding a flashlight approaching their position. The Somali yelled, "American boys, American boys," and Shrader, out of ammunition and out of ideas, cautiously approached the man. The excited Somali said, "UAE, UAE is here," as he pointed toward a United Arab Emirate armored personal carrier. For Shrader and Alliman it meant their terror was over, but it would be a long time before their wounds would heal.

This incident prompted an immediate requisition for sufficient rapid-fire M4 carbines to equip each aviation crew member. Aviation soldiers had been trapped on the ground armed with nothing more than

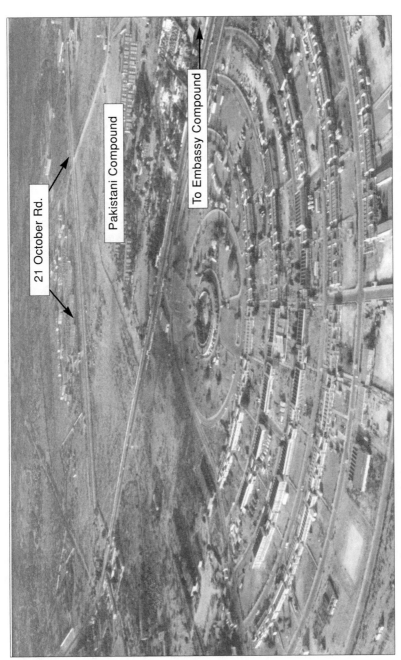

21 October Rd.

Pakistani Compound

To Embassy Compound

The University of Mogadishu, home of the 2-14th Infantry and UN Logistics Support Command

9mm pistols to protect themselves, which was unacceptable. It was now a little over a week later, and although personal weapons would be key to our soldiers' survival this day, their use was the furthest thing from my mind.

The activity in our TOC resembled a beehive. Everything was orderly and deliberate, but at a lightning pace. I still could not believe a helicopter was down near the Olympic Hotel. Bendyk began to list our courses of action. We had two AH-1F Cobra attack helicopters on a 15-minute strip alert and the Quick Reaction Company (QRC) was standing by at what was left of the University of Mogadishu. The university complex, which consisted of structures aligned in curved rows forming a semicircular campus, was adjacent to the embassy compound.

COL Ed Ward, the UNOSOM U3, or operations officer, had alerted the brigade earlier to place the QRC on a higher state of alert in response to TF Ranger activities. This was standard operating procedure when the Rangers were conducting an operation. Charlie Company Tigers, 2-14th Infantry, commanded by CPT Michael Whetstone, once again found themselves as the QRC. Whetstone's men were combat hardened, having just a week earlier participated in a fierce firefight while retrieving the charred remains of the Courage 53 crew: that fight cost him three seriously wounded soldiers.[3]

Here we were confronted with a downed helicopter in the middle of a city 8 days after Captain Whetstone's "Lightfighters" sustained their injuries securing a crash scene. I was frustrated by how this was happening again and by the lack of information at our disposal.

The next call we received was from BG Greg Gile, 10th Mountain Division's assistant division commander for operations. He said that MG William Garrison, commander of TF Ranger, "wanted the QRC now!" And General Gile wanted the force displaced to Garrison's location at the Mogadishu airport (General Gile had arrived in Somalia 5 days earlier to participate in my change of command). Gile just happened to be visiting TF Ranger when its operation had begun. General Montgomery immediately directed Gile to remain in place, facilitate the planning with Garrison, and keep the UNOSOM deputy commander informed.

Responding to Gile's directive, I immediately ordered Lieutenant Colonel David to move the QRC out. David's tactical command headquarters would accompany the QRC, and he wanted to take the bypass road to the airport instead of driving the more direct route through the heart of the SNA-occupied city near the K4 circle (a traffic circle forming the nucleus of five main boulevards, which spanned the city like the spokes of a wheel). I agreed. The additional time to traverse the by-pass road far outweighed the possibility of the QRC being ambushed before it got to the airport. This was the first of many decisions that later would be questioned.

What some lost sight of that day was the delicate balancing act of getting Lieutenant Colonel David and his troops to the stranded TF as fast as possible to save lives versus getting his force to them at all. Bill David would later say, "I always tried to err on the side of doing all we could to ensure we 'got there'—even if it meant . . . more soldiers dying. It was the rescue of the entire element that was the main effort."

The control of David and his QRC was transferred, or "chopped," to TF Ranger. This had been directed previously by UNOSOM II Headquarters at the urging of TF Ranger and the approval of U.S. Central Command (CENTCOM) headquarters. The brigade staff was aware of this command and control lash-up, but I had been in country a couple of weeks and somewhere during the in-briefs I missed it. I didn't like it, and I immediately called Colonel Ward.

Ward, a burly armor officer with a common-sense approach to problem solving, appeared somewhat befuddled at my challenge to the placing of 2-14th Infantry under the task force's control. He shared my concern, but stated that this was agreed to weeks before and now was not the time to change. I was angry, but he was right, so I acquiesced.

As we were trying to sort out the exact location of the downed aircraft and determine the Rangers' objective, the size of their force, and what actions they were taking, a call came informing us a second Black Hawk had been shot down. There was a momentary pause throughout the entire operations center. The silence was accompanied by looks of disbelief. I remember breaking the stillness by saying, "What the hell is going on?"

I directed Lee Gore to launch his strip-alert AH-1 Cobra helicopters to position them for immediate response. Lee had anticipated my directive. He had been down this road before, and he knew the only fire support our ground forces had were the direct fires from his attack helicopters. He also knew that the Somalis respected the Cobra gunship. They called it "the big bird with the long tail that spits stones," and they had plenty of opportunity to see and feel firsthand the sting of the 20mm rounds from the muzzle of the Cobra's flexible turret.

The strip-alert aircraft were airborne as Gore received the order. The two Cobras were accompanied by an OH-58C scout aircraft piloted by CPT Bill Metheny, Coyote 06. CWO Dave Coates, Raven 33, was in the lead gunship accompanied by his wingman, CWO Scott

MacDonald, Coyote 25. Chief Warrant Officer Coates, a highly re-spected instructor pilot, flew the Cobra as if he and the aircraft were one: he knew that he and his wingman might be the only difference be-tween success and failure for the soldiers on the ground. The three air-craft took up a racetrack pattern over the southwest portion of the city.

My thoughts briefly turned toward the circumstances that had brought the special operators to the theater and thrust them into this predicament.

Notes

1. The German "Red Devil Brigade" (paratroopers) were headquartered in Beledweyne. Duty in Somalia was the first deployment of the German military outside its borders since World War II—a controversial decision that was emotion-ally debated in Germany.

2. "Slain Sergeant Was Living a Dream," *Washington Times,* 9 October 1993, p. A12.

3. One of those wounded soldiers was a 24-year-old sergeant named Christo-pher Reid, a soft-spoken Jamaican immigrant who had attained U.S. citizenship the previous year. During that fateful night, he was standing next to a building as Cap-tain Whetstone's company secured the site. An RPG detonated inches from him. The explosion ignited the propellant in Reid's AT4 antitank weapon, which was slung over his shoulder, severing his right hand and leg, rupturing his eardrums, and leaving him temporarily blind. Traumatized, Reid reached for his right hand with his left—there was nothing. He called out to his buddies, "I'm hurt, I'm hurt. Help me!" His buddies did help, and he was quickly evacuated. Their fast think-ing saved his life.

4

TASK FORCE RANGER

The courage of the soldier is heightened by the knowledge of his profession.
—*Vegetius*, Military Institutions of the Romans, A.D. 378

On 5 June 1993, a contingent of Pakistani soldiers en route to inspect a weapons storage facility in Mogadishu was ambushed and twenty-four soldiers were brutally massacred. The UN Security Council passed a resolution on 6 June authorizing the "arrest and detention for prosecution, trial and punishment" of those responsible. All indications pointed to Mohammed Farah Aideed and his SNA militia. On 17 June the Security Council passed UN resolution 837, which directed the apprehension of Aideed for questioning. The UN operation in Somalia, under the leadership of the UN Special Envoy U.S. Admiral (retired) Jonathan Howe, immediately issued an arrest order for Aideed and spiced the pot with a $25,000 reward for his capture. Later that day President Clinton declared: "The military back of Aideed has been broken. A warrant has been issued for his arrest." Unwittingly, the United Nations hinged its success on Aideed's capture, and U.S. and UN troops stopped being peacekeepers and became one of the warring parties.

Initial UNOSOM II plans called for the QRF to apprehend Aideed. Determining where he was hiding and his movements was to be the QRF's biggest challenge. The QRF headquarters was provided timely human intelligence from the U.S. Central Intelligence Agency and from the many sources the QRF intelligence officer maintained. Although accurate intelligence is always a challenge, particularly when you are looking for one man who remains on the move, it was the realization that the QRF was not trained, nor was it equipped, to undertake such a task that prompted Howe to ask for special operations forces (SOF).

MG William F. Garrison, commander of Joint Special Operations Command at Fort Bragg, North Carolina, got the order. Garrison was the leader of the elite Delta Force made up of seasoned soldiers, sailors, and airmen called "operators," and Delta Force was the key ingredient in any attempt to "snatch" a belligerent. As the commander of Central Command, General Hoar insisted that he maintain control of General Garrison's forces: the force was and would remain a strategic asset. Additionally, I suspect Hoar did not want a repeat of what had occurred in Panama and the early stages of Operation Desert Shield when SOF had operated throughout the theater without the theater commander in chief's knowledge.

I was never privy to Garrison's thinking, but it is my understanding that his initial plan called for a small group of Delta Force operators and army special operations aviators numbering fewer than thirty to be deployed to Mogadishu. But as hostilities increased and Aideed's well-armed militia became more aggressive, the planned force grew to 450 troops consisting of a squadron from Delta Force, a Ranger company, and elements of the army's special operations aviation unit, Task Force 160.[1] Despite the U.S. Army Rangers' making up only a third of the force, the collection of diverse special operators became known as Task Force Ranger. The media would later make it sound as though everyone involved that night was a Ranger.

On 8 August 1993, four U.S. Army military policemen were killed on Jialle-Siaad Street in the Madina district of Mogadishu when their Humvee was destroyed by a command-detonated mine. Later that day President Clinton ordered TF Ranger to Somalia.

The early afternoon of 3 October was like any other day for members of TF Ranger, with the exception of those who chose to attend a Sunday morning religious service. Many of the soldiers were wearing only shorts, enjoying the warm rays of the midday sun within the confines of the Mogadishu airport. Periodically, the pungent odor from the adjacent smoldering dump irritated the senses, the prevailing southeastern sea breeze guaranteeing the presence of the caustic aroma throughout the sprawling manmade landscape.

It was shaping up to be another hot day in the East African coastal city. Most of the TF troops were participating in routine activities or enjoying a game of volleyball or cards. At 1 P.M. the TF leadership received information that two of Aideed's top lieutenants, Abdi Hassan Awale and Omar Salad Elmi, would be attending a gathering later that afternoon near the Olympic Hotel. By 1:30 P.M. LTC Danny McKnight, the Rangers' battalion commander, was well on his way to completing his plan to snatch Aideed's lieutenants and advisors.

General Garrison quickly informed General Montgomery of his intentions. Montgomery cautioned the senior Ranger about the dangers of the area and labeled it a bad place. He likened it to the post–Civil War cavalry marching into "Indian country." Garrison acknowledged the warning.

To identify the meeting place, one of Aideed's followers, turned TF Ranger informant, was to stop his car on Hidwadag Street in front of the target building, get out, and lift the hood to view the engine compartment. This would signal the meeting place. The activity was observed a couple of kilometers away by the crew of a modified observation helicopter equipped with electro-optics that "down-linked" or "beamed" a television image back to TF Ranger's operations center at the airport.[2] The clandestine signal was also observed overhead by a high-flying navy P-3 Orion modified with electro-optics and a down-link to the operations center. A steady stream of video information was flowing to the headquarters.

After the signal was observed and passed, the TF, which was pumped, ready, and had its target location in hand, quickly boarded its MH-60s only to be placed on hold when a question arose about the location of the meeting place. The mission was eventually postponed for more than half an hour because the SNA turncoat confessed that because he was so nervous, he hadn't parked directly in front of the target building. The objective, a squared off, three-story, pale-white building, was one block north of the Olympic Hotel on Hidwadag Street. The agent's admission forced the task force to delay the mission; the TF sent him back into the city to verify the target and modify their plan.

TF Ranger's mode of operation involved a heavily armed, lightning-fast strike from both air and ground: the intended result was complete surprise coupled with overwhelming force. But success of the operation was predicated on time-sensitive information and actions. First, the task force required real- or near-real-time intelligence to react quickly to a meeting of the SNA leadership. These meetings, like Aideed himself, were constantly moving, and this drove the task force to rely on its spies, communications intercepts, and a fleet of overhead and stand-off electro-optic eyes.

Second, the TF needed to strike fast and get out promptly before losing the advantage of shock, numbers, and firepower. Figuring that the time on the objective would be a matter of minutes, the decision was made to leave night observation devices and canteens of water behind to lighten the soldiers' loads—a decision that would later come back to haunt the leadership.

Task Force 160 Little Birds parked on the ramp at the Mogadishu airport

Perched on benches attached to each side of four MH-6 Little Bird helicopters, the Delta troops darted across the city and abruptly settled on the streets around their objective at 3:40 P.M. The troopers, launching from the Little Bird skids and fighting the dust and debris churned by the rotor blades, dashed into the building. Simultaneously, Rangers began dropping out of the sky employing a technique called fast-rope, which is similar to rappelling. The troopers were secured to long thick nylon ropes attached to MH-60s, and in an instant had slid to the ground or building tops to establish their security perimeter and blocking positions around the objective (a Black Hawk's full complement of soldiers could be unloaded in a matter of seconds). The operation was being executed like clockwork with no problems, other than the helicopters' down-wash causing clouds of dust to billow from the streets and alleys—and obscure the ground and blow an occasional tin roof from a building.

Then PFC Todd Blackburn, securing the fast-rope, lost his grip and fell nearly 50 feet to the street below. He was critically hurt, suffering internal injuries. After being carried down a dusty trash-littered street, Blackburn was evacuated in a heroic three-vehicle dash to the airfield by Delta operators and Rangers. This was but the first of many things to go wrong that day.

Weeks earlier on 23 August, Major General Garrison, a tall, muscular officer with a close-cropped Ranger haircut, had arrived in Mogadishu under the cloak of secrecy. A small advance party had accompanied him, and its inconspicuous arrival concealed the magnitude of the operation. Garrison's presence was to remain secret. To reduce the visibility of the operation and minimize speculation about the task force's arrival on the scene, the media were led to believe that TF Ranger reported to Major General Montgomery.[3] In reality, the task force worked for General Garrison, who reported directly to General Hoar (Figure 4.1). Garrison had an obligation to consult with Montgomery prior to a task force operation to make sure that no UN personnel were in harm's way. This arrangement worked, but failed to support unity of U.S. command in Somalia. Fortunately, both men had a mutual respect for one another, and in their short time working together had developed a close friendship.

The preponderance of the task force arrived in Mogadishu on a half-dozen C-5 transport aircraft on 26 August and quickly occupied an old and dilapidated hangar near the airport terminal. The task force was prepared for action by 29 August, but Aideed's whereabouts remained unknown, and he had not been seen for nearly a month. From 7 September

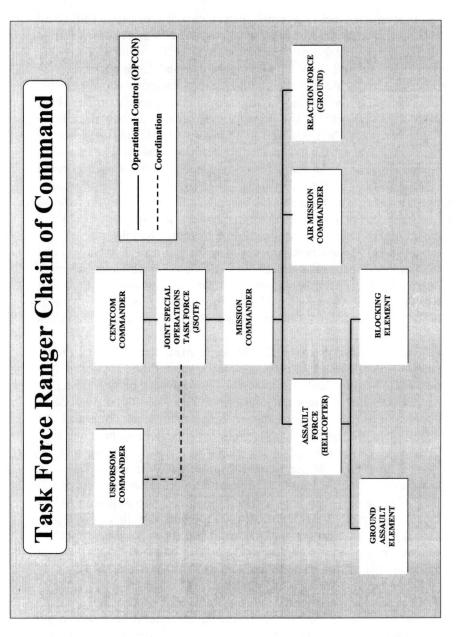

Figure 4.1 Task Force Ranger Chain of Command

the TF would hunt more than Aideed. Prior to October 3 the task force executed six missions, with results that ranged from embarrassment in the 30 August assault on the Lig-Ligato house that captured eight suspects who turned out to be working for the UN Development Program, to the successful 21 September capture of Osman Hassan Ali (known as Atto), suspected chief financier and number two man in the SNA. Atto would spend the next 5 months in secret captivity on a tiny island off Somalia near the city of Kismayu. The QRF maintained a small communication contingent on the island—a task that was not necessarily within the scope of our mission, but certainly within our capability and expertise.[4]

The complexity of the mission, the congestion and diversity of urban terrain, and the heavy reliance on near-real-time intelligence drove TF Ranger to a templated approach for the accomplishment of its task. The basis for its tactics was the conventional cordon-and-search operation with the Delta Force operators assaulting the objective to search and seize their target(s), while the Rangers manned a security cordon around the objective, all the while being supported by helicopters overhead. Garrison and his task force attempted variations to mask their procedures, but repetition and consistency had unintentionally telegraphed their mode of operation to those who were interested.

This is not to say that the task force didn't try deception. I recall nights when the airspace above Mogadishu, defined by the GRG grids, was off limits to our aircraft. I would walk outside the white-stucco building at the embassy compound that doubled as my office and living quarters and peer into the clear desert night. Soon I would hear a low roar in the distance that gradually grew louder and more pervasive as the blacked-out Task Force 160 aircraft, packed with soldiers whose legs dangled from the aircraft, filled the night sky just feet above the rooftops. This practice, taking the tight-knit formation of aircraft throughout the city, was known as "signature flights." Its purpose was to intimidate, deceive, and confuse the SNA, although I have my doubts as to its effectiveness.

On 3 October the SNA showed no sign of being intimidated or fooled. Private First Class Blackburn's untimely 50-foot fall proved to be a momentary setback. But the hunt for Aideed's lieutenants near the Olympic Hotel continued, as the operation's momentum was maintained and proceeded with the speed and efficiency known only to the special operators.

The Rangers quickly secured the perimeter around the target building. For U.S. Army Ranger Carlos Rodriguez and his squad, the trip down the fast-rope and subsequent movement to their security position went as planned. Rodriguez had concerns as they moved down the street, and he later described the perils and how his part in the operation quickly went from participant to spectator. "It was bright daylight, there were windows and doorways all around us, and you can't watch all of them all of the time. All of a sudden the Somalis just opened up on us . . . small arms and grenades. There was shooting from all directions, and we couldn't see who was shooting at us. I saw a muzzle once, sticking around a corner, and I shot at it." Shortly after he fired toward the corner Rodriguez was shot in the right hip. He went on, "I got some shrapnel in my left foot and a little in my face. It broke some bones and I was down. Our squad leader got hit too. It got pretty confusing."[5]

Members of his squad pulled Rodriguez, his squad leader, and two other Rangers into a room of a nearby house. Rodriguez recalls that "there were four of us in there wounded and some others in other rooms nearby. We were calling back and forth to each other. I was bleeding pretty good." After a medic placed inflatable pressure pants on Rodriguez to immobilize the limbs and stop the bleeding, he said, "We just waited and waited."[6] Rodriguez and his comrades would wait for 8 more hours before help would arrive.

Back on Hidwadag Street the Delta operators secured their objective and captured the SNA in the building, but the operation took much longer than they had anticipated. The operators were receiving fire from all directions, and although they had encountered stiffer resistance than they had anticipated, they had accomplished their objective. The TF operators had scooped up twenty-four Somali prisoners and were preparing to transport them directly back to the airport. The truck convoy arrived on the scene at 4 P.M.

At 4:20 P.M. an MH-60 Black Hawk, Super 61, piloted by CWO Clifton Wolcott and Donovan "Bull" Briley, was orbiting 100 feet overhead providing fire support from its three on-board snipers. A single RPG grenade pierced the helicopter and sent it lurching forward, nose low, spinning out of control. Wolcott managed to regain enough control to align the fuselage with a narrow alley about 300 yards east of the target building, but the rotor blades hit the surrounding dwellings and the aircraft flipped, striking cockpit first, and coming to rest against a stone wall—collapsing the fuselage around Wolcott. Both pilots were killed and their five crew members injured.

This single event changed the entire complexion of the operation, and as one young Ranger, SGT Randy Ramaglia, who witnessed the crash and then later became a casualty himself, said, "Wait a minute you know this isn't . . . it's not suppose to work like this. We're Americans!

We're the ones dictating the game here."[7] It was a shock to everyone and despite the downing by an RPG of Courage 53 a week earlier, the TF had not anticipated the full consequences of a crashed aircraft in the city. The TF had planned and rehearsed for such an event, but everything was predicated on a timely extraction taking minutes, not hours.

Rangers quickly maneuvered from their security cordon through the narrow streets and alleyways toward the crash site to secure the aircraft's occupants. Delta operators, having completed their part of the mission, also dashed to the crash site. These brave soldiers, trapped in a fight to the death, fought every foot of the way. The volume of fire directed at the soldiers as they maneuvered, especially from RPGs, shook even the seasoned troopers. They were fighting for their lives, while Americans halfway around the world back home were just starting their Sunday morning routines.

Simultaneously, a search-and-rescue Black Hawk received rotor blade damage from militia ground fire as it steadied over Freedom Road, unleashing a fifteen-man security team near the crash site. Meanwhile, Lieutenant Colonel McKnight, readying his convoy of 5-ton trucks and Humvees to return to the airfield with his precious cargo of prisoners, was diverted by Garrison to reinforce the helicopter crash site. McKnight never made it. The maze-like streets and convoluted city layout caused McKnight and his Rangers to lose their way as they received automatic-weapons and RPG fire at every turn. At one point an RPG struck one of the vehicles, decapitating the operator. Casualties were mounting, and McKnight, who was receiving directions from TF Ranger's command center, found himself driving in circles. Concerned for the wounded and the security of the prisoners, Garrison consented to McKnight's appeal to return to the airfield.

At 4:40 P.M. while ninety-plus Rangers and Delta operators consolidated around the Black Hawk crash site, a second Black Hawk orbiting overhead, Super 64, piloted by CWO Michael Durant, was struck by an RPG in the tail rotor, severing 2 to 3 feet of vertical-fin assembly. Crippled but briefly under control, the Black Hawk was headed by its aircrew in the direction of the airport. Moments later, its tail rotor came apart and the aircraft went spinning out of control, hurling itself onto several tin-roofed shanties, flattening the fragile structures. Things were getting worse by the minute, and this latest aircraft downing complicated the mission immeasurably.

Garrison indeed had a problem. Aircrews were down at two different locations in the city. Because Durant's aircraft sustained flight for a short time, it had traveled more than a kilometer from the fighting and the focus of the SNA's attention. The militia did not immediately converge on this crash site, but sympathizers did—Somalis, loyal to Aideed, who were fed up with UN and U.S. involvement.

The Little Birds circled above the second crash site, but they were getting low on fuel. LTC Thomas Matthews, the aviation commander, was confronted with refueling the aircraft, maintaining fire support at the first crash site, and responding to Chief Warrant Officer Durant's crash. In addition to Matthews's challenges, neither of the crash sites could support an MH-60's landing.

Super 64 had augered in and created its own landing zone out of Habr Gidr shacks. Some of the Little Bird pilots wanted to attempt a landing and retrieve their comrades just as they had done when Chief Warrant Officer Wolcott's helicopter went down, but their request was wisely denied. It was too risky, although it didn't stop one crew from landing a couple of hundred meters from the crash site—but neither Durant nor his crew appeared. There just wasn't a suitable place to land anywhere near the wreckage. The Little Birds continued to circle overhead, as they would do throughout the night at Wolcott's crash, preventing hundreds of Somalis from overrunning the site.

Garrison immediately dispatched an MH-60, Super 62, flown by CWO Michael Goffena to the crash site of Super 64. Goffena had been Wolcott's wingman and on board his helicopter were two Delta snipers, MSG Gary Gordon, age 33, and SFC Randall Shughart, age 35. Goffena located a confined clearing cluttered with debris a little over 100 meters from the crash site, where he hovered as the two snipers jumped to the ground below. After lifting off, he flew toward the crash site and paused long enough for Master Sergeant Gordon and Sergeant First Class Shughart to get their bearings. The last thing Goffena and his crew saw of the two operators was their thumbs-up signal as they stood in a deserted, trash-littered alley.

Gordon and Shughart reached the crash site. The aircraft was for the most part intact. The hostile crowd had finished off most of the Super 64 occupants who hadn't been killed upon impact. Warrant Officer Durant was the only one left, and he had sustained back injuries and a broken leg. He positioned himself away from the crowds on one side of the wreckage, and the two operators quickly occupied the other side and kept the hostile mob at bay, until the two guardians ran out of ammunition. The U.S. warriors succumbed to what we termed the swarm effect, which had been experienced before during clashes between UN forces and Somalis on the city streets. Within minutes the Somalis, coming from surrounding neighborhoods, would swarm around their victims, eventually overwhelming them. Out of ammunition, first

Gordon and then Shughart died. But before Shughart met his demise, he retrieved Gordon's CAR-15 automatic rifle and handed the loaded weapon to the pilot. Shughart told Durant "good luck" and, armed with an M16 retrieved from the wreckage, continued the fight until he was gunned down.

Gordon and Shughart's efforts were not in vain. They ensured that Durant would live. A militia member in the crowd realized the political value of keeping Durant alive, and he was somehow able to drag Durant from the clutches of the mob. Injured from the impact and beaten by the partisans, Durant was taken prisoner by the SNA.

Michael Durant, along with a Nigerian soldier, was released 11 days later on 14 October. Umar Shantali, the 20-year-old Nigerian soldier, had spent 5 weeks in captivity. His life was spared when facing sure death upon his capture, he had begun to pray to Allah and the Somalis realized that he was a Muslim. Religious preference didn't discourage his captors from later dislocating his ankles so that he wouldn't escape. In the first few weeks of Shantali's captivity, the SNA had kept him chained to a chair, naked and locked in a dark room, forcing him to eat and sleep in his own excrement. He was certain he was going to die. Durant's treatment was more humane, but no less terrifying.

Gordon and Shughart received posthumously the nation's highest award for military valor, the Congressional Medal of Honor. Durant would later tell reporters that the real heroes did not come home. "Those guys [Gordon and Shughart] came when they had to know it was a losing battle. There was nobody else left to back them up. If they had not come in, I wouldn't have survived." During the ceremony to honor these courageous soldiers, President Clinton told their widows, "Sergeants Gordon and Shugart died to give Durant and others a chance to live. They were part of a larger mission—a difficult one— that saved hundreds of thousands of innocent Somalis from starvation and gave that nation a chance to build its own future."[8]

Task Force Ranger's headquarters was having a difficult time. There were two aircraft down; not quite 100 Rangers and Delta operators under siege; and a makeshift platoon-size quick-reaction force made up from the remnants of the extraction convoy that had evacuated Private First Class Blackburn, as well as task force support personnel, all caught in an ambush. And now the special operators' headquarters was about to have the UNOSOM II ground QRF bogged down in an intense firefight in the center of Mogadishu at K4 circle. Added to their troubles was the sporadic distress signal the headquarters was receiving from one of Super 64 crew member's survival transmitters. TF Ranger headquarters knew their comrades needed help, but they were unable to provide it.

Notes

1. Task Force Ranger arrived on six giant C-5 Galaxy cargo planes in Mogadishu on 26 August 1993. Task Force 160 aviation consisted of MH-6 and MH-60 troop transport helicopters and AH-6 Little Bird attack helicopters for a total of sixteen aircraft.

2. An OH-58D equipped with video down-link was provided to the special operators from a Fort Hood, Texas, aviation unit.

3. The real security concern centered on keeping secret the presence of the Delta component of the task force.

4. The QRF mission was "on order respond to hostile threats and attacks that exceed UNOSOM II military force capabilities."

5. "Anatomy of a Disaster," *Time,* 18 October 1993, p. 42.

6. Ibid., p. 42.

7. Ambush in Mogadishu, an interview with SGT Randy Ramaglia, PBS Frontline Web site: *www.pbs.org,* 1998.

8. "Medals of Honor," *Soldier,* July 1995, p. 5.

5

FAILED ATTEMPT

It is self-evident that it is the defender who primarily benefits from the terrain. The defender's superior ability to produce surprise by virtue of the strength and direction of his own attacks stems from the fact that the attacker has to approach on roads and paths on which it can easily be observed.

—*Clausewitz, On War*

Major General Montgomery was acutely aware of the dangers associated with fighting without armor in a city. Montgomery, an armor officer with extensive command experience, knew both the firepower and protection such forces could bring to the fight. His worst fears were being realized.

Our ground QRF were transported by 5-ton trucks reinforced with sandbags and sheets of plywood lining the floors of the troop areas—techniques of the Vietnam era. Augmenting the force were hard-shell Humvees. The hard shell provided minimal protection from small-arms fire and no protection against RPGs, although some did glance off the rounded surfaces of the vehicles.

In early September, General Montgomery dispatched a message to General Hoar outlining the need for an augmentation task force consisting of Bradley Fighting Vehicles and M1 tanks supported by artillery to supplement the QRF. Excerpts from the message outline his intent for the reinforcements: "It [the requested force] would protect local logistics traffic, long-haul convoy, key installations and the Mogadishu by-pass observation posts. And it would provide critical roadblock clearing for vulnerable, thin-skinned US vehicles. I would use it in conjunction with other QRF operations only when necessary."

Hoar, balancing the needs of the field commander and the political implications of increasing the number of forces in theater, which was coming under increased scrutiny, supported Montgomery's request but excluded the artillery.

General Colin Powell, the chairman of the Joint Chiefs of Staff, endorsed the request and forwarded it to the secretary of defense, Les Aspin. Aspin disapproved the request—a decision that many would later say cost him his job.

As Lieutenant Colonel David met with General Garrison, General Montgomery made an urgent request to the Italians of UNOSOM for their armor. A regiment of tanks was located northeast of Mogadishu in the town of Balcad. The Italian commander agreed after conferring with Rome, and directed his tank crews to make the 3-hour journey to an assembly area on the outskirts of Mogadishu. Military commanders receiving direction from their capitals was commonplace and served to undercut the military commander's authority. As one frustrated senior UN official commented, "You can't have 30 different hands on the tiller. You can't have directions coming from capitals saying do this, don't do that. You have to have a commander with authority to command his units." It was not the way to prosecute war and certainly had no place on the battlefield. The night of 3 October would be my first taste of such warfare—operational participation constrained by national persuasion.

Garrison directed David to take his QRC up through the K4 circle. Bill David had little time: his objective was limited to the southern crash site. Garrison felt that TF Ranger had adequate organic assets to extract personnel from the northern site. David did not have a solid fix on the exact location of the southern site, so the plan was to move to the general location of the downed aircraft and have a special operations helicopter vector his outfit to the site.

I was opposed to the route through the K4 circle for the same reasons that David and his troops were not routed past the intersection earlier when ordered to the airport. It was the gateway to Aideed territory, and his followers surrounded the traffic circle. My intelligence officer, CPT John McPherson, was adamant about not going near the traffic circle, and I had based my earlier decision on his insistence.

If anyone knew the Somali people and the SNA, it was John McPherson.[1] A wiry, quick-witted officer, he was consumed by the study of Somalia, its people, and their culture. It was as if he possessed a sixth sense about their behavior, which resulted in his uncanny ability to predict their actions. In my opinion, John was the best intelligence officer in theater. By the time we heard of the decision to send David and his QRC via the K4 circle, they were in a fierce firefight.

Time was of the essence, and General Garrison had already dispatched a small force of Rangers and Delta operators in Humvees and

5-ton trucks—representing his own reaction force—into the city to re-inforce their stranded comrades. It was a platoon-size force made up of support soldiers (cooks, clerks, and mechanics) and the troops who had extracted Blackburn and returned him to the safety of the airfield. The ad hoc reaction force would meet stiff resistance and would not reach its destination.

Although UN intelligence estimates had placed the SNA militia strength at 950–1,000, there were thousands of Habr Gidr SNA sympa-thizers in southern Mogadishu who were organized by neighborhoods and city blocks to prevent any penetration of their safe haven. These sectors represented SNA military districts manned by a duty officer at all times.

After the Ranger reaction force passed the K4 circle, it proceeded north on Via Lenin. It received small-arms fire almost the entire route, and just as it turned east on National Street the route erupted with ma-chine gun fire and explosions. Somali gunmen were shooting at the column from building windows and rooftops on both sides of the street. This was the same route the original Ranger twelve-vehicle con-voy extraction force had taken to reach the target building near the Olympic Hotel.

The Somalis were adept at the emplacement of obstacles, and were known to employ everything from burning tires to derelict CONEX containers. Their tactic was elementary: allow the enemy force to pro-ceed far enough down the street until it confronted an impassable ob-stacle, and then quickly obstruct the enemy's rear to trap the force. Ob-stacles of varying complexity were always scattered all along a route.

Suddenly, what was left of the battered extraction convoy led by a wounded LTC Danny McKnight appeared on the street. Just as quickly, a Humvee burst into flames after being struck by two RPGs, which in-jured three Rangers, and the vehicle came to a stop on the side of the street, billowing smoke and flames. The Ranger reaction force, now joined with the extraction convoy, off-loaded many of the wounded from the bullet-riddled vehicles. Most of the trucks and Humvees in McKnight's convoy were barely able to move, riding on flat tires and broken differentials.

Unable to proceed even if they had wanted to, the Ranger reaction force and what was left of McKnight's convoy were forced to reverse direction and fight back to the K4 circle. Automatic-weapons fire and RPGs inundated them. The fray was bloody, and the intensity and noise of the incoming projectiles filled the air like a swarm of angry bees. Racing back toward the airport in their thin-skinned Humvees and

5-ton trucks, the Rangers sped right through the lead elements of Bill David's QRC.

Charlie Company reported to David that it was taking fire 300 meters north of the K4 circle, receiving heavy fire from both sides of the street. Simultaneously, 50 meters to David's front an intense ambush opened up on more of his vehicles, this being plunging fire from second- and third-story windows and rooftops. Green and red tracers were flying everywhere as David jabbed his driver, SP4 Scott Davis from Fort Walton Beach, Florida, to tell him to take cover next to a wall. Meanwhile, the lead QRC elements pushed through the ambush kill zone and turned on National Street toward the crash sites. The hostile fire intensified.

David and his soldiers were having a tough time. I was monitoring David's command net, and the dialogue between him and his lead element reflected the intensity of the fight. Reports from David of a Pakistani armored personnel carrier (APC) and a Ranger Humvee burning arrived at the operations center as we were receiving reports that the airfield was taking sniper fire. Lieutenant Colonel David and his soldiers had dismounted and were fighting both sides of the street when the makeshift Ranger reaction force and the remnants of the extraction convoy blew through David's positions toward the airfield. This initially resulted in confusion about who was who, but the Ranger force didn't slow down long enough to become intermingled and make a difference. David's radios lit up with frantic calls attempting to determine who the unknown force was, then subsided just as quickly once the Rangers were clear of his position. Fortunately, the momentary confrontation of friendly forces did not result in fratricide.

It was quickly becoming apparent that David and his QRC were not going to penetrate the force securing the streets leading to the crash sites from the direction of K4 circle. There was too much resistance, and RPGs were in abundance.[2] David's thin-skinned force was too small and outgunned.

Brigadier General Gile, whose call sign was Mountain 05, called me on the radio and said that Montgomery wanted David and his outfit chopped back to the QRF headquarters. Montgomery, in the old embassy building, was communicating with Garrison and Gile via secure telephone. Gile told me that Montgomery, in his capacity of deputy commander UNOSOM II, had directed the Pakistani contingent at 6:30 P.M. to relocate their four M48 tanks from a position near the airport to the New Port. Montgomery had also asked the Malaysians to support the effort. Coupled with the QRF, he wanted a combined effort in order

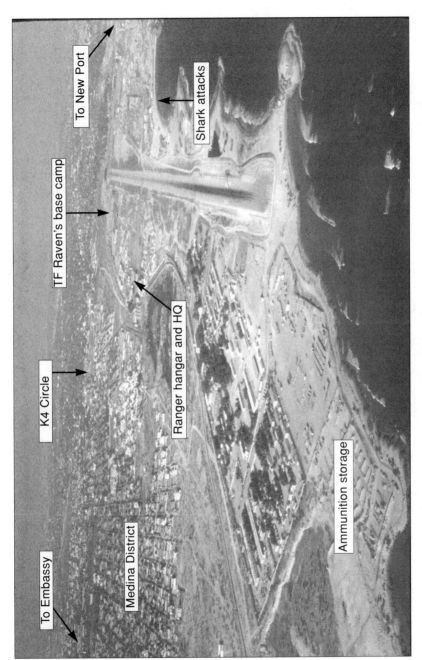

To New Port

Shark attacks

TF Raven's base camp

K4 Circle

Ranger hangar and HQ

To Embassy

Medina District

Ammunition storage

Mogadishu airport

not to "piecemeal the rescue force." The Malaysians were dispatched to the New Port with twenty-eight APCs loaded with infantry.

The New Port was just that, a seaport and center of commerce that provided access to Mogadishu and central Somalia. It was called the New Port because it had been constructed sometime after the adjacent old port outgrew its usefulness and became obstructed by a half-submerged derelict ship.

It was Montgomery's intent for us to hastily develop a plan using the QRF and Pakistani and Malaysian forces. The plan would later include what was left of TF Ranger, a platoon-size force. I directed David back to the airport. He requested more time. There were a couple of disabled vehicles to his front, and he was concerned that they may still be occupied with Rangers or have Rangers dismounted nearby. I agreed and 10 minutes later he called and said he was withdrawing.

Bill David later recalled that before this failed attempt, he was pretty concerned whether he was going to live or die that day. This was not his first experience of close combat, having fought building to building on the streets of Mogadishu just a couple of weeks earlier. But this was different. For David, "hearing the roar of the battle getting louder as we made our way into the city, it was quickly becoming apparent this was something much, much, much greater than anything previously experienced." He feared the stiff resistance meant a long night ahead—and he was right.

As David returned to the airport, he said an "Our Father" followed by a "Hail Mary." These were the last prayers he would say all night. From that point on he genuinely believed he would personally be OK, and he would not again experience any fear for his well-being.

Although special operations' AH-6 attack helicopters attempted to support the effort, the aviators were unable to tell friendly forces from the enemy because of the close proximity of Colonel David's soldiers and the militia. David and I would later receive criticism for not using either the Little Birds or our own attack helicopters during his fight near K4 circle.[3] When David was asked later why he chose not to employ attack helicopters, he expressed his concern for collateral damage. The densely populated area could have led to the injury or death of innocent bystanders—people who became less visible as the night drew on.

Casualties were being evacuated from the airfield by UH-1V Medevac and MH-60 helicopters to the 46th Combat Support Hospital a few minutes away at the embassy compound. Task Force Raven's physician would later receive a call from the 46th asking why all the handles were sawed off the litters used to transport the wounded. He pointed out that the NATO-standard litters were too long to fit width-wise into the MH-60 helicopters, so field expedience was necessary.

Notes

1. Captain McPherson was replaced a few months later with an equally capable officer, CPT David Tohn, who was not only instrumental during the closing days in Somalia, but later proved crucial to our success in Haiti.

2. Mohammed Saddig Odeh, a suspect in the August 1998 U.S. Embassy bombing in Kenya, told Pakistani intelligence officials upon his capture that Saudi millionaire Osama bin Laden, in an effort to expand his worldwide anti-American terror network, had helped bankroll Aideed and provided weapons in 1993.

3. Task Force Little Birds were supporting ground forces and they owned the airspace. This led to frustration for the TF Raven attack helicopter pilots who were airborne but unable to enter the airspace.

6

THE PLAN

The main thing is always to have a plan; if it is not the best plan,
it is at least better than no plan at all.
—*General Sir John Monash, 1918*

It was almost dark. The sky reflected the faint glow of an African sun,
which had set a half-hour earlier. Accompanied by Major Bendyk and
Captain McPherson, I climbed into a running Black Hawk at Jaybird for
the quick trip to the airfield and Task Force Ranger headquarters. When we
arrived at the airfield, the sky had been consumed by the black of night.
We hurriedly walked across the tarmac toward TF Ranger headquarters.
The noise from running helicopters and power generators contradicted the
lack of action outside of the headquarters. There was little activity and this
initially surprised me, until I realized most of the task force was committed in the city. As we walked toward the headquarters Lieutenant Colonel
David met us, and Lieutenant Colonel Gore arrived simultaneously.

We all walked toward the headquarters, which occupied a partially
roofed two-story dirty-white-stucco building scarred by past fighting.
Characteristic of the city, there were no windows, just the remnants of
what once was. Cut pieces of canvas, camouflage ponchos, and vehicle
tarps covered the voids in the walls. After entering the front of the
building, we were escorted down a hallway to the operations center.
Many of the Rangers and Delta Force operators occupying the operations center were in their black gym shorts. This was the standard uniform when they were not on a mission.

Major General Garrison stood near an operations map attached to
the wall. He and his staff had the advantage of viewing the battle on
television monitors as it unfolded, thanks to the imagery "beamed" from
an observation helicopter and a navy four-engine P-3 Orion. This ability to watch at firsthand the mission take a turn for the worse, followed

by the constant barrage of garbled and confused radio transmissions had taken its toll. You could see a look of gloom on many of the soldier's faces as the disaster was being played out in front of them on closed-circuit TV. Others were trying to communicate and effect coordination. Every radio net was operating at full capacity—orders being barked—not heard—repeated. The unthinkable had happened right before their eyes: two birds down, a bunch of dead and wounded soldiers, and no end in sight.

Garrison was a capable leader who had over the years earned the respect, admiration, and loyalty of his special operators. Despite his imposing physical size and presence, you could see the stress on his face. But the horrific circumstances did not detract from his ability to lead his force.

Task Force Ranger's leadership and staff were professionals who represent the best of our military. The actions I observed that night in the operations center were typical of any command confronted with a trapped force, and possessing no means to rapidly reach out and extract their stranded troops. TF Ranger's aviation was doing everything possible to fend off the onslaught of militia on the position, but the circumstances essentially forced the headquarters to become a bystander until a creditable ground rescue force could be organized.

The Rangers and Delta operators were experiencing plenty of casualties—something they were not accustomed to—and it clearly affected everyone in the headquarters.

Once in the operations center, we gathered at one end of the room viewing the operations map. Brigadier General Gile was also present. He appeared calm and, although I'm sure he was concerned about how new I was to the command and the theater, he let me do my job. This attitude prevailed throughout the remainder of the battle. His parting words were, "Let David do his job."

Garrison wanted Colonel David's force to depart the New Port and travel to the crash site areas using Tanzania Street, which came close to satisfying the truism that the shortest distance between two points is a straight line. Considering that time was paramount, and was slipping away, the decision made sense. There was risk: it took David's force directly through SNA occupied city. General Garrison agreed that his headquarters would inform General Montgomery of the selected route. There was little else said.

Throughout the day and night, the special operators repeatedly tried to prod us into doing things faster. At times we felt pushed, but their pressure was understandable—their comrades' lives were in jeopardy and seconds did count. But Bill David captured the rescue preparation best: "We had to be sure, had to be right, couldn't afford to make a mistake in haste—because if we failed, there was no one else—then they [trapped soldiers] would really be screwed."

David and I returned to his Humvee where his operations officer, MAJ Mike Ellerbe, met us. Ellerbe's military bearing and physical presence were overshadowed only by his superior tactical competence and exceptional analytical skills. Before that night was over, Mike Ellerbe's superb physical condition would be sorely tested by the wounds that earned him the Purple Heart.

We huddled over an acetate-covered map of Mogadishu spread over the hood of Colonel David's Humvee. At the same time, Alpha Company (Terminator), 2-14th Infantry, commanded by CPT Drew Meyerowich, closed on the airfield from the university, increasing David's force to over 350 soldiers. With flashlights in hand David laid out his plan. It was straightforward: his outfit would depart the New Port with the fresh troops of Alpha Company in the lead. The objectives consisted of each crash site: Alpha Company effecting a link-up with the stranded Rangers at crash site one in the north, and Charlie Company searching for survivors at crash site two in the south. David would position himself between the two sites along National Street (numbers and types of coalition armored vehicles at our disposal were not yet known). The airspace would be divided using National Street as the boundary between Gore's QRF aviators working the boulevard and south, while Lieutenant Colonel Matthews's TF 160 aircraft remained to the north supporting the Rangers at crash site one.

I could feel the heat radiating from the Humvee engine. The lighting was poor and the tactical map showed its wear, smeared with ghost images of past operations, tattered on the edges, and creased from its many folds. It was David's personal map and it was apparent the map had spent a lot of time in his desert camouflage pants pocket. The crash sites and primary and secondary routes were depicted on the map by black felt-tip pen.

Once again John McPherson found himself in opposition to the route selected by the leadership. John vehemently disagreed with the route selection because of the number of suspected SNA sympathizers along the route. He recommended a roundabout way that gave wide birth to the SNA and approached the objective area from the east. I respected John's professional assessment, but time was critical, and a lot of time had already passed. I concurred with Garrison and David's route selection.

Major General Montgomery was also concerned about the proposed route and intervened to deny the use of Tanzania Street. A new route was selected using Via Roma to the east, to Via Londra, and then north on Via Jen Daaud through Strongpoint 69 to National Street. This would bring David's force in from the east and past Pakistani Strongpoint 207 located on National Street. John McPherson breathed a sigh of relief.

The Pakistani tank platoon and Malaysian APCs arrived at New Port shortly after nightfall where they linked up with their U.S. QRF liaison team. The team consisted of a lieutenant or captain, staff sergeant, and specialist/private first class with a Humvee. The use of U.S. liaison teams with the coalition forces proved very effective. It provided an English-speaking direct link to us, which aided in the QRF's ability to react quickly and with the appropriate force. This was especially critical when responding with attack helicopters, which was the support of choice. Additionally, the coalition force became a little more assertive and self-assured with the presence of Americans. They knew that if they needed help, the presence of an American guaranteed they would get it.

I left David and Gore so they could brief their leaders. I made the short 3-minute flight to the New Port to discuss the mission with the on-site Pakistani and Malaysian leaders. It was pitch black as the Black Hawk came in low over the ocean to the dockside at the New Port. Upon landing, I made a beeline to a white UN Toyota pickup surrounded by a group of soldiers. There were two Pakistani officers—a major and a captain—and three Malaysian officers—two captain company commanders and a major, their operations officer. I asked who was in charge. The operations officer stepped forward and said he was in charge. All of the officers spoke marginal English; I found myself speaking in almost a pidgin English. The Pakistani major kept insisting on flying with me in the helicopter. He said he was the armored unit commander and was persistent in his demand to accompany me in the air. I told him that if he was the commander of the tankers, he needed to lead from a tank. I ended up directing my comments to the young Pakistani captain who was going to accompany his soldiers.

Several months later while I was attending a farewell for the Malaysian commander, Col. Abdul Latif Ahmad, and his battalion, a young Malaysian captain approached me and reminded me of my comment to the Pakistani tank commander. The captain said he would never forget my exchange with the major and that it made a lasting impression on him. I thanked him and told him the entire night made a

To Mogadishu Airport

Entrance to New Port

Site of marine humvee mining

Stacked sealand container wall

To Old Port

New Port

lasting impression on me. With a wide grin and a firm handshake, he agreed.

Surrounded by coalition troops dockside, I provided them a brief overview of the operation and told them to stand pat for Lieutenant Colonel David and his force. They would work directly for David and he would arrive soon with the details. The Pakistanis were hesitant to lead with their tanks, and the Malaysians were not at all pleased with the prospect of replacing their infantry in their APCs with U.S. soldiers. Both countries' officers were going to have to speak to their superiors, and that could mean contacting their country's political leadership.

The soft-spoken Montgomery was highly regarded by the coalition forces, and from UNOSOM headquarters his influence, along with some on-site coaching by Bill David, promptly settled both issues. The Malaysians off-loaded their infantry from the wheeled APCs, leaving only the vehicle commanders, drivers, and 12.7mm gunners for the twenty-eight white-painted Condors. The Pakistani tanks, which were U.S.-built M48s, did lead the column as far as their first strongpoint along the route, Strongpoint 69. After that David's fellows would take the lead.

Although coalition armies and soldiers came with varied degrees of professionalism, expertise, and training, my time in Somalia taught me that a coalition partner had to be assigned only tasks that exploited its strengths. Sometimes that proved to be a challenge. On one occasion, a certain coalition unit's integrity and professionalism came into question when it was given the mission of conducting a cordon-and-search operation in concert with two other coalition partners. The day prior to executing the mission, the unit's commander dispatched his force to the objective and advised members of the Somali militia occupying the compound that this unit was coming the next day to search for arms. The unit's commander called this a rehearsal, but in reality his actions guaranteed the avoidance of any confrontation. Fortunately such conduct was the exception.

Before I moved to the airfield and linked up with Lee Gore, we attached our night-vision goggles (NVGs) to our helmets (later, I would discard my helmet in favor of the comfort of the standard VIP headset). We quickly boarded the rear of a fully fueled Black Hawk for the trip back to the New Port. The pieces were almost in place, but it was taking a long time.

The congestion and chaos at dockside in the New Port was reminiscent of a shopping mall parking lot during the Christmas season. David and his leaders were trying their best in the dark of night to configure a tactical convoy: Alpha and Charlie Company vehicles; a forty-man ranger detachment made up of cooks and clerks and their vehicles; and the vehicles of the Malaysians and Pakistanis. David also had a platoon of Charlie Company, 1-87th Infantry, 10th Mountain soldiers who were part of his original task force in lieu of military police. Adding to the congestion in the confined space was a number of UN pickups and transports, and, of course, the 200-plus displaced Malaysian infantrymen. This chaotic period consumed a lot of precious time.

It was during the dockside turbulence that Captain Meyerowich was approached by Special Forces LTC Lee Van Arsdale, who, with a couple of Delta operators, invited himself along. One of the operators had been to the northern crash site earlier—a plus for Meyerowich, who was charged with penetrating the site.

It was also at the port that you could feel the apprehension in the air. These brave young Lightfighters, with tense expressions, stomachs in knots, and wide eyes reflecting both a sense of concern and staunch determination, were each in his own way struggling to confront his fears. These troops knew what was ahead of them—they could hear it, smell it, and see it in the distance. The fight had been going for some time and they knew they were going to take casualties. Yet without hesitation, they marched into one of the most intense battles in our history.

7

THE RESCUE

But the bravest are surely those who have the clearest vision of
what is before them, glory and danger alike, and yet notwith-
standing go out to meet it.
                    —*Thucydides,* History of the Peloponnesian War

It was now 11:10 P.M. on 3 October and Bill David along with his coalition task force departed the front gate of New Port onto Via Roma,
seven hours after the downing of Super 64. The city was dark. Without the
aid of NVGs you could barely see your hand in front of your face. This
immediately presented a problem. Our coalition partners were not
equipped with night-vision devices. This was one of the reasons the
Pakistani tank commander had earlier resisted leading the convoy down
the narrow streets of Mogadishu. The Pakistani tank leading the convoy
would have to proceed with white lights, and the Malaysian APCs would
have to be guided by their American passengers viewing the roadway
through NVGs: a formidable task considering the language barrier. A
major lesson learned is that if you are going to fight with a coalition force
on equal footing, possess comparable capabilities. Additionally, the
Lightfighters quickly discovered that their radios would not penetrate the
thick skin of the Malaysian Condor APCs, making communication nearly impossible and plaguing the soldiers throughout the operation.

I was airborne in a UH-60 along with Lee Gore. The aircraft's
cabin presented a dim glow from the cockpit's NVG compatible blue-
green lighting. The crew's call sign was Courage 54, and CW2 Bill
Kellogg and WO1 Tony Blackburn piloted the helicopter. These fellows, along with the other professional aviators and crew members flying the Black Hawks, were from B Company, 9th Assault Helicopter
Battalion, 101st Aviation Regiment. This Fort Campbell, Kentucky,
unit was but one of many units that provided structure and people that

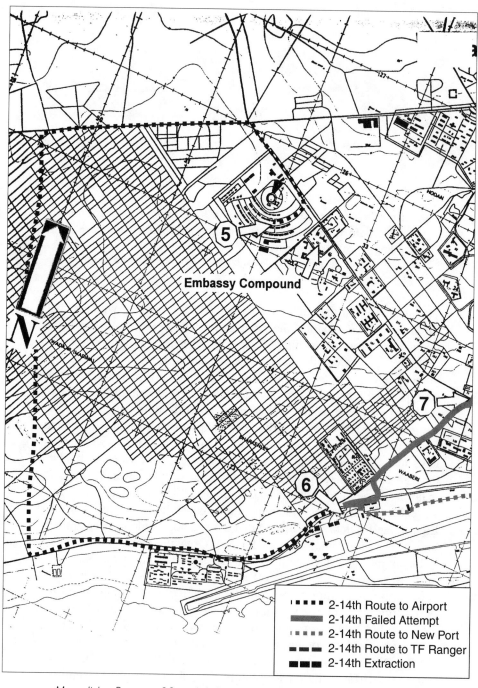

Mogadishu: Rescue of 3 and 4 October (see Chronology on pp. 62–64)

Legend:

- ▪▪▪▪ 2-14th Route to Airport
- ▬▬▬ 2-14th Failed Attempt
- ▫▫▫▫ 2-14th Route to New Port
- ▬ ▬ ▬ 2-14th Route to TF Ranger
- ▬▬▬ 2-14th Extraction

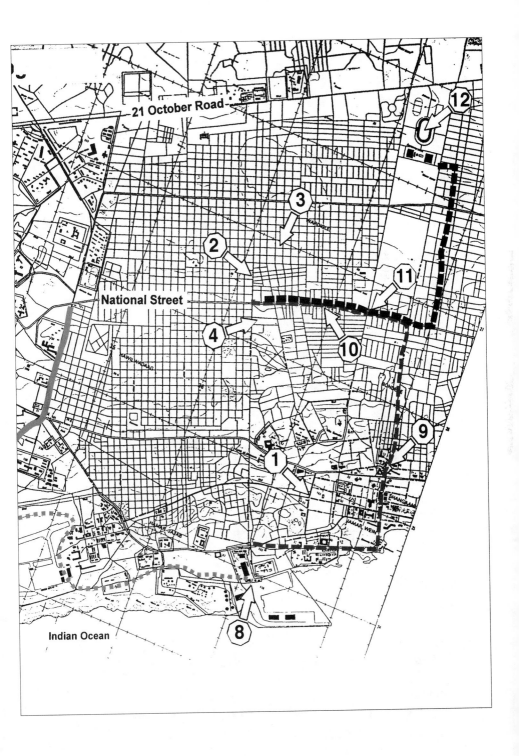

21 October Road

National Street

Indian Ocean

Chronology of Events:
Mogadishu 3 and 4 October

25 September

Map Location 1
- 2:00 A.M.   Courage 53 piloted by Chief Warrant Officer Shrader crashes in an attempt to reach the safety of the New Port after being struck by a rocket-propelled grenade.

3 and 4 October

Map Location 2
- 1:00 P.M.   TF Ranger receives word that two of Aideed's top lieutenants would attend a gathering near the Olympic Hotel.
- 3:40 P.M.   TF Ranger's Little Birds land operators near the Olympic Hotel while Rangers fast-rope to cordon off the objective.
- 4:00 P.M.   TF Ranger's truck convoy arrives at the target house near the Olympic Hotel to extract twenty-four Somali prisoners.

Map Location 3
- 4:20 P.M.   Super 61 piloted by CWO Clifton Wolcott is shot down.
- 4:40 P.M.   Rangers consolidate around Wolcott's crash site.

Map Location 4
- 4:40 P.M.   Super 64 piloted by Chief Warrant Officer Durant is shot down.

Map Location 5
- 4:55 P.M.   Lieutenant Colonel David and his Charlie Company QRC depart for the airport.

Map Location 4
- 5:20 P.M.   Gordon and Shughart arrive at Durant's crash site.

Map Location 6
- 5:25 P.M.   David and soldiers arrive at TF Ranger headquarters.

Map Location 7
- 5:50 P.M.   David and his force pass K4 circle, where they are ambushed enroute to Durant's crash site.

Map Location 8
- 6:30 P.M.   Four Pakistani M48 tanks relocate to the New Port.

Map Location 6
- 7:05 P.M.   The remainder of the 2-14th Infantry repositions from the university complex to the airport.

Map Location 8
- 9:30 P.M.   2-14th Infantry, Malaysian APCs, and Pakistani M48 tank crews link up at the New Port.
- 11:10 P.M. David and his rescue task force depart the New Port.

Map Location 9
- 11:20 P.M. David and his force pass Checkpoint 69.

Map Location 10
- 12:00 P.M. Two Malaysian APCs turn south on the wrong street and become separated from David's force.

Map Location 3
- 1:55 A.M.   Alpha Company, 2-14th Infantry links up with trapped Rangers at northern crash site (1). They remain until first light as they join the Rangers in freeing Wolcott's body.

Map Location 4
- 2:30 A.M.   Charlie Company, 2-14th Infantry reaches southern crash site (2). Shortly afterwards they reach the soldiers from the two lost APCs.

Map Location 3
- 6:05 A.M.   David's troops and the Rangers consolidate south of this location on National Street in preparation for relocating to Pakistani stadium.

Chronology of Events (cont.)

Map Location 10
- **6:08 P.M.** Task Force Raven's AH-1 Cobra attack helicopters hit disabled Malaysian APCs a couple of blocks west of this location.

Map Location 11
- **6:12 P.M.** The rescue force and TF Ranger pass Checkpoint 207 en route to Pakistani stadium.

Map Location 12
- **6:32 P.M.** David and his convoy reach the Pakistani stadium.

formed Gore's aviation Task Force Raven. Lee's unit was truly an all-army outfit comprising not only Fort Campbell soldiers, but troops from Fort Drum, New York; Fort Bragg, North Carolina; Fort Hood, Texas; Fort Stewart, Georgia; Fort Riley, Kansas; Fort Eustis, Virginia; Fort Rucker, Alabama; and Fort Lewis, Washington. These soldiers, some arriving as part of an organization and others as individuals, melded in Somalia over a brief 2-week transition with the outgoing task force.

We circled the New Port at 1,000 feet as David and his force departed the front gate. I peered out the side door of the aircraft at the city stretching below. Without the aid of NVGs, the city was a black hole with the random flickering among the ruins of small campfires lit by refugees and displaced persons. Occasionally, a generator lighted a walled house, and you couldn't miss the UN compounds with their massive floodlights illuminating their perimeters and the night sky above. It was eerie—a city so large with no lights.

This once thriving metropolitan area on the shore of the Indian Ocean had been reduced to roofless walls and potholed streets littered with thousands of plastic bags and debris. The Mediterranean-style city had been the pride of President Mohammed Siad Barre, the ex-army chief who had seized power in a bloodless military coup in 1969, espousing scientific socialism. Twenty-one years later he was driven from the country when civil war broke out. The city had once supported half a million people and had been host to the Pan-African games. Now its Olympics-sized stadium, arena, and pool were reduced to shambles, and the population had swelled to over a million people—Ethiopian and Somali refugees who flocked to the city to escape the famine, bandits, and fighting in the outer provinces.

I flipped my goggles down, and the view of the city virtually went from midnight blackness to green-hued daylight. The relief of the buildings became discernible, with the many shadows created by the angular terrain providing a ghost-like image. It was a surrealistic scene. In the distance I could see the sporadic camera-like flash of the infrared strobe lights positioned by the stranded Rangers and Delta operators to mark their perimeter. The strobe lights could not be seen with the naked eye, therefore the SNA was unaware of their presence. On the other hand, the special operations AH-6 helicopters providing continuous fire support from above could easily distinguish the encircled troops' position. I was able to simultaneously view both the Rangers' perimeter inundated by a steady stream of incoming and outgoing tracer fire and David's rescue force departing the entrance of the New Port. The distance between the two forces seemed like 100 miles, not the 3 kilometers it actually was.

Gore's aviation plan called for an OH-58D helicopter to observe the route in front of the convoy as it moved through the narrow streets of Mogadishu. With its stabilized mast-mounted 30-power sight that houses a thermal-imaging system, low-light television, and a laser range finder/designator, the OH-58D Kiowa could reconnoiter the route for any obstructions or enemy activity without exposing David's approach or the aircraft to hostile fire. Escorting the convoy from the air was, once again, the team of Metheny, Coates, and MacDonald. The Cobra attack helicopters took up a racetrack pattern adjacent to the convoy. Metheny in his unarmed OH-58A, a Vietnam-vintage airframe that has little in common with the modern OH-58D, flew low and on the flank of the rescue force.

The convoy had not cleared the gate at the New Port when the lead Pakistani tank came upon debris scattered across Via Roma from the marine Humvee that had struck the mine that morning. The twisted metal, tires, and canvas were no match for a tank, but the Pakistani tank commander stopped abruptly and refused to displace the unexpected obstacle. Sixty-plus vehicles were strung out like an immobilized snake through the ruins of the city and back through the entrance of the port facility.

The radios were silent up to this point, then all of a sudden David asked his lead element why it had stopped. LT John Breen, an artillery officer who was a liaison to the Malaysian force, was near the front of the column. He began yelling at the tank commander to break through the barrier. Out of frustration, Breen verbally threatened the tank commander, and the result was a speedy breach of the obstacle without incident. The soldiers were fortunate the impediment was not covered by enemy fire—a luxury not to be experienced again.

During this delay, Metheny flew circles around the lead elements to determine what the holdup was and whether there was any enemy activity. I too found myself directing my aircraft over the contested area at an altitude well above Metheny's. As the rescue force proceeded, thoughts flashed in my mind of soldiers from the past I had served with and respected. Soldiers who had been mentors before the term was in vogue. Soldiers with names like Colegrove, Lawrie, Fletcher, Gauthier, and Craig, who shared with me the foot soldier's life in Vietnam. How movement through the dense jungle was often times controlled by the anxious colonel barking orders while he flew overhead in a helicopter. Although it was never said, I sensed frustration and anger in these men as they took orders from a commander who was removed from the rigors and challenges of the terrain, and the anxiety and fear of close violent combat.

And here I was, 22 years later, the "colonel" flying overhead in the helicopter as the brave young Lightfighters negotiated their way toward the center of hell. I decided right then that I would say little to Bill David, and instead direct my energies toward ensuring his receiving every ounce of support our brigade could muster. I recall someone saying keep routine decisionmaking decentralized and save the important ones for yourself. I wasn't sure if routine applied to anything this day, but the philosophy was sound. I also remembered the questions LTC Hal Moore, commander of the 1-7th Cavalry, who had fought the battle of Ia Drang in Vietnam, kept asking himself. What's happening? What's not happening? How can I influence the action?

The convoy turned north on Via Jen Daaud and made an abrupt 90-degree turn away from Via Londra and an adjacent 20-foot coral drop-off to the ocean. The roadway led toward Checkpoint 69 and the heart of the city. David's force had a couple of kilometers to go before reaching National Street. The route was narrow and lined on each side with one-, two-, and three-story structures. This was Ali Mahdi Mohammed territory of the Abgal clan, a subclan of the Hawiye. Ali Mahdi was the leader of the United Somali Congress and a rival of Aideed and the SNA, so passage through this stretch of the route went without provocation.

David's force was moving quickly past one intersection after another. Gore's helicopters were keeping a close eye on the route, and his Cobra gunships were flying parallel racetrack patterns waiting to pounce on any threat to the Lightfighters.

Lee directed the crew of Courage 54 to position our aircraft just south of National Street. We were flying 500 feet above the city, which put me in the best place to observe both David's approach down National Street past checkpoint 207 and, later, Charlie Company's progress to Durant's crash site two and Alpha Company's link-up at Wolcott's crash site one. Additionally, our airborne position enabled Gore to easily orchestrate his forces with those of Matthews's special operations aircraft. Despite my earlier qualms about commanding from above, I was in the best position to influence the action if necessary.

I was impressed with Gore's approach to doing business. His deep voice, accented by a touch of southern inflection, was firm, and his thoughts focused and methodical as he delivered instructions to his commanders and their aircrews. He had developed a solid plan, and he demonstrated his flexibility and willingness to do whatever was needed to accommodate David on the ground and Matthews in the air.

The rescue force, with Malaysian APCs in the lead by this time, turned west onto National Street and proceeded 200 meters to the Pakistani Checkpoint 207. This checkpoint marked the beginning of Habr Gidr territory, and represented the separation between the SNA sympathizers and the indifferent. Checkpoint 207 consisted of a U.S.-made M113 APC and a sandbagged position. Bill David's force was about to enter the Black Sea. As David's lead APCs passed the checkpoint, the SNA and their followers opened with a barrage of automatic-weapons fire and RPGs that raked both sides of the vehicles. Soldiers riding inside later said it sounded like being in a tin shack during a heavy rain.

To make matters worse, about 200 meters from where the force was to turn north off of National Street toward crash site one, the two lead APCs turned south. Soldiers from Alpha Company's 2d Platoon were inside. As the two vehicles traveled farther south, the remainder of the convoy, now with a Pakistani tank in the lead by default, continued west on National Street for a short distance. The tank suddenly stopped dead in its tracks, and the tank commander refused to go any farther.

About the same time, an RPG struck the first of the two lost APCs about 1,000 meters south of National Street, from where the two had mistakenly turned. The driver's compartment was penetrated, throwing the driver back among the U.S. soldiers. The Malaysian soldier was only wounded, but later would receive additional wounds from a second RPG that led to his death. 1LT Mark Hollis, 2d Platoon leader, was in the second APC, which was hit by an RPG in the engine compartment, sending smoke billowing from the vehicle. Hollis quickly led his men to shelter in the rubble of a nearby building. Hollis knew he was isolated and in trouble. He and his soldiers would experience some of the fiercest combat of the battle until their rescue by CPT Mike Whetstone's 1st Platoon some 4 hours later.

Back on National Street, Captain Meyerowich ordered the Pakistani tank to move forward. The tank did not budge. It held its ground despite being in the center of the ambush kill zone. The tankers did continue to fire, and the engagement was one of the few times the Pakistani tanks used their main guns.

The entire column was held up, and it stretched back past Checkpoint 207 and to the intersection of Via Jen Daaud. David and Meyerowich were trying desperately to get the convoy going, but the tank still was not moving. Finally, it cautiously edged forward. This attempt to keep the convoy moving and heading in the right direction was not an isolated incident. Every time the lead tank received small-arms fire it would abruptly stop, bringing the convoy to a halt. David and his leaders were continually prodding the Pakistani and Malaysian soldiers to maintain the momentum. It occupied much of their time, and the frustration in their voices was clear.

The view from above showed a steady stream of small-arms fire covering the lead elements of the convoy and an equally intense flow of fire from the convoy back into the buildings. It was close combat in the extreme. This fire-hose flow of automatic fire stretched several hundred meters, and was happening within a matter of feet between the sides of the vehicles and the two- and three-story buildings that lined National Street. Everything, from 5.56mm to the Malaysian's 12.7mm heavy machine guns, was firing in all directions. Ricochets went everywhere and arced into the sky only to disappear and fall back on the city as the tracers dissipated. The only interruption to the intensity of the automatic fire was the explosions from the militia's RPGs and the Americans' MK19 grenade rounds. The soldiers would later called this trip down National Street as "The Bullet Car Wash."

The green glow in my NVGs and bright streaks of automatic-weapons fire, coupled with the curt radio calls that were barely audible because of the deafening gunfire as the backdrop, captured the intensity of the fire fight. The goggle image gave the impression of viewing a poor-quality video. I could only imagine what David and his troopers were experiencing.

It was during the movement down National Street that David's vehicle driver, Specialist Davis, received a grazing gunshot wound to the left arm as the command and control Humvee passed an alley. After being hit Davis began to yell, "I'm hit, Goddammit—I'm hit!" David's command sergeant major, Gerry Counts, a tough "hard-charging" professional respected by the best, quickly assessed the wound as superficial. He sternly barked back, "Shut the fuck up and drive!" As far as Counts was concerned, the arm was still attached so obviously the wound wasn't that bad.

With all the ricochets, Metheny and his Cobra team flying just above the building tops found themselves dodging rounds that were not intended for them. That did not last for long. Coates initiated an attack from a tight pattern he had established south of National Street. With the 700-plus rounds-per-minute 20mm cannon mounted on the flexible turret and a laser beam boresighted to the gun, Coates and his copilot/gunner, CW2 Eric Jacobsen, were able to place fire with pinpoint accuracy on the source of the militia salvos. Each time they circled around to engage, they received more fire directed at them. This prompted Coates to modify his pattern and approach the target from National Street, directly over the top of the convoy. Establishing a shallow dive, Coates engaged the target with 2.75-inch rockets, while Jacobsen engaged with the 20mm cannon. Coates's wingman, MacDonald, followed by sending additional rockets and 20mm rounds into the target buildings.

The use of 2.75-inch rockets in a city was controversial. We were employing a rocket with a high-explosive warhead, referred to by the pilots as a "10-pounder," that had a burst radius of 10 meters. Unlike a missile, rockets are unguided and tend to go wherever they are last pointed and to a distance determined by their propellant. They do not possess the ballistics of a rifled round, and they are greatly influenced by the turbulence created from the helicopter rotor disk. A rocket's aerodynamics are especially affected during hover flight. During forward flight the rocket encounters what is called "clean air," that is, air undisturbed by the helicopter's rotor system. Therefore, diving or running fire by the aircrew assures a more accurate delivery and reduces the risk of collateral damage. Cobra pilots in Vietnam, who fired daily, had been known to place their lethal spears through window openings. That takes a lot of practice and the experience of firing hundreds of rockets.

The decision whether or not to employ 2.75-inch rockets and TOW missiles was always difficult. Although the TOW missile is a point-weapon system, our Cobra helicopters were not equipped with night TOW-firing capability. Out of the thousand or so Cobras in the army inventory at the time, approximately fifty C-NITE (Cobra night-integrated target enhancement) attack helicopters were able to fire TOW missiles at night without the aid of artificial illumination. These forward-looking infrared (FLIR)-equipped aircraft were located in Korea. The lack of night-missile-firing attack helicopters in theater was, in itself, a hotly contested issue. It certainly invited the question of where the night-fighting Apache helicopters were. This was never adequately answered and was clearly another indication that our leadership outside the theater did not fully understand or grasp what was occurring in Somalia.

Earlier in the evening during the planning process, I had made it clear to Lee Gore that if we had to employ rockets we would. They would be used as a last resort. I wanted to remain prudent in their use, but I also wanted Bill David to have everything at his immediate disposal. We had Americans trapped and their very existence was in jeopardy. I would do whatever was necessary to protect our soldiers.

Two months later I found myself in a small, recently renovated building outside of the embassy compound. Sitting in the center of a large sterile room with a new tile floor and freshly painted white walls, I responded to questions about the use of the appropriate level of force. A UN commission empowered to investigate the military activities on 3 and 4 October directed the questions. A Finnish lieutenant general, a Zimbabwean brigadier, and a UN special envoy led this official inquiry. They were investigating allegations that we (the QRF) had used excessive force that evening. One of their concerns was the use of rockets.

Our approach for determining the appropriate level of force was based upon what was known as graduated response. That is, we would employ the lowest level of force to overcome the immediate threat, then ratchet up the force as we met more resistance—force predicated on an arsenal that included psychological operations (PSYOPS) loud-speakers on the low end to TOW missiles on the high end. On the night of 3 October, we employed everything at our disposal with the exception of mortars.

Accompanied by my legal officer, I answered the commission's questions forthrightly. There was no doubt in my mind that we employed the appropriate level of force given the circumstances. Although the atmosphere was cordial, I sensed that the commission members did not comprehend the gravity of the 3 October fight. In any event, the interview was brought to an abrupt conclusion and nothing ever came of the investigation.

I had inherited from my predecessor a superb staff judge advocate officer, Charles (Chuck) Pede, a warrior at heart. Chuck had been involved, right along with the S2 and S3, in the planning and conduct of QRF combat operations. I found this a most interesting development in staff integration, but a necessary one. I've never been a fan of attorneys. Maybe because over the years they have cost me more money than I care to recall, but Chuck's knowledge and legal perspective of the rules of engagement were beneficial when we considered collateral damage associated with a preplanned operation. On more than one occasion, he served as my conscience as I arrived at a critical decision.

On this day of 3 October decisions were easily made—our troops on the ground were in big trouble, and every passing minute exposed the aviators trying to help from above to the lethal fire from below.

As Coates and Jacobsen approached over the convoy and down National Street, they began to take heavy fire. As Coates described the completion of his gun run, "I made a left break at about 120 knots. There were tracers going past us all around the aircraft—to the left, right, above, and below. Six or seven RPGs were fired at us, and one exploded right under the aircraft, causing it to shudder." Jacobsen added, "You could hear the shrapnel pinging on the bottom of the aircraft."[1] The crew returned to the airfield to exchange their damaged helicopter for another. This would be the third aircraft for the crew. Hours earlier Coates had replaced a Cobra that had experienced power problems.

MacDonald remained on station receiving targets from Chief Warrant Officer Neely piloting the sophisticated OH-58D. The aircraft's superb night acquisition capability could easily identify what targets needed to be neutralized. The problem became getting the message to the attack helicopters. Normally grid coordinates from a map are used to locate a target; but, failing that, there is no better way than to physically mark the target—a common practice during Vietnam. By placing smoke, some other pyrotechnic, or ground fire on the target area the pilot confirms its color or description and engages the target. Furthermore, it is imperative that the aviator know the friendly troops' location. But grid coordinates in a city do not provide the accuracy needed, and distances are difficult to estimate. Shades of smoke, coloration of buildings, or any description requiring color or texture is nullified by the use of NVGs. Even placing ground fire was ineffective because the battle was intense and exchanges with the militiamen were occurring in all directions.

Neely did the next best thing. He took a hand-held laser pointer and illuminated the areas where David's force was receiving the heaviest fire. The laser designator was only a little larger than a pencil, but reached out as far as 1,000 meters to mark targets with a dot of light that could easily be seen by NVG-wearing Cobra crewmen. This technique not only proved effective for the attack helicopter crews, but later aided the soldiers on the ground in locating the right street to turn north toward crash site one.

Down on National Street things were not getting any better. Instead of dashing down National Street, the convoy moved in spurts. It would travel 50 to 75 meters and stop. When it finally reached the intersection to turn north, the Pakistani tank was confronted with a makeshift roadblock. It was now 20 minutes past midnight and Meyerowich took matters into his own hands. He dismounted his vehicle and along with his fellow Lightfighters peered around the corner at the Olympic Hotel. They then commenced to dismantle the roadblock. Shortly thereafter, the Pakinstani tank commander, refusing to displace north off of National Street, occupied a position at the intersection, while Meyerowich and the remainder of the force moved toward crash site one.

The Malaysians were not being any more cooperative. With the lead tank remaining on National Street, the Malaysian vehicle commanders did not want to proceed. LT John Breen later expressed his frustration: "The Malaysians just wouldn't go. We're fighting with them and fighting with them, and they won't go."[2]

Mike Ellerbe, occupying the same Humvee as David, was stalled with the convoy on National Street. All of a sudden the vehicles came under attack from 60mm mortars. Ellerbe observed the impact of the rounds occurring one after another toward his position. He ordered driver Scott Davis to back up just in time to see a round hit 25 meters to the front, and then a second hit 25 meters to the rear. A third explosion missed their Humvee, but destroyed a nearby vehicle, hurling the 10th Mountain troopers to the ground. The next series of mortar rounds hit close, and Ellerbe was a recipient of a dozen small fragments of a shell's hot, jagged shrapnel, most of which struck him in the left inner thigh. Ellerbe shrieked from the pain of the sizzling metal penetrating his leg. David quickly turned toward Ellerbe, who was bleeding near the groin, and asked him if anything had hit his balls. Ellerbe checked and confirmed with a distorted grin that "all mission equipment was present." David then told him to "take another dip of Copenhagen [smokeless tobacco] and get back to work."

Rick Atkinson, who at the time was with the European bureau of the *Washington Post,* weeks later had an opportunity to interview the SNA commanders involved in the battle of 3 October and he confirmed the SNA's use of mortars. According to Atkinson's report, Col. Sharif Hassan Giumale was commander of the SNA forces, and upon the urging from a displaced group of Habr Gidr who still had relatives in among the trapped rangers, he decided to direct his mortars only toward the 10th Mountain reinforcements. Regrettably many Somalis became casualties as a result of the erratic mortar fire.

Meanwhile, Kellogg had repositioned our aircraft to a higher altitude and to a pattern farther south of National Street. Although the militia members were initially unable to see the helicopters flying above them, the late moonrise provided a faint backdrop to the blacked-out flying machines. Our aircraft had been the target for a number of RPG gunners, and some of the lethal projectiles had come too close for comfort. Even at the higher altitude we were still the subject of ground fire.

The higher flight pattern was making it difficult for me to view the battle through goggles. My inability to see the fight, coupled with the aircraft congestion created by Lee Gore's attack team and Matthews's Little Birds, prompted me to relocate farther south near the New Port. First we needed to refuel the aircraft. Kellogg repositioned the Black Hawk to the airfield rapid, or "hot," refueling point. While the aircraft ran at full throttle, the petroleum handlers quickly pumped JP4 aviation fuel into the aircraft. I remained plugged into the aircraft by a 50-foot "mic" cord to monitor the radios while I stepped a few paces away from the helicopter to relieve myself. A few minutes later, the grounding cables were disconnected and we were airborne. Later we would again land for fuel, but this time Lee and I would hastily occupy a fully fueled aircraft with a fresh crew waiting for us to continue the mission.

Kellogg positioned our aircraft in a racetrack pattern at about 1,000 feet over the New Port and along Moscow Street. The voices on the radios were intense, especially on Bill David's command net. With the abundance of radios in the helicopter, I had the luxury of monitoring any number of nets. There was little doubt that David's force had encountered stiff resistance. The transmissions degenerated into shouting, followed by the hurried response of "say again?" This was usually followed by a beep and the rushing of squelch as the secure transmissions stepped on each other. As the Lightfighters "keyed" their radio handsets, the crackle of automatic gunfire and the explosions from RPGs and mortars obscured their voices. The sounds were deafening to the soldiers on the ground.

Suddenly, a frenzied call to Bill David, Dragon 06, from one of his officers burst on the net. He was excited: his voice was several octaves above normal, and his radio transmitter accentuated his rapid breathing. Rapid gunfire and sporadic explosions near the frantic caller painted a desperate predicament. The officer was unable to move his APC, unsure of his position, and he had taken several causalities. His speech was so fast and his voice so high that he was barely audible.

I found my own pulse increase just listening to the soldier. But Bill David quickly reached through the radio transmission speaking with an absence of emotion. His voice was calm and filled with confidence and strength as he instructed the young officer "to hold the course, remain steady, and keep pushing forward." There was a brief pause, then the officer responded with a natural, calm, "I'm in charge" voice, "Roger, Dragon 06, everything is under control."

In a matter of seconds Bill had been able to bring the frightened, excited young officer from a high hover back down to earth and place him back in charge of his unit. And he did so merely by the tone of his voice and making it perfectly clear he (David) was in charge of the situation. I knew right then that nothing could replace voice transmissions when you are in the middle of a fray. It certainly highlighted the limitations of a "digitized army" and the importance of steadfast, quality leaders.

Overhead, Gore's aviators continued with their relentless pursuit of SNA crew-served weapons and the buildings with their concentrations of militia. During one of the Cobra's attack runs, a 23mm antiaircraft weapon engaged the aircraft. This came as a surprise to the pilots even though it should not have. We knew the SNA possessed such weapons, but their lack of a night-sighting capability and the militia's poor level of training lulled us into thinking the guns would not be employed, or if they were, they would be ineffective. The latter fortunately proved the norm.

Chief Warrant Officer Neely in his OH-58D observed the origin of the steady flow of tracers streaming past the Cobra and exploding above in a newly formed scud layer of clouds. Neely marked the location of the antiaircraft gun with his laser spot so Chief Warrant Officer MacDonald flying the Cobra could engage. As MacDonald approached the target area, he was unable to acquire the laser spot in the clutter of the city. Neely placed the designator spot in an open area next to the compound where the gun was located. On his second pass, MacDonald acquired the laser spot and followed it to the target as Neely walked the spot to the gun's location. MacDonald engaged with a pair of 2.75-inch rockets, hitting squarely on the target and ending the gun's usefulness.

Fighting in or above a city is not easy. The confines of the structures and streets placed the Cobra's 20mm rounds near David's lead forces. As the "danger close" friendly rounds exploded near the APCs, the drivers and vehicle commanders were slowing down or stopping to secure their hatches and seek the cover of their vehicles. This further impeded the rescue column's momentum, and eventually led to directing the Cobra gunships to back off and assume an orbit in close proximity for quick response.

There were scattered debris and makeshift barricades blocking the Lightfighters' route as they went north toward the Olympic Hotel. The order was given to dismount the Malaysians' Condors and proceed on foot. The "sappers" from the U.S. 41st Combat Engineer Battalion were the first to dismount and immediately began the task of clearing a path for the vehicles. The Condor APCs would be needed to remove the wounded and ensure a quick departure to safety—a task that would be hampered by the loss of four Condors in the early hours of the fight. Additionally, the vehicles' heavy machine guns provided a much needed rapid volume of fire.

Assisting the sappers in clearing the debris was a 19-year-old infantryman, PFC James H. Martin Jr. from Collinsville, Illinois. Martin was a 2-14th Infantry assistant machine gunner and the son of a Korean War veteran. His M60 gunner, SP Andrew Boynton, was providing cover for the clearing effort from a doorway on their flank. As the clearing team moved deliberately from one obstacle to another, Boynton cautiously paralleled their movement along the street ducking in and out of doorways. As they approached the charred remnant of a ranger 5-ton truck in the middle of the street, they observed the movement of several figures. The team scurried to cover in nearby doorways.

Boynton soon found himself sharing his small space with Martin and SSG Richard Roberts. Then the street exploded with automatic-weapons fire, with bullets flying everywhere. Assuming the prone position, Boynton returned fire and then turned to get more ammunition from Martin. Martin was lying on his back with a small bullet hole in the center of his forehead just beneath the brim of his helmet. Boynton, who had gone through basic training with Martin and shared their first assignment together, thought, strangely, "That must have hurt." In reality, Martin probably didn't know what hit him. Boynton would later say about his comrade Martin, "It was. . . . a loss. He was a good friend."[3]

Martin was replaced by one of the combat engineers as the 2d Platoon of Alpha Company continued to press toward the objective. U.S.

soldiers had not experienced the intensity and such savagery of close combat in over 20 years.

Martin was one of two Falcon Brigade soldiers who would sacrifice their lives during the rescue attempt, the second being SG Cornell L. Houston of the 41st Combat Engineer Battalion. A native of Mobile, Alabama, Sergeant Houston was the father of five children, the youngest an infant. He was attached to Alpha Company and was in the first of the two lead Malaysian APCs that made the wrong turn off National Street.

The disoriented soldiers, led by LT Mark Hollis, had taken a number of casualties. Hollis knew they had to consolidate their position and, if possible, work their way back to the main force. As they ran to the security of some rubble near a house, two of the troopers, Private Xiong Ly of the 41st Engineers and Sergeant Houston, were hit by gunfire and shrapnel. Ly would recover from his wounds, but Houston was not so lucky. He had taken a fragment in his abdomen that destroyed his liver. He died 2 days later in Landstuhl Army Medical Center in Germany.

Over a year later, I would attend two building dedication ceremonies in honor of both of these great young Americans. The 10th Mountain Division sponsored a first-class tribute to them for their families, friends, and comrades. Martin and Houston each had buildings in their respective battalion areas at Fort Drum named in their honor. The observances were very emotional for everyone involved, as all of us struggled with our personal thoughts of the events that had led to the taking of these two men's lives. As I left the ceremony I couldn't help but think, "What a hell of a way to get your name on a building."

Elements from the 1st Platoon, Charlie Company, led by LT James K. Haynes, finally reached Ly, Houston, and their fellow troopers just in time. They quickly loaded up two of Haynes's APCs with the hollow-eyed soldiers pulled from the terror of fighting an overwhelming enemy for more than 4 hours.

Minutes earlier, Haynes had led his platoon to the location of the second crashed aircraft, the site where there was still hope of finding Gordon, Shughart, or Durant and his crew. Traveling in four armored vehicles, Lieutenant Haynes was unable to locate the wreckage because of the alleyways and trails that crisscrossed the shantytown section of Mogadishu. At one point, when he and his Lightfighters dismounted, they were met with intense small-arms fire. Unsuccessful in his attempt to locate the crash site, he solicited the aid of a helicopter overhead to point the way. Again using the hand-held laser, the aviator was able to

Somali militiamen near the Juba River in southern Somalia

guide the men of Haynes's force, now back in their vehicles, to the crash site some 200 meters from their position. Once there, the only thing they found were a few Somalis sifting through the rubble, and trails of blood. Haynes's soldiers fanned out and called names, but to no avail.

After Lieutenant Haynes had collected the Alpha Company soldiers, he linked up with Captain Whetstone for their rendezvous with the remainder of David's outfit. There was one problem—the Malaysian APC drivers had other ideas. From their perspective, the mission was complete and it was time to return to the safe haven of the New Port. The Malaysians had the blessing of their chain of command. To the astonishment of Captain Whetstone, the convoy of Condors transporting Charlie Company Lightfighters raced down National Street past David and Checkpoint 207 to the security of the New Port and stayed there.

David was infuriated at what was happening and demanded that Whetstone stop as the Condors continued to rumble past his position.

Whetstone responded helplessly, and his frustration was reflected in his radio transmission. He was incensed.

North of National Street Captain Meyerowich replaced his lead platoon, the 2d Platoon, with the company's 1st Platoon. The 2d Platoon had been the tip of the spear for hours, and its causalities and dwindling numbers attested to its contribution and the stiff resistance.[4] Meyerowich was smart in moving fresh troops into the lead, because the fighting was savage and the tempo of the combat was at its apex as the Lightfighters neared the Rangers.

The militiamen were proving to be enemies to be respected, but their stamina was blunted by their generous use of *khat,* also known as *mirrah. Khat* is a mildly narcotic leafy plant that when chewed in a bovine fashion provides a high. Although *khat* chewing is over six centuries old in neighboring Ethiopia and across the Gulf of Aden in Yemen, it only dates back a couple of generations in Somalia. The militia leaders would feed it to their young gunslingers to stabilize their nerves and divert the fighters' attention from their empty bellies. The glassy-eyed militiamen with their yellow, khat-stained teeth were fighting hard and with little fear, but their fervor was diminishing.

A number of unflattering nicknames were hung on the Somalis. The most common were "Skinny" or "Sammy," I suppose spawned by their lean physiques and the offensive tale of *Little Black Sambo.* I did not condone these labels and found it perplexing that soldiers, regardless of ethnic origin or skin color, used them. During night operations, the aircrews referred to the Somali as "moon crickets," because of their nighttime appearance while viewed from above through NVGs. Despite these references, the fine-boned, thin East Africans were lethal, and it had little to do with their body weight and stature. This night, women and children joined the male warriors in the fierce fighting, urged on by the militia's insistence that a foreign army was invading Somali soil that they must defend at all cost.

Above the encircled task force, the Little Birds continued providing their deadly accurate fire from their Vietnam-vintage miniguns. These small six-barreled electric-drive guns spit out 4,000 to 6,000 rounds per minute, and were once again proving their lethality some 25 years later. Unlike the Cobra with its flexible turret, the AH-6 fixed gun required the centerline of the aircraft to be pointed at the intended target. The pilots were flying just above the building tops, slow and sideways to engage the attackers.

As the aircraft circled in a racetrack pattern over the compressed battlefield, once again the sky was lit up with a stream of 23mm antiaircraft fire. The rounds appeared as a brilliant stream of beads swaying in a breeze against the night sky as they passed near the small helicopters. The low altitude flown by the Little Birds provided only brief exposure to the antiaircraft fire and permitted the pilots time to fire their miniguns.

David set up his tactical ops center along National Street just short of the point where Alpha Company had turned north to crash site one and Charlie Company turned south toward crash site two. This placed him at a central location, which afforded him the best command and control and the option to quickly go where he was needed.

As both companies continued their push toward the objectives, Garrison's headquarters requested Gore's aviators to back off. Congestion was becoming a concern, and Matthews's aviators with their Little Birds would continue the support around and near both objectives. It made sense, and Lee directed his attack team to reposition to a block of airspace over the New Port. We were approaching 1,500 feet above ground level in the command-and-control UH-60, when Metheny and his team repositioned 500 feet below us.

Meyerowich was one of the first to spot the infrared strobe lights marking the position of the trapped Rangers. The Lightfighters finally reached the perimeter at 1:55 A.M. on 4 October. There were some tense moments as each side attempted to link up in the middle of a storm of bullets and explosions. It was by the grace of God and sound discipline of both groups of soldiers that someone did not get killed or injured by friendly fire during the link-up. As Alpha Company poured into and expanded the Ranger perimeter, tempers briefly flared over who was in charge. Meyerowich along with his first sergeant, Dave Mita, had no doubts that it was Meyerowich. The Ranger company commander, CPT Mike Steele, naturally had other ideas. After some raised voices, profanity, and the flexing of muscles, it was agreed that Meyerowich would be in charge. For the next $3^1/_2$ hours the 14th Infantry, the Rangers, and the Delta operators worked side by side fending off the militia as they struggled to free the remains of Chief Warrant Officer Wolcott from the wreckage of the Black Hawk.

Bill David's instructions to Meyerowich were "to stay the course—we will fight here as long as it takes. We will not leave any of our soldiers on the battlefield." David turned to Mike Ellerbe and told him they were not going anywhere until the mission was complete. For Ellerbe at that moment David's words had a calming affect, and it meant that the mission would come to closure. But there was much to be done.

Bravo Company, commanded by CPT Mark Suich, along with the remainder of the 14th Infantry was at the New Port in reserve. David was confident that the militia would never expect another U.S. Army company-size element to enter the fight—an assessment I supported. If Alpha Company got into a pinch, David was prepared to bring Bravo Company forward to bail it out.

The angels of the night were the medics. Their sheer determination, heroic actions, and expertise saved many lives. David had the medics divided into Team Alpha led by the battalion's surgeon, MAJ Chris Marino, and Team Bravo led by 2LT Michael Flaherty. Marino and his team accompanied Meyerowich, and upon their arrival at TF Ranger's location the medical soldiers quickly began triage of the wounded. Marino's actions this night would earn him the Bronze Star for Valor. He later commented that "we found a lot of people severely injured and killed packed into two buildings." One of the medics would later lament, "Every medic wishes he could go through combat to have the experience, but after you go through it, you don't want any part of it. You've seen enough for a lifetime." A profound statement shared by everyone that night.

The radios were unusually quiet and our aircraft was now holding at 2,000 feet above the New Port. Lee Gore had just completed a call with his battle captain when suddenly three white flashes exploded in succession on the starboard side of the aircraft. We were jolted, but more by pilot control inputs than the lethal flak. Although our attacker could not see where we were, he evidently could hear the helicopters flying somewhere over the New Port. That was enough for the militia to reposition a 23mm near the New Port and start shooting at the source of the noise. The enemy gunner had plenty of targets—my aircraft, Metheny's scout helicopter, and the two Cobras.

A soldier viewing the engagement from the airfield said it "was a double-barreled stream of fire. The rounds shot straight out over New Port, and about 500 meters after tracer burnout they would airburst in a white explosion." This engagement took place several kilometers south of National Street and the crash sites.

Metheny didn't waste any time relocating his attack team southwest of the airfield, and we pushed farther out from the airfield and over the ocean.

I've never been fond of flying over the ocean, and I thought that second only to the nightmare that Bill David's Golden Dragons and the TF were experiencing in the middle of Mogadishu would be crashing and spending the night battling the rough surf and predators of the Indian

Ocean. Therefore flying over the churning sea brought me little comfort. The ocean had already claimed six UN personnel from shark attacks, and the sharks didn't discriminate in their prey. Their victims ranged from a Swedish nurse to a Russian helicopter pilot. The fifth shark attack had been in late September, the victim being SP4 Edward J. Nicholas of Houston, Texas, a Falcon Brigade soldier who failed to follow an order.[5]

This night there would be little problem with U.S. soldiers following orders. David's force was consolidated, and his efforts were now directed toward securing the sixty-plus armored vehicles strung out along National Street and up to the Ranger perimeter, and the Herculean effort to dislodge Wolcott's remains from the twisted wreckage. One of the teams accompanying the 10th Mountain soldiers brought a battery-powered super-saw for cutting metal, but it proved no match for the collapsed airframe. They were still unable to free his body. In frustration, the soldiers tugged and pulled as they applied their brute strength against the contorted alloy. The fuselage and pilots' console were wrapped around and into Wolcott's lower body.

The southern crash site was clear, as was all of the terrain south of National Street. The only things left were the wreckage of Super 64, four disabled Condor APCs, and the still missing Gordon, Shughart, and the MH-60 crew. With crash site two clear, Matthews directed all of his aviation support to the northern crash site.

The airspace south of National Street free of TF 160 helicopters allowed Gore's aviators to maneuver into positions where they could destroy the four abandoned APCs. It was important that we leave nothing behind of any use. As it was, we were short Super 64 and her crew.

The night advantage was about to slip away. The cloak of darkness would soon give way to a bright African sun, and the militia's erratic and inaccurate fire would have a better chance of finding a target. At 5:15 A.M., the faint luminescence from a sun still beyond the horizon was just beginning to radiate. There was no breeze, and a thin layer of brown-gray dust, smoke, and propellant hung low over the center of Mogadishu. Despite a night of fighting the city was beginning to stir, and David, his soldiers, and the Rangers were smack-dab in the middle of the million residents.

The soldiers, exhausted and nearly out of ideas, finally attached a nylon cargo strap to a Humvee and then wrapped it around Wolcott's body. It worked. With Wolcott's remains secure, Meyerowich and the Rangers had accomplished what they had set out to do—*leave no one behind.* Now it was a race against Mother Nature's clock, the sun. The

14th Infantry and the Rangers started loading the APCs to make the dash to friendly lines.

Notes

1. CPT Christopher Hornbarger, "TF Raven's Role on 3 October," December 1993, p. 11.

2. "The Charge of the Light Division," *Watertown Daily Times,* 20 October 1994, p. G3.

3. Ibid., p. 6.

4. The extraordinary physical and mental demands Lieutenant Colonel David placed on his battalion during predeployment training at Fort Drum resulted in soldiers able to cope with the rigors and demands of prolonged close combat.

5. General Montgomery had issued an order prohibiting swimming in the ocean shortly after the first occurrence. Unfortunately, there were those who chose to disregard the order and accepted the risk of getting attacked. Nicholas was a turbine engine mechanic assigned to H Company, 159th Aviation Regiment, an Intermediate Maintenance Company that was part of TF Raven. Nicholas was with two buddies, and after spending the better part of the day filling sandbags, they decided to stop by a beach located within the confines of the airfield security. The beach was designated for sunbathing only, but the soldiers decided to take a swim. They were wading in the surf when suddenly Nicholas yelled, "Shark! Shark!" Nicholas's comrades immediately started toward the shoreline when Nicholas pleaded, "Don't leave me! Don't leave me!" Those were his last words. The terrified soldiers abruptly turned around and grabbed for their wounded friend, who was engulfed in a plume of blood. For a moment, they were in a tug-of-war with the shark. Finally, the two soldiers were able to free Nicholas from the grasp of the shark's bite, but not before the creature had inflicted its fatal wounds. In less than 4 feet of water, the shark's first bite had taken most of Nicholas's calf muscle. The second attack ripped away his thigh muscle and a portion of his buttock. He lost consciousness from his profuse loss of blood. Nicholas was taken to the Romanian hospital located at the airfield. He received a large infusion of blood and was eventually transported to the U.S. field hospital. Fifty-six units of blood and hours later, he was prepared for evacuation to Germany. A week later, Specialist Nicholas, who never regained consciousness, died with his bride of 2 months and his mother at his bedside. It is such a tragedy that the young soldier paid the ultimate price for not following orders.

8

"MOGADISHU MILE"

Look at an infantryman's eyes and you can tell how much war he
has seen.
                              —*Bill Mauldin,* cartoonist

General Montgomery had directed the Pakistani contingent to prepare
the athletic stadium on 21 October Road for the returning rescue
force. The stadium was home for a Pakistani infantry battalion and was
referred to as the "Paki" stadium. He also directed the Pakistanis to secure
the route from Checkpoint 207 back to the stadium. Meanwhile, Gore had
placed four Black Hawks on standby for the evacuation of wounded upon
their return.

The UNOSOM II medical community, led by U.S. physicians, had
been forced into a mass-casualty drill 10 hours earlier because of the
number of wounded received from the afternoon encounters. Now, on
4 October, they were readying for the influx of new casualties. Anyone
who had any medical training was assigned a function as medical
teams were formed, priorities were established, and preparations were
made. The medical leadership had had the foresight to request a
standby Air Force C-141 Medevac aircraft that was on strip alert near
Cairo. It made the 5-hour journey and arrived in Mogadishu by first
light. It would be used to transport the most seriously wounded to medical facilities in Germany.

The Lightfighters and Rangers were loading the Malaysian Condor
APCs near the perimeter with the dead and wounded. There were more
people than vehicles, so many of the dead were placed on top of the armored vehicles. It was a morbid sight—the soiled white UN vehicles
with corpses stacked on top. Some bodies were missing pieces and
others did not resemble a cadaver. The able-bodied formed into two
columns as they escorted the vehicles down the roadway, using the

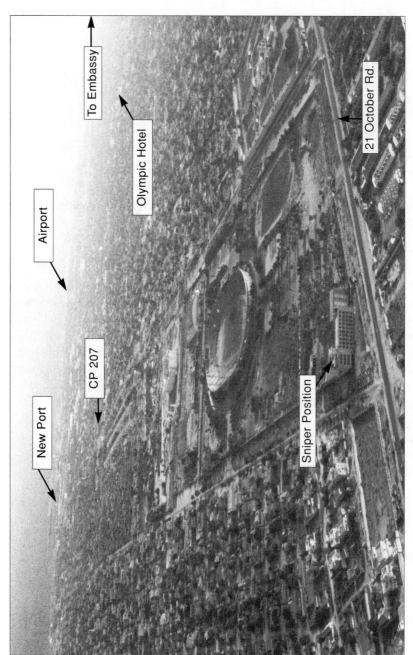

Pakastani stadium

armored personnel carriers as protection as they passed the Olympic Hotel. At least that is how it went until the vehicles operated by nervous Malaysian drivers quickly outpaced the soldiers. The sniping was sporadic as the surviving troopers scurried toward National Street and the waiting column of armored vehicles.

Overhead, the Little Birds continued low passes to suppress any sign of enemy fire on the retreating force. At one point, the AH-6s started receiving a concentration of 23mm antiaircraft fire coming from a courtyard just north of National Street. The fire was ineffective, but threatening nonetheless. Bandit 15, an OH-58A observation helicopter, crewed by CW2 Jeff Fraher and SGT Jeff Webb and his attack helicopter team, was repositioning south of National Street to destroy the abandoned Condors when the crew observed the origin of the antiaircraft fire. Brief coordination between Gore and Matthews resulted in the Little Birds' repositioning to the north of 21 October Road, thus allowing Fraher and his guns to engage the lethal intimidation.

Fraher directed his wingman, a Cobra crewed by 1LT Chris Lynch and CW2 Tom Haskell, toward the target. Their first pass on the target resulted in two misplaced rockets. Haskell, concerned about collateral damage, conducted his second attack employing his 20mm cannon. He approached the courtyard low and fast and with deadly accuracy. His third pass ensured that the antiaircraft gun would not be a threat again. Matthews's AH-6s returned to their close-in support of the withdrawing Lightfighters, Rangers, and special operators.

When Meyerowich and his comrades turned onto National Street, all hell broke loose. The militia and their sympathizers had regrouped and positioned themselves along the street. They were engaging the Americans in one final battle with everything they had. The soldiers started piling into and onto the Condors, and on the few command-and-control Humvees in the rescue force. Some of the Humvees had ten to fifteen soldiers dangling from them, but with the shortage of vehicles there was no alternative.

Lieutenant Colonel David looked to his TF Ranger liaison officer, MAJ Craig Nixon, to confirm through the Ranger's radio channels that everyone was accounted for. Once given the thumbs up, David directed Meyerowich to withdraw. David's task force began the race through the gauntlet of Somali fire toward Checkpoint 207. The troops would later refer to the sprint as the "Mogadishu mile." Suddenly, Brigadier General Gile's voice broke into David's command net alerting him to Rangers who were literally running for their lives to catch up to the speeding column that had left them behind.[1] This took everyone by surprise.

Located at Task Force Ranger's tactical operations center (TOC), Gile had the advantage of an observation helicopter monitoring the rescue from a safe distance and transmitting the television image to the TOC.

David immediately halted his force to wait for the trailing Rangers, while several lead vehicles with nervous coalition drivers opted to continue on to the Paki stadium. The convoy was still under heavy fire from both sides of the street. Finally, with the trailing Rangers on board, the last element of the rescue force sped past Checkpoint 207 and on to the safety of the stadium a couple of kilometers away. Matthews's AH-6 Little Birds provided aerial security all the way.

Chief Warrant Officer Fraher and his two Cobras returned to deal with the four abandoned Condors APCs, which were at two separate locations. It was after 6 A.M., and the sun was well above the horizon. The rays of sunshine filtered through the smoke and haze that continued to hang motionless over the battle area. The Cobras initially engaged near the vehicles with their 20mm cannon to disperse the hundreds of Somalis, who were scavenging anything of value. Minutes later, the two gunships placed eight TOW missiles into the hulls of the Condors, producing a huge fireball and rendering them useless.

At 6:32 A.M., fourteen and a half hours after Private First Class Rodriguez had slid down the fast-rope from the hovering Black Hawk, the Rangers were finally able to enjoy the safety and security of the stadium sanctuary. And for Bill David and his 14th Infantry, it was the culmination of 13 frustrating and hard-fought hours rescuing their stranded comrades.

David was relieved he had everyone accounted for and lamented that he "felt terrible about the guys who gave their lives." He later reminisced, "I knew what had happened that night was something really big. I just didn't know how big."

The odor of cordite and burning debris lingered in the air as the Paki stadium resembled a scene from the movie classic, *Gone with the Wind*, where the wounded lay in the smoldering aftermath of Sherman's march through Atlanta. With the black and gray smoke billowing from the battlefield just streets away, the cluttered arena was filled with the body bags of the dead, while the doctors triaged the wounded. Dispersed throughout the stadium were the exhausted soldiers whose pale faces reflected the anguish and horror they had experienced. They had the thousand-mile stare. Little was said between these brave young warriors, for they had lived through a hell that night—one known only to them.

These troopers had seen it all, and one of their aviation comrades, a Cobra pilot, 1LT Bob Kokorda, expressed his admiration for these selfless foot soldiers in a letter to his parents. "In retrospect, I realized that no matter how intense it was in our cockpit, it became blindingly obvious that the soldiers on the ground had been in the very center of Hell. . . . I gained the utmost respect for the United States infantry."[2]

Matthews's MH-60s, along with Gore's UH-60s and UH-1 Medevac aircraft, were shuttling the wounded from the stadium to the 46th Combat Support Hospital (CSH) and to the airfield. Those transported to the airfield were stabilized and readied for their journey to Germany. The MH-60s were also retrieving the Rangers and Delta operators and returning them to the airfield. Later that morning David and his troopers returned to their start point, the university compound. Some went directly by helicopter and others by vehicle, taking a route through the desert north of Mogadishu and away from any further hostility. The 30-minute drive seemed like hours to the exhausted and anxious Golden Dragons.

The fight was over, and the city reflected the hustle and bustle of an ordinary day in Mogadishu. A layer of pollution still permeated the air above the city. Throughout the urban landscape, there were structures smoldering from errant rounds that had randomly left few areas of the city untouched by the night's events.

My lips were chapped and my mouth was cotton dry. Sitting on the helicopter's nylon troop seat with my head down, back arched, and forearms resting upon my knees, I glanced over at Lee Gore and wondered if I appeared as tired as he did. The lines in his face were pronounced, and his sunken eyes were bloodshot and accentuated by dark rings. I suppose we both looked well beyond our years at that moment. What Bill David and his troops looked and felt like, I could only imagine. Lee looked at me and said," Sir, are you ready to call it a day?" I responded, "Yep!"

Notes

1. Brigadier General Gile did not exert his presence. He successfully worked the seams and filled in the gaps whenever he saw a need.

2. CPT Christopher Hornbarger, "TF Raven's Role on 3 October," December 1993, p. 12.

9

AFTERMATH

This was no police action. It was fucking war.
—*Sergeant First Class Richard Knight*
2d Battalion, 14th Infantry Regiment

Mohammed Farah Aideed was not captured. In fact, he was nowhere near the Olympic Hotel or the target building when Task Force Ranger swooped down on the clandestine gathering. But detaining a number of his key lieutenants inflicted a blow to Aideed's movement, and their absence was felt.

It was a costly battle, but, considering the reactive nature of the operation, the urban environment, and intensity and length of the fighting, casualties could have been far worse. A total of twenty U.S. and coalition soldiers were killed and eighty-eight wounded. Task Force Ranger sustained sixteen killed in action and fifty-seven wounded in action. The QRF sustained one soldier killed in action (Martin) and one died of wounds (Houston), while twenty-two others were wounded in action. Twelve of the twenty-two QRF soldiers were returned to duty. Our coalition partners paid a price as well: the Malaysians had two soldiers killed in action and seven wounded, while the Pakistanis incurred two wounded.

In all fairness to the coalition soldiers who fought alongside their American brethren, they served above and beyond the call of duty. I have heard much criticism about their performance over the years, but at the risk of being labeled a hypocrite I say the fact remains they were there when they were needed.

I once overheard a couple of U.S. soldiers disparaging the coalition soldiers for their performance the night of 3–4 October. I asked them point-blank, "Would you pull your infantry out of your Bradley fighting vehicles and not only replace them with Malaysian soldiers, but place the Bradley and M1 tanks under the control of a Pakistani commander for the purpose of rescuing Pakistani and Malaysian soldiers? Think about it, would American soldiers do that?" They said no more. Despite the difficulties encountered, we owe much to those two armies.

The number of SNA militiamen and sympathizers killed or wounded ranged from 500 to 1,500, depending on whom you listened to. Because of his accessibility to the SNA leadership shortly after the fight, Rick Atkinson's published Somali casualty figures probably represent the most accurate estimates—312 killed and 814 wounded. Whatever the numbers, there was little doubt that the blood flowed freely in the streets of Mogadishu on the night of 3–4 October.

There were plenty of heroes then, and the awards and medals would come later. The most coveted recognition an infantryman can earn is the Combat Infantryman's Badge (CIB). It signifies that you have been in combat and exposed to hostile fire. Army Regulation 600-8-22 specifies that "a recipient must be personally present and under hostile fire while serving in an assigned infantry or special forces primary duty, in a unit actively engaged in ground combat with the enemy." Bill David was judicious with his recommendations for who should receive the recognition. If you weren't directly engaged in the fight that night, you did not qualify. Most commanders would have blanket-issued the badge for their entire unit. Desert Storm reflected such abuses, where entire battalions were awarded the prestigious recognition without even crossing the Saudi Arabian border into Iraq.

David did want to make an exception to the regulation for an officer who had seen combat in an earlier operation. A Chemical Corps lieutenant, Mike Rogney, was the platoon leader for 2d Platoon, Bravo Company, 2-14th Infantry. David had deviated from the norm and assigned Rogney as a platoon leader some 10 months earlier because "he was such a 'stud' with loads of innate leadership ability." An older officer, he had prior enlisted service and was seasoned beyond his years.

Rogney and his soldiers experienced combat on 13 September during an intense firefight near the Madina hospital, where the young lieutenant proved time and again that he possessed the mettle of a combat infantryman. Bravo Company had three soldiers wounded in action that day—one of them was another platoon leader. Lieutenant Rogney's troops would receive the CIB, but he would not. He had been leading a platoon whose men had fought for their lives and our army could not see fit to bend the rules. Much to the misfortune of Lieutenant Rogney, the army regulation stipulates that "personnel with other than an infantry or special forces MOS are not eligible, regardless of the circumstances. . . . Commanders are not authorized to make any exception to this policy." I fully supported Bill David in his request for an exception to the regulation feeling that if there was ever a soldier who deserved the recognition, it was Mike Rogney. The JTF commander later denied the request. Rogney had to pay for the past abuses in faraway lands where soldiers had received the CIB without a shot fired in anger and an inflexible regulation. Ironically, all he'd wanted to do was become an infantry officer.

We continued with heightened security at our compounds. In the aftermath of the action we could be considered vulnerable, so it was essential to remain vigilant. I knew we had hurt Aideed and his SNA followers, but I refused to underestimate what they were capable of doing. To ensure that we were prepared to continue our mission, Bravo Company of the Golden Dragons became the ground QRC.

With our security concerns satisfied, my attention shifted to our wounded. Sergeant Major Brown was already at the field hospital. Like Brown, I had to visit the wounded soldiers. I passed through our operations center and headed for the 46th CSH. The 46th CSH was a maze of environmentally controlled tents that were all connected to form the hospital, and if you didn't have instructions or a guide, it was easy to get lost.

I was led to a ward where many of the troops were recovering from surgery. The arched tent was filled to capacity with soldiers in various states of consciousness. I approach a young Asian American lying in a bed. His left arm had a transparent intravenous tube; his legs were bandaged, as was his right arm and hand. The bandages were stained with blood and a yellowish disinfectant that all contrasted with the sterile white coverings. His faded blue medical gown was open at the top exposing cuts and tears to his upper chest and lower neck. His face was bruised and marred by superficial gashes and scrapes, and his left eye was blackened. The teenage soldier's dark eyes were not of a naive 19-year-old, but of someone much older who had seen more than most. I reached out and grabbed his left hand. I squeezed it and asked how he was doing. The energy in his response startled me. He burst out with, "A lot better than most of these guys—sir! Did we kick their ass? Huh, sir. Did we kick their ass?" I paused and thought, "Where do these guys come from?" Controlling my emotions and with a strained voice, I responded, "Yea! We kicked their ass."

What magnificent soldiers. It was never more evident than at that moment, that these troopers from places like Long Beach, California; Davenport, Iowa; and Reading, Massachusetts are what make our army and our country the best in the world.

That afternoon, I found myself standing at attention on the airport tarmac across from Major General Garrison and his commanders as we paid tribute to our dead soldiers' remains being loaded onto an awaiting C-141 transport for their journey home. It was a warm, sunny day with an occasional gust of wind blowing across the apron from the ocean. The wooden staffs bearing the American flag and unit colors flexed in the breeze and pulled at the flag bearers as they stood perfectly erect. All the U.S. leadership was present for this solemn tribute, and everyone's face reflected the anguish of the moment. One by one, the aluminum alloy containers were marched between Garrison and me by soldiers who had volunteered to make the last walk with their comrades. We held our salutes until the last container had passed through the aircraft's large aft clamshell doors and was secured on the plane's floor. It was a moment I shall never forget.

Back in the United States, the citizens and politicians were in an uproar. The vivid images captured on video of U.S. service members' naked and battered bodies being dragged through the streets of Mogadishu were flashed on televisions across the country, bringing the brutality and savagery into everyone's home.[1] The news coverage provoked repulsion and visceral reactions. The graphic coverage had a chilling effect on our country, with this single event captured on film bringing the entire nation to its feet.

The battle of 3 and 4 October ignited a heated debate and calls for the immediate withdrawal of U.S. forces from Somalia. Critics of our involvement reacted sharply to the incident. Senator Robert Byrd (Democrat-West Virginia), one of the more vocal opponents, said, "Americans by the dozens are paying with their lives and limbs for a misplaced policy." The home support for any type of mission in Somalia was crumbling.

On this day, foreign policy was at the forefront of U.S. politics and at the core of every American's conversation. Although Americans were dying in Somalia, an even more ominous scenario was unfolding in Russia. President Boris Yeltsin's leadership was being challenged, and his failure could have more far-reaching affects on world affairs than Somalia. The 2-week standoff between Yeltsin and former Vice President Alexander Rutskoi, barricaded in the parliament building, finally flared into violence. Moscow turned into an open-air shooting range for Rutskoi's ragtag army of Communists, neo-Nazis, and just plain hooligans dedicated to restoring the old Soviet Union. On Monday 4 October, President Yeltsin responded by shelling the parliament building and quashing the rebellion.

But despite the world's attention to events in Russia, U.S. Congress leaders were asking why we were in Somalia in the first place, and demanding to know why there was no U.S. armor in theater. Because of his denial 10 days earlier to the request by the field commander for armor forces, Secretary of Defense Les Aspin was openly criticized and there were bipartisan calls for his resignation.

After two decades of brainstorming over defense spending and theoretical war in the House, Aspin was facing his first real-life test—and some in the Pentagon and in Congress said he flunked. Aspin never did provide a good reason for not approving the armor request, and this and other controversial issues during his stewardship of the Defense Department led to his resignation in January 1994.

During the early morning hours of 4 October, approval was given to dispatch the initial reaction company from the 24th Infantry Division at Fort Stewart, Georgia, to Mogadishu. The company was a mechanized company team consisting of two platoons equipped with Bradley fighting vehicles and an M1 tank platoon. The mechanized unit would arrive $3^1/_2$ days later via C-5 aircraft, and was the first wave of a massive force buildup that would change the complexion of the QRF and how we would conduct future operations.

On Thursday, 7 October, President Clinton placed a mark on the wall. He announced that U.S. forces would be out of Somalia not later than 31 March 1994. At the same time, he vowed that he would not "cut and run" from the war-torn country. Clinton demonstrated his resolve by approving a force that would double the number of troops on Somalia soil and position large numbers off shore. The additional army soldiers would triple the size of the brigade. Along with our brigade, a joint special operations task force (JSOTF) and a PSYOPS task force would come under the operational control of a joint task force (JTF) headquarters yet to be formed.

The JTF, referred to as JTF-Somalia, would, when directed, have tactical control (TACON) of Commander Task Group (CTG) 156.1 composed of the navy aircraft carrier USS *America* battle group; CTG 156.3 with the helicopter carrier USS *New Orleans;* and Commander Task Force 158, built around the 13th Marine Expeditionary Unit. The naval forces included 7,084 sailors and 1,996 marines for a total of 9,080 additional service members at the JTF commander's disposal. There would be plenty of combat power in theater, but it wasn't there yet.

While the politicians were debating the merits of the president's decision, the army forces readying for deployment, and the navy/marines steaming toward Somalia, we were still in the thick of it. Monday night remained relatively quiet, but Tuesday night saw sporadic fighting and mortar fire. Our pilots performing the Eyes over Mogadishu mission were busy flying from one compound to the next responding to potential perimeter penetrations. Although it never materialized, there was an intelligence report that an assault on one of our compounds was imminent.

We were flying our OH-58D aircraft entirely during the hours of darkness. Between this reliable flying observation platform and two ground-based telescopic FLIR-equipped sensors called "Night Stalker" (not to be confused with the special operations TF-160 Night Stalkers), we were able to keep an eye on most of the trouble areas. We employed the OH-58D in a high hover between 800 and 1,000 feet above secure terrain, which usually meant over a compound. We were concerned with the single-engine capability of the aircraft and vulnerability to ground fire. These tactics gave the pilot a secure place to land in the event of an engine failure or mechanical problem, as well as protecting the aircraft from taking an unwanted round in the belly. I would be damned if we'd have a repeat of Sunday's events.

Hovering a helicopter over unsecured terrain had always been a concern of mine. Army field manuals over the years have depicted scout and attack helicopters hovering near a ridge line or hill mass, engaging the flank of the approaching enemy armored column. Every exercise I had ever participated in, with the exception of my training at the Army's Joint Readiness Training Center, seemed to conveniently assume away anyone who might be below your aircraft. It makes little difference if you are over trees or buildings, you don't know what is underneath unless a "friendly" force is occupying the ground. The "zipping" in and out of terrain that isn't secured by the infantry is mighty risky, unless you are in the middle of the desert. In the desert, as demonstrated during Desert Storm, the aviator has the latitude to hover and pause over the dirt below and know what is beneath and to the flanks of his aircraft.

The lesson of secure terrain came to me as a flash of the obvious when I was a young captain. As I occupied the front seat of a G-model Cobra during the annual Team Spirit exercise in Korea, my copilot and I were working our way up a meandering gully toward an attack position.[2] He was at the controls and I was navigating, directing him through the mountainous terrain by taking cues from a map folded on my lap, when I glanced diagonally 20 feet above our rotor disk toward a ridge sprinkled with scrub. To my dismay, I saw an aggressor soldier nonchalantly set his C-rations down and pick up his M16 rifle and point it at us. I could see that the soldier was simulating firing his rifle by his jerking motion that replicated the weapon's recoil. There was no way to validate the engagement, but I knew that had it been for real, one Cobra would be lying on its side at the bottom of the gulch with two dead aviators. It was an encounter that produced some insight.

Wednesday, 6 October, started out as a typically warm Somalia day. It later turned ugly. TF Ranger, which was jammed into the old hangar at the airfield, was the object of a late afternoon mortar attack. First reports reflected the uncertainty about the origin of the attack or the weapon employed: it was either an RPG fired indirectly or a mortar. It turned out to be a single mortar round and it was lethal.

Thirteen soldiers from TF Ranger received wounds; one—SFC Matthew L. Rierson, a Delta operator from Nevada, Iowa—died later. Among the wounded was a Special Forces medical officer, MAJ John O. "Bob" Marsh. Marsh, the son of the former Army Secretary John O. Marsh Jr., had an artery severed in his leg. Although this was a serious injury, he would fully recover and, like his fellow soldiers, would bear the scars of the jagged metal fragments from the mortar's warhead.

Our brigade was equipped with the highly accurate AN/TPQ-36 Firefinder weapon-locating radar (which we referred to as the Q36). The Q36 is a countermortar radar system designed to track high-angle trajectories, specifically mortar-type targets. The manufacturer's literature gives the system's range as 18–24 kilometers, but our area of concern was much closer. This radar has a stationary antenna that sweeps a rapid sequence of beams along the horizon, forming an electronic radar curtain over a 90-degree area. Any high-angle round penetrating this curtain triggers an immediate verification beam; upon verification, an automatic tracking sequence begins and the target's origin is determined. Also, the system has the capacity to track and determine multiple targets. We had two Q36s positioned at the extremes of the airfield, and this positioning afforded us complete coverage of our compounds and a view of Mogadishu. We received a third system later as a backup.

The soldiers who physically manned the system and worked in the target acquisition cell in the brigade headquarters were good. They could pinpoint the origin of a mortar round in a matter of seconds. Our challenge was to quickly neutralize or destroy the mortar and its crew, which was nearly impossible. Although we had clearance for countermortar fire with the 2-14th Infantry's 81mm mortars, their use was only preapproved for two locations habitually used by the militia. The sites were preapproved targets because they were in the center of large open fields providing little chance for collateral damage. But the militia's tactic for mortar employment was simple. They would hurriedly erect their mortar in some innocent party's backyard, fire no more than four to six rounds, and quickly disperse.

There was little we could do. With a continual helicopter presence overhead, we were able to get eyes on the mortar sites quickly, but normally not quick enough. I know of two incidents where we were able to eliminate the mortar after the fact. Once, during the dark of night, a Special Forces soldier, equipped with night optics and a Barrett .50-caliber sniper rifle suspended from the troop compartment ceiling of a Black Hawk, was able to place a couple of armor-piercing rounds through the tube of an abandoned 120mm mortar, rendering it useless. The mortar crew fled in haste upon hearing the approaching helicopter. The second success was a Cobra's using its 20mm cannon to shoot a fleeing mortar crew shortly after the militia had fired the mortar. (The latter incident was in response to the Wednesday attack on the task force hangar.)

The lone mortar round that struck the Rangers' living area came from the Madina (Wadajir) district. This Mogadishu suburb was north of the airfield and adjacent to the university and embassy compounds. Madina's residents were of the Abgal clan, adversaries of the Habr Gidr SNA loyalists. (The United Nations had once had living quarters in the district, as did some of the contributing nations.) After our target acquisition cell had provided the mortar's location, one of our airborne Cobra gunships was promptly dispatched to Madina to ferret out and destroy the perpetrators.

During this Cobra-mortar engagement, I received my first lesson on the operational challenges presented by the press. En route from the operations center to Jaybird helipad, I stopped by my office to retrieve my gear. On the television near the desk was CNN "World News." I noticed that the screen depicted a colored illustration of the Horn of Africa, highlighting Somalia; the country was portrayed in light brown with the adjacent Indian Ocean and the Red Sea in blue. In the upper right corner of the screen was a still photograph of the reporter doing the talking, Tom Watkins of the Toronto *Star.* Watkins had been bouncing around among Kenya, Ethiopia, and Somalia for some time, and he had the distinction of being the only Western reporter within hundreds of miles during this tense period. Meanwhile, the remainder of the Western press corps was still trying to figure out how to get back to Somalia.

The world media had abandoned the country after the 12 July killing of four journalists by an angry crowd. The correspondents had been trying to cover the story of the QRF's heliborne attack on the Abdi House, an SNA command and control center, when an unruly crowd surrounded the reporters, bludgeoned them to death, and then displayed their bodies for the television cameras.

Watkins was the lone holdover, and during the mortar attack on the Rangers he was in downtown Mogadishu reporting via his satellite connection to a CNN anchor. The dialogue went something like the following. "Well, Tom, what's going on over there?" Watkins responded, "There has been some type of attack down at the airfield. I believe there have been causalities." As I listened to Watkins, I heard from my doorway the thump, thump, thump from a Cobra's 20mm cannon. (Although the rules of engagement [ROE] allowed the pilot to employ his turret weapon at his discretion providing the ROE parameters were met, I knew I would be receiving a call on my field telephone from the TOC reporting the engagement.)

No sooner did the attack helicopter's burst of 20mm stop than Watkins excitedly exclaimed on the TV, "Wait a minute! There is a Cobra helicopter firing its 20mm machine gun over in the Madina district." Just as Watkins was through with his outburst, my field phone rang and it was MAJ John Bendyk: "Sir, one of our Cobras just engaged a mortar position in the Madina district." I responded sarcastically, "You're late, John, turn on CNN and you can get the grid coordinates."

Watkins' voice report had traveled via satellite to CNN headquarters in Atlanta, and then the voice and image were retransmitted via a satellite to my television in Mogadishu—quicker than the Cobra pilot less than a kilometer away could report to me through our operations center. As a field commander, it is difficult to compete with that level of responsiveness. If the commander in chief himself was watching the news report along with the rest of the world, he knew where the attack originated before my operations officer. But despite the split-second transmissions beamed back inside the Beltway, the president's attention was on finding a reputable negotiator for the mess in Somalia.

In Washington President Clinton appointed Robert Oakley as his emissary. As a former ambassador to Somalia from 1982 to 1984, and having recently enjoyed diplomatic success during the UN Task Force (UNITAF) period, he was more than qualified. The outspoken Oakley knew Somalia, its people, and the culture better than most. On 10 October he arrived in Mogadishu as Aideed, seizing on a sudden about-face in U.S. policy, said he wanted a cease-fire with UN forces. The United Nations and the United States did not agree to Aideed's unilateral cease-fire, so from their perspective it was business as usual—but it really was not.

Notes

1. The Somalis desecrated the bodies of all five Americans slain near Super 64. It was later determined that they had been shot dead before their corpses were defiled.

2. Team Spirit was an annual, spring training exercise involving U.S. and Korean forces. The exercise was terminated in 1993 to enhance relations with North Korea.

10

THE CAVALRY ARRIVES

There is unmatched power in the synergistic capabilities of joint operations.

—*General Gordon R. Sullivan,*
Chief of Staff of the Army (1991–1995)

The first battalion-size reinforcement to arrive in Mogadishu was the 10th Mountain Division's 2d Battalion, 22d Infantry. These Light-fighters quickly fell in on the many U.S. compounds throughout the area of operation to provide added security and force protection. LTC Eric Smith, a talented, dynamic young infantry officer who had a propensity for detail, commanded the light infantry battalion known as the Triple Deuce. I referred to Eric as "Task Master," a nickname I got from one of his officers.

Shortly after the arrival of Eric's outfit, the special operations community had dispatched four AC-130 Spectre gunships to Mombasa, Kenya. These heavily armed aircraft can reach out of the sky and touch an enemy with deadly accuracy using its 105mm howitzer, 40mm cannon, or 20mm Gatling gun. On 10 October 1993, an AC-130 demonstrated its lethality by thumping derelict weapons in a former SNA weapons storage compound north of the city. The site was purposely selected because its close proximity to Mogadishu afforded the city's residents a view of the destructive capability that could rain from the sky.

The AC-130 was feared and respected by the SNA, and it was a comfort to us on the ground. The deadly aircraft had been in theater once before, shortly after the June ambush of the Pakistani soldiers, but the scarce resource had soon departed for more pressing assignments. When I would walk out of the operations center or my "hooch" on a starlit night, I would listen overhead for the low monotone hum of the aircraft's four turbo-prop engines as its crew orbited a few thousand feet above and acted as our airborne guardian.

Even with Spectre overhead, I still slept with my 9mm pistol at my
side and a concussion or "stun" grenade within arm's reach of my cot.[1]
I really didn't know whether anyone really cared about killing or
snatching me, but Major General Montgomery had a price on his head,
so I only assumed as the QRF commander I might too. One day, I saw
a Somali who could have passed for Aideed's twin brother near my living area. It wasn't him, but just the thought, along with the presence
of so many Somali workers moving freely inside the compound,
brought me little comfort in our security arrangement. Any non-Amer-
ican in our area was always escorted, but with fifteen-plus nations represented on the embassy grounds, Somali workers were everywhere.

Lieutenant Colonel Smith's outfit was followed by Task Force 1-64
(1st Battalion, 64th Armored Regiment, 24th Infantry Division), commanded by LTC Robert Clark. Clark, a conscientious armor officer, worked hard
educating me on M2 Bradley Fighting Vehicles and M1 Abrams tanks. My
previous experiences in five infantry divisions, three of them light, one
motorized, and one a composite in Korea, had hardly prepared me to deal
with the maintenance nuances of the heavy firepower. Terms like *Florida
plate* when discussing the steel plate that secures the front drive-wheel of
an M9 armored combat earthmover (ACE) vehicle and acronyms like
UCOFT (unit conduct of fire trainer) became part of my vernacular.

Task Force 1-64 was big. Its five armor and mechanized company-
teams, a 155mm self-propelled artillery battery, an engineer company,
and many other supporting elements totaled nearly 1,100 soldiers.

Accompanying TF 1-64 was the 43d Combat Engineer Battalion
(Heavy) from Fort Benning, Georgia.[2] LTC Larry Davis commanded
this diverse battalion. Davis typified the engineer. He was bright, hard
working, and loved making things. I've always admired engineers, especially civil engineers, partly because my father and brother are civil
engineers and partly because I have always felt that engineers can
stand back from their work and view their accomplishments—see the
tangible results of their efforts. On the other hand, I have destroyed
more things than I have made.

The 43d Engineer Battalion had been earmarked for inactivation
when this mission breathed new life into the unit's soldiers. The battalion had the capacity for both vertical and horizontal construction. An
amazing organization, I don't believe there was anything the engineer
troopers couldn't build. I often thought how every brigade commander
should have such an engineer battalion at his disposal.

LTC Jack Weiss and his 46th Support Battalion were augmented
with a robust slice from the 24th Infantry Division to support the influx

The author (front row, 2d from right) and his battalion commanders

of armor. Jack and his Lightfighter support troops would have their hands full with the heavy force, but nothing they couldn't handle.

Larry Davis and his battalion's primary mission was to construct a base in the middle of the desert to house themselves and the 1,100-plus soldiers of TF 1-64. The site selected was an abandoned Soviet anti aircraft missile site about 4 miles north of Mogadishu. The location afforded 360 degrees cleared of any obstructions, and a place from which the highly mobile force could rapidly enter the city from any number of approaches. In 30 days' time, Davis and his engineer troops cleared the area of discarded antiaircraft missiles and erected the compound, appropriately named Victory Base after the 24th ("Victory") Division.

Not every unit had been preparing for the upcoming months in Somalia. One in particular was heading home, many of its soldiers thinking not soon enough. On 17 October, just 51 days after they had set foot in Somalia, the men of Task Force Ranger boarded C-5 transports and departed Mogadishu just as they had arrived—with no fanfare or speeches. The Rangers, special ops aviators, and Delta operators were there one day and gone the next, leaving behind a few sandbagged aircraft revetments and a deserted hangar. Just days before, Major General Garrison had sent a handwritten note to President Clinton accepting full responsibility for the actions of 3 October.

By early November, the 10th Aviation Brigade headquarters had shed the designation of QRF and became known as the Falcon Brigade. It had grown to six battalions with more than 3,600 soldiers equipped with thirty Abrams tanks, forty-eight Bradley Fighting Vehicles, eight 155mm self-propelled howitzers, fifty helicopters, and more than 800 assorted pieces of rolling stock.

The Somalia QRF mission was a historic milestone for army aviation. On 27 July the nucleus of the aviation brigade headquarters had been deployed to Somalia. The brigade headquarters assumed command of the QRF mission on 7 August from the 10th Mountain's 2d Infantry Brigade headquarters. Acceptance of the mission represented the first time ground maneuver forces were placed under the direct command of an aviation headquarters during combat operations. Since the inception of the army's aviation branch in April 1983, aviation leadership had touted the aviation brigade headquarters as the division commander's fourth maneuver headquarters, attempting to place it on equal footing with the infantry and armor maneuver brigades. Our doctrine supported the use of the aviation headquarters in this manner, and some commands exercised their fourth maneuver headquarters during division field and command post training.

Despite the doctrine and training exercises, the reality was, and still is, that few commanders exploited the aviation brigade headquarters—some because of their lack of confidence, but most because the headquarters has thin resources, possesses little depth, and lacks some essential staff functions.

The 10th Aviation Brigade, using staff augmentations, overcame these shortcomings. Our headquarters mirrored a separate brigade with everything from a plans shop in the S3 to civil affairs and PSYOPS. This cleared the way for the division leadership to provide the aviation brigade the opportunity in Somalia to operate as a maneuver headquarters, much to the displeasure of some fellow combat arms officers. The skeptics and the critics continue to disseminate their doubt. Infantry Lieutenant Colonel Bolger, in his book entitled *Savage Peace,* writes the following about the aviation headquarters in Somalia and why it was selected for the mission:

> An aviation brigade is not organized or structured as well as other types of maneuver brigades for the command and control of what is, predominantly, a ground maneuver force. Soldiers knew this. But 1st and 2nd Brigades had just done their turns. So, as the books say, 10th Mountain "accepted risk" and put pilots in charge of riflemen.[3]

I was not present when the decision was made to send the aviation brigade headquarters to Somalia and assume the QRF mission, that being well before my time. I do know that because the 10th Mountain Division was a division of two infantry brigades, MG Steve Arnold, the commander, routinely called on his aviation brigade to perform missions that were traditionally reserved for ground maneuver brigades. This occurred during field and command post exercises, as well as the division's deployment in response to Hurricane Andrew in which the aviation brigade was provided a sector of responsibility. The sharing of traditional missions was motivated by a combination of necessity (Arnold was short a brigade) and the trust and confidence he had in my predecessor. It was apparent the leadership and soldiers of the aviation brigade had demonstrated they could do the job.

But in Somalia the brigade headquarters was confronted with another challenge—integrating over 2,000 additional soldiers and three more battalions into the brigade. And along with the added capability, came a realignment of command relationships. The brigade would no longer report directly to Major General Montgomery. JTF-Somalia, commanded by MG Carl F. Ernst, would be layered between Montgomery and myself (Figure 10.1).

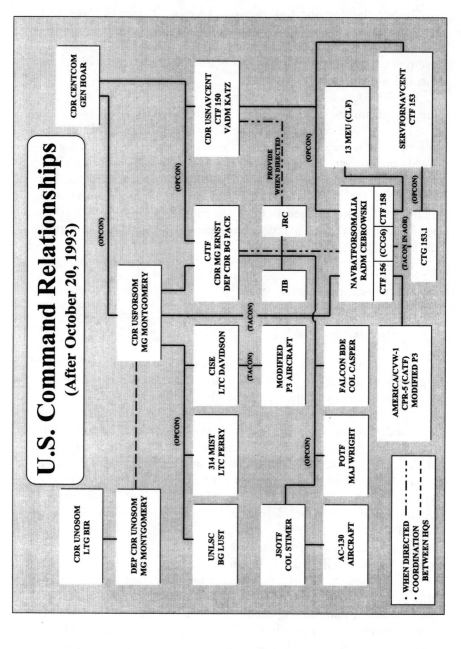

Figure 10.1 U.S. Command Relationships, Somalia (after 20 October 1993)

Ernst had been recently promoted to MG and arrived in late October from the army's Training and Doctrine Command headquarters at Fort Monroe, Virginia. He was a staunch infantryman with both airborne and mechanized infantry experience. With a thin, wiry build and pronounced facial features, Ernst was extremely fit and one of the most technically and tactically competent officers I have met.

The nucleus of Ernst's staff was derived from the 10th Mountain Division, with additions tagged from all four services and all parts of the world. His deputy was Marine Corps Brigadier General Pete Pace, a bright, expressive officer whose demeanor provided a refreshing balance to Ernst's more intense personality. Pace's youthful collegian appearance concealed the many years he had faithfully served the Corps.

One of the more colorful officers on his staff was the J3, Colonel Buck Bedard, a Somalia veteran. Bedard was a hard-charging marine who looked and acted the part. Upon meeting him, you would swear he was the weathered, leatherneck gunnery sergeant from a World War II John Wayne movie. A gravelly voiced, large-framed marine whose biceps always appeared uncomfortably constrained by the tight sleeves of his desert camouflage uniform, Bedard was an officer to be reckoned with. With his usual half-smoked cigar in the corner of his mouth, I viewed him as a marine's marine. He knew his business, and if there was anything you could count on from Buck Bedard, it was that he would "tell it like it is."

En route to Mogadishu, Major General Ernst had traveled through Central Command (CENTCOM) headquarters in Tampa, Florida, where he received his marching orders from General Hoar. I was not privy to what was discussed between the two, but Ernst arrived in country ready for a fight. He immediately energized his staff.

The majority of his staff had arrived earlier under the leadership of a newly appointed chief of staff, COL Zannie O. Smith—a fellow I came to respect and rely heavily upon for advice and counsel. Smith and his staff were dealing with everything from basic living and working arrangements to how the headquarters should be organized and function. We did our part to ease their transition, but it was a hectic time for the JTF headquarters personnel.

Initially the brigade staff had resented the JTF staff. As expected, JTF personnel were viewed as the new guys on the block, asking for everything, telling us what to do, and restricting our access to the UNOSOM II staff—the latter creating the biggest discord. During the previous 3 months, QRF headquarters personnel had walked a couple of hundred yards across the embassy compound to the UNOSOM II headquarters to conduct business with staff counterparts. Now there was another headquarters literally jammed in between, and it irritated the brigade staff like a chipped tooth.

I, too, found myself feeling annoyed and cut off. I was accustomed to talking with General Montgomery daily and attending his morning meetings with my fellow coalition commanders. After the JTF headquarters stood up I rightfully reported to my new boss, but I was no longer on an equal footing with the other twenty-one contingent commanders. General Ernst had that distinction.

I attended Ernst's 5 P.M. daily meeting at his headquarters, which was about 100 meters from the brigade and consisted of a series of mobile trailers lashed together and surrounded by sea-land containers providing force protection. Once inside, you went along long air-conditioned hallways ending in 90-degree turns to another corridor. One of the trailers was designated as the briefing room. During the nightly update, I would sit in the front row along with Ernst, Pace, and U.S. Air Force Colonel Stimer, the JSOTF commander, while to our rear were forty or more straphangers from the staff.

As the briefing officers worked their way down the routine sequence of topics, I always braced for the portion that covered equipment readiness. It was almost humorous, because all of the equipment (twenty or more types) briefed belonged to the Falcon Brigade, with the exception of the AC-130s. In fact, the readiness briefing mirrored my own staff's briefing that had occurred an hour earlier. I could always count on a question or two about the availability of a particular type of vehicle, aircraft, or electronics gear. One day, I leaned over to General Pace and whispered that I thought there were a few thousand marines in theater somewhere, and I wondered why their equipment status wasn't scrutinized? Pace smiled, and at the next day's update marine equipment availability rates were given. I suddenly experienced a significant reduction in questions, while a substantial number were directed to the marine liaison officer. It was also at this forum where I discovered that navy and marine aviation routinely declare "no-fly" days, when no aircraft fly. This was a good example of the culture differences among the services: our aviation flew every day of the 8-month Somalia deployment. For me to declare a no-fly day would have been heresy to the army leadership; Montgomery and Ernst would have strung me up.

Before Ernst's arrival in theater, I had experienced some tension in my relationship with Brigadier General Gile. Because of the volatility of the situation in Mogadishu, Major General Meade had acceded to

Montgomery's request for Gile to remain in theater for a while. With a new commander at the helm of the QRF and the division's reputation on the line, it seemed the prudent thing to do. This was an easy request to support, for Meade made it a point to provide Montgomery with whatever help he needed.

Gile kept his distance from the brigade for a couple of days after the 3 October fight. Gradually he began to exert his influence—a natural thing to do for an operator—and as the force grew, he began attending my staff updates and meetings. It wasn't long before he became the center of attention. General Gile is a quality officer for whom I have the utmost respect, but he was in a tough spot to make things happen. He too was probably frustrated, given the circumstances, but his presence placed me in an even tougher position.

With the imminent arrival of Ernst, Pace already on the ground, and Gile lingering about, Montgomery had more chiefs than Indians. He assured Major General Meade that things were in good hands, and directed Gile's return to Fort Drum.

Among the new arrivals to Somalia were the international media. The brigade had its own media officer, a young Chemical Corps captain, Andy Mazur, working in his functional area of public affairs. Although the news media demanded some of my time and that of my commanders, we found ourselves expending a great deal more personal energy on briefing and escorting the many visitors who were showing a renewed interest in Somalia.

Everyone visited us, from the newly appointed chairman of the Joint Chiefs, Army General John M. Shalikashvili, to a plethora of congressmen and their staffers. It was a distraction, but necessary. I understood the importance of keeping the military and political leadership informed, and we were the right people to do it—not a staff officer at CENTCOM headquarters or a bureaucrat back in the Pentagon. One question habitually asked by the visiting dignitaries was, "What can we do for you?" And invariably the soldiers' response was, "Qualify us for the combat tax exclusion like you are doing in Kuwait." To the visitor they firmly asserted, "We will get that done for you if it's the last thing we do." It never happened!

Senators John Warner (Republican-Virginia) and Carl Levin (Democrat-Michigan) of the Senate Armed Services Committee were two such visitors. They were very much interested in what had occurred on 3 October and the soldiers' morale. Both men were very pleasant, and on a number of occasions throughout their visit they expressed their genuine concern for the troops' well-being. I was flying with the senators and Major General Montgomery from the airport to the embassy when the pilot made an approach into Jaybird from the southwest. This approach took the aircraft over the university complex and near the Swedish hospital. It was a warm, sunny afternoon, and as the aircraft slowed for its approach to land, we all couldn't help notice several of the female Swedish nurses on the roof of the hospital sunbathing topless. This created a bit of a stir in the helicopter troop compartment and a long pause in the conversation as we all did a double-take. I looked at Senator Warner, and we both smiled. I thought he might be thinking, "Just how hard do they really have it over here?" I found out later that the appealing scenery was a routine occurrence and known to the aviators. During subsequent landing approaches into Jaybird I never once influenced which way the pilots landed, but there were a few times I considered it.

The brigade headquarters was busy receiving the follow-on forces. Daylight hours were spent greeting and unloading troops and equipment, which were arriving by air force and charter planes, as well as by ship. Mogadishu was soon bustling with soldiers and equipment, but there were still many areas into which the U.S. forces chose not to venture.

Despite the enclaves we placed off limits for routine movement, it was still very important that we demonstrate our presence. From my days as a young Officer Candidate School student I remembered my company commander, CPT Bob McCredy, saying that "every once in a while you have to flex your muscles to let your soldiers and your enemy know who is in charge. You must have presence!" I viewed presence as self-preservation—as had occurred in mid-October, when the AC-130 fired at decaying war machines on the outskirts of Mogadishu within view of clan elders, and placing tanks and Bradleys at key intersections. Flexing our muscles caused the SNA to think twice about more hostile acts toward Americans.

But we still considered every movement outside of a secure area as a combat operation. It didn't make any difference if you were the chaplain delivering mail or the support platoon leader hauling water, you couldn't exit a compound if you had fewer than three vehicles and two crew-served automatic weapons. I gave to the Headquarters Company soldiers a routine pitch: "When you leave the sanctity of the compound, I want you to think that everyone outside wants a piece of you. Always remain alert, point your weapon at chest level—not in the air or toward the ground—and never look away from the stares of the Somali people. I don't care if they are six or sixty, you don't talk, you don't smile, you don't wave; you show no compassion. You look them straight in the eye like you're going to reach into their chest and rip out their heart." Although a bit melodramatic, my intent was to make our vigilant soldiers appear unapproachable, and the longer we remained in Somalia the more important it became.

On 25 October, Aideed's militiamen and those of rival warlord Ali Mahdi Mohammed clashed for the first time in 19 months. The fierce fighting occurred along Mogadishu's Green Line, which separated the areas controlled by the feuding warlords. It resulted in ten Somalis killed and forty-five wounded. The skirmish in the heart of the city illustrated the further erosion of UN influence in Somalia's affairs.

Aideed was still "wanted" by the UN, but there was little enthusiasm to ferret him out from the center of Mogadishu. With Robert Oakley on the scene as U.S. emissary, the dialogue between the United States, the SNA, and Ali Mahdi Mohammed's United Somalia Congress (USC) was reestablished. The USC and Ali Mahdi were willing to work with either the United States or the United Nations. Aideed, on the other hand, wanted nothing to do with the United Nations.

Back in the United States the first political casualty was the State Department's Robert Gosende, special envoy to Somalia. Gosende strongly supported the policy of barring Mohammed Farah Aideed from talks on Somalia's political future and he embodied the U.S. commitment to armed pursuit of Aideed. Gosende had sent a cable from Mogadishu to the State Department on 6 September, stating, "Any plan for negotiating a 'truce' with Aideed's henchmen should be shelved. We should refuse to deal with perpetrators of terrorist acts."[4] President Clinton had discarded this policy when he dispatched Oakley as his envoy.

Gosende had gone back to the United States in late September with the intention of returning to Somalia. It never happened. Richard Bogosian, a career diplomat and former ambassador to Chad, replaced him. But before Bogosian's arrival in the country, Oakley had been working hard to reach some sort of agreement among the clans. Despite the political maneuvering at home and abroad, the soldiers of the QRF still had their mission to perform.

The QRF's mission had been to respond to hostile threats and outright attacks that exceeded UNOSOM II military force capabilities and to assist in military operations that were beyond the capabilities of UNOSOM II military forces. As Falcon Brigade, the mission remained essentially unchanged as the theater reserve with the exception of providing combat forces to secure lines of communication. This added mission meant we had to be prepared to commence offensive operations—to fight!

Notes

1. A concussion grenade produces no fragmentation but, rather, a blast concussion and a flash to temporarily stun, blind, and disorient.

2. The preponderance of equipment for Task Force 1-64 and the 43d Engineers arrived some days later by ship.

3. Daniel P. Bolger, *Savage Peace: Americans at War in the 1990s* (Novato, Calif.: Presidio Press, 1995), p. 304.

4. "U.S. Replaces Envoy Associated with Discarded Somalia Policy," *Washington Post,* 27 October 1993, p. 28.

11

PREPARING TO FIGHT

Peace enforcement operations are combat operations normally executed under the constraints imposed by the rules of engagement.
—*Platoon Sergeant*, 2d Battalion, 14th Infantry Regiment

Under the direction of the JTF headquarters, we began working on a
series of contingency plans to regain control of lost lines of communications (supply and transportation routes). Along with the planning
came a number of training exercises followed by mission rehearsals.
Major General Ernst was the energy behind these initiatives. The operations brought to bear the tremendous combined-arms capability and firepower of the brigade.

Synchronizing the battlefield operating systems became paramount. The brigade staff developed battle drills and planned rehearsals
to ensure that our OH-58Ds could move throughout the battlefield from
one predesignated battle position to another, thereby ensuring that the
lasing angle was within tolerance for Copperhead artillery or marine
heliborne Hellfire missiles destined for predetermined targets. Additionally, the OH-58D's highly accurate navigation system permitted
precise target location that could be handed off to other engagement
systems via the airborne target handover system.[1]

Special operations AC-130 gunships were incorporated into all
operations—their gunners acquiring targets off knee-board sketches
of the city depicting numbered buildings. All helicopter crews, artillery forward observers, and key leaders down to the platoon leaders
carried these sketches. Coordination and communication were tested
as targets were identified and lased by OH-58D aircraft and ground
designators for smart-bomb delivery by navy A-6 Intruders. Obstacles
were in place, and routes for armored and mechanized forces were
reconnoitered.

Although training the force was given priority, we continued to conduct daily operations in support of UNOSOM II. We maintained and frequently exercised a battalion strike force comprising infantry, armor, and aviation. The strike force headquarters was rotated among the three ground maneuver battalions. Conducting convoy escorts and manning and improving compound perimeters were daily occurrences, as was securing the main supply route, a bypass road that skirted Mogadishu to the west. Though an engineering accomplishment, the bypass road physically represented the complete failure and hopelessness of the UN effort in Somali. After 9 months in country, the United Nations was compelled to construct a road to circumvent Mogadishu and preclude the Somalis from sniping and ambushing convoys. Insult was added to injury by placing infantry on the roadway for security.

The bypass had been constructed in August and September and was initially secured by one of Bill David's rifle companies on a rotational basis. The infantry unit on duty was deployed in a series of strongpoints along the 5-mile stretch of roadway, culminating in checkpoints at either end—an extremely boring mission for the officers, NCOs, and soldiers of the battalion. We were relieved of the labor-intensive mission by a newly arrived Indian mechanized brigade. The early morning relief occurred without incident until someone on the UNOSOM staff realized that the northernmost checkpoint near the U.S. support compound, Hunter Base, was adjacent to the Pakistani brigade sector. Considering the political differences between India and Pakistan, UNOSOM decided that the Falcon Brigade should continue to man the single checkpoint, thereby providing a physical buffer between the two rival armies. UNOSOM headquarters didn't want to risk coalition soldiers shooting at each other.

One day while I was in my Humvee driving out to visit the soldiers occupying the checkpoint, I passed a sight that epitomized the ignorance and destitution that the United Nations and the nongovernmental humanitarian organizations were trying to overcome. A small child, no more than 2 years old, was sitting at one end of a pool of stagnant water not much larger than a big puddle found after a thunderstorm, while a few feet away a cow was urinating into the same pool. A herdsman stood by oblivious to the dangers posed to the child. The sight pulled at my heartstrings: children are a people's future, and that child had no future. A helicopter in the distance caught my eye and I shifted my thoughts to our operations.

Lee Gore was flying his aircraft literally 24 hours a day in support of the Eyes over Mogadishu mission, and rarely a day went by without his outfit conducting a mission called Wide-body Escort. A novel mission, it involved army helicopters escorting air force and large wide-body (747 or DC10) charter aircraft during their final approach to and initial departure from the Mogadishu airport.

From the first time I had met General Montgomery, he harbored a legitimate fear that a wide-body aircraft could become the target of the SNA or some other disgruntled Somali with an antiaircraft missile. There were reports of SA-7 missiles in country, but it was pretty much concluded that they were inoperable. Such missiles that had been uncovered during the cordon-and-search operations bore out this conclusion.

However, depending on the level of tension in the city, the wide-body flights were often canceled or delayed. One day, someone got the idea that if a helicopter with its ALQ-144 antimissile jammer blasting away flew next to a heavy transport, the emitter might be able to deflect or confuse a hostile missile—a rather naive idea that was short-lived because the system was designed to protect the helicopter and nothing more. But there was merit in randomly launching a helicopter 15 minutes prior to a wide-body's arrival or departure to provide airborne presence and observation along the northern perimeter of the airfield—essentially conducting a screen operation. The Indian Ocean provided the security to the south. But, still, there was much debate about the utility of the mission when considering the inordinate number of flight hours consumed.

I had always felt that if the SNA wanted to destroy an aircraft, it could easily do so with a mortar or RPG round from the Madina district, similar to the earlier attack on the Rangers, and in fact we had experienced a number of damaged helicopters from ill-placed mortar rounds. But shelling the airfield and destroying a large transport aircraft would have closed the airport for a long time, and I didn't think any of the political factions could afford the fallout, especially the SNA. The United States was on the record for departing Somalia not later than 31 March 1994, so it made little sense to initiate something that would disrupt the timeline.

Training was the name of the game, and we were busily constructing ranges and maneuver areas for the force to exercise. A cluster of rubble-strewn buildings, which had fallen prey to war and looting on the outskirts of the city, was reconfigured as a training site for military operations in urbanized terrain, referred to as MOUT. Here the soldiers could hone their close-combat skills through a series of blank-fire and live-fire training exercises without the fear of militia reprisal.

But more than the militia posed a threat to our soldiers. One day in particular reinforced how Somalia itself is a hostile land. It was a typical crystal-clear, warm, sunny day accented by a light breeze, and Bill

David had dispatched a rifle company several kilometers southwest of Mogadishu to conduct demolition training. With the demolition charge prepared and the troops shielded from the blast, the explosive was detonated. Much to the horror of the soldiers, the result of the explosion was a swarm of enraged bees. They had disturbed an underground beehive, and the bees swiftly attacked the troops with the fury of a desert sandstorm. The dark cloud of enraged insects enveloped the soldiers, inflicting pain on any and all exposed skin. The soldiers eventually were able to escape the wrath of the bees, but not before many were covered with welts. Three troopers were hospitalized with over 100 stings. Fortunately the episode did not result in any fatalities, but it served to remind us how unforgiving the environment was.

While rigorous collective training was challenging the brigade soldiers, we experienced a rash of accidentally discharged weapons. Few had to do with training. I had little patience with the term "accidental discharge" and less with the mishaps. Weapons went off accidentally because soldiers either did not have their "head in the game," or they didn't follow the correct procedures.

I view accidental discharges as a problem with discipline, training, or just lack of familiarity with handling a loaded weapon. Although the majority of incidents occurred soon after soldiers' arrivals in the country, the discharges were not limited solely to the green troops. The brigade experienced accidental discharges in everything from the 25mm Bushmaster cannon on a Bradley Fighting Vehicle to an MK19, 40mm rapid-fire grenade launcher mounted on a Humvee. How we didn't kill or injure someone in those incidents I'll never know. We weren't so lucky with two follow-on occurrences.

In mid-December, as the Golden Dragons were departing the university complex in vehicle convoy traveling to the airfield for their journey home, a young soldier with an M60 machine gun released the charging handle of his weapon and fired a single 7.62mm round squarely into the chest of a Tunisian sentry, killing the coalition soldier instantly. All of the sacrifices the Golden Dragons had made and the great things they had accomplished were tarnished by that single shot. The 14th Infantry troopers were sick with grief and disappointment. One of the toughest tasks I had to perform was apologizing to the Tunisian commander. I was embarrassed for our soldiers, our army, and our nation. Upon my arrival at the Tunisian headquarters, I was greeted with all the courtesies due my rank and position. The young Tunisian lieutenant colonel kept saying, "Mistakes happen, Sir," as if to reassure me. The sentry was married and had three children. I never again wanted to look a fellow commander in the eyes to say "I am sorry."

Late one February night a lone Cobra helicopter crew was conducting a routine Eyes over Mogadishu mission. One hour and 10 minutes into their mission at an altitude of 1,000 feet over the shoreline, the front seat gunner/copilot decided to test his laser designator, a requirement at the start of any Cobra mission. Looking through the headpiece of the telescopic sight unit, he aimed his crosshairs 45 degrees off center at a flickering light near the Old Port. When he squeezed the trigger to unleash the beam of laser energy, the aircraft's 20mm cannon fired a four-round burst. The light he had targeted was coming from the sleeping area of a Nigerian battalion. So at 2 A.M., four high-explosive 20mm rounds lashed out of the sky and struck the walls of an old set of ruins that surrounded the tents of the Nigerian sleeping quarters. The shrapnel from the rounds, mixed with chunks of plaster and brick, rained on top of fifty sleeping soldiers. They were lucky. Only two soldiers were hit, and fortunately their wounds were superficial. The worst was from a small piece of metal that found its way into a soldier's buttock.

Much to my displeasure and discomfort, I found myself at the Nigerian compound standing eye to eye with the battalion commander. Again, there was a formation of soldiers greeting my arrival, and again I was afforded the correct reception. An older lieutenant colonel, the Nigerian commander, appeared to be trying to make me feel better about the incident. At one point he said, "Colonel, I thought it was the Pakistanis." During this period, the Pakistani contingent was in the process of receiving AH-1S Cobras in preparation to assume the attack helicopter mission from us. I responded, "No, it was my soldiers."

I found myself thinking how I represented the finest army in the world and here I was apologizing for accidentally shooting a fellow coalition soldier. It made me sick!

Joint training occurred daily, and as the weeks progressed Falcon Brigade's preparedness increased proportionally. We were aggressively planning and training for offensive operations, but by late December the brigade began a deliberate and methodical withdrawal.

The focus had changed. Although subtle, the tone of the entire force had shifted to one of caution. Much of this was propagated by the UN release on 6 November of sixteen of the fifty-nine militia detainees. Despite this shift in attitude, the rigorous combat training continued even as the initial withdrawal was executed.

Ernst had a bright young officer on his staff who led the planning effort: LTC Harry Scott, an infantry officer, with whom I had been pleased to work some years earlier when he was a brigade operations officer in the 25th Light Infantry Division. A stickler for detail and a meticulous planner, Harry produced a theater-level withdrawal plan that rivaled any produced by Fort Leavenworth's School for Advanced Military Studies, whose graduates were called "Jedi Knights," and Harry Scott was one of the best.

The plan called for a phased withdrawal of forces, a pause for an assessment, and then a continuation with the next phase. This was not a redeployment; it was planned and executed as a withdrawal that might have to be executed under enemy pressure at any point. Although Ernst's initial concept was out of sync with Montgomery's, the two generals' intent was to guarantee protection for the remaining forces by maintaining a flexible hard-hitting infantry, armor, and aviation package to the end.

Ernst would not see the plan executed to its end, for his departure came sooner than that of Montgomery. Highly respected officers, Major General Ernst and Major General Montgomery had a strained relationship. Both Vietnam veterans, these intelligent, strong-willed men approached the mission in Somalia from opposing perspectives.

Montgomery had seen his fair share of combat in both Vietnam and Somalia. The result was a consummate soldier-statesman. Montgomery was a student of the Russian language, and he had spent much of his 30 years as a soldier in commands in Europe where he routinely worked with allied forces and their governments. Serving as the number two coalition soldier in Somalia under Lieutenant General Bir, Montgomery was in his element working with soldiers, and occasionally diplomats, of the twenty-two donor nations.

Ernst, on the other hand, was focused entirely on warfighting. He lived and breathed maneuver warfare and had rarely served away from troops. He knew weapon nomenclatures down to the minutest detail, and his many trips to the army's National Training Center in Southern California and Joint Readiness Training Center in Arkansas made him a master of battle systems synchronization.[2] General Ernst had arrived ready to fight, and championed the notion that it was time to "retake the city"—an idea that was not the least bit appealing to the soldiers who had experienced firsthand the horror and brutality of fighting in the streets of Mogadishu.

Montgomery proceeded slowly and methodically, keeping in the forefront the notion that the U.S. force would be out of Somalia by the end of March. He also knew that many coalition soldiers would remain well past March and he had a responsibility to them.

The two generals' distinct approaches to the operation were apparent in the information flow from the two headquarters. Shortly after Ernst's arrival in the country, when I interfaced with both headquarters,

I would hear one thing from Montgomery and turn around and hear the same thing with a totally different slant from Ernst. Ernst and his staff communicated directly with CENTCOM headquarters, as did Montgomery and his staff. I could only surmise that by the time the information got to me, it had been processed through two different filters (headquarters), and therefore it was skewed. An example was our involvement in the planning to forcibly reopen 21 October Road. (Although a rather odd name for a roadway, the date had significance. It was 21 October 1969 when Siad Barre had successfully seized power and established the Somalia Democratic Republic.)

The brigade's mission statement was expanded to the reopening of the lines of communication, and 21 October Road at one time had been a critical main supply route for the resupply of coalition forces in central and northeast Somalia. After the roadway had been plagued by a number of ambushes and obstacles, a bypass road was constructed several miles to the north of Mogadishu. With the completion of the bypass, 21 October Road lost its importance.

Despite the new roadway, General Ernst and his staff set out to retake control of the disputed portion of the road, which ran between Lenin Street and the Pasta Factory. This two-mile stretch of roadway was controlled by the SNA, and was cluttered with debris and makeshift roadblocks. The south side of the road was lined with one- and two-story buildings and constituted the densely populated northern boundary of Mogadishu. The northern side of the roadway was predominantly desert with a few buildings scattered about.

The plan was rather elaborate (Figure 11.1). We would approach the roadway from the desert to the north with two battalion task forces on line. Lieutenant Colonel Clark and his TF 1-64 would be on the northeastern flank with Lieutenant Colonel Smith and his TF 2-22d Infantry, beefed up with armor, on the western flank. Bill David and his 2-14th Infantry would remain in reserve at Victory Base.

Adjacent to TF 1-64 was the 22d Marine Expeditionary Unit (MEU), which had replaced the 13th MEU in theater. Col. Larry Outlaw, a Marine helo aviator, commanded the 22d. Outlaw and his outfit would come ashore east of Mogadishu and travel north-northwest in a large semicircle, ending up on Clark's left flank approaching Balad Road from the north. Balad Road intersected 21 October Road and led to the outlands of central Somalia.

A Pakistani infantry battalion equipped with U.S.-made M113 APCs and M48 tanks would proceed east on 21 October Road from Lenin Street as the clearing force. AC-130s would be supporting from

FALCON BDE D-DAY TIMELINE
(DRAFT)

	D-6	D-5	D-4	D-3	D-2	D-1
JTF	JTF OPORD (D-7) TRANSFER SWORD/ HUNTER SECURITY TO LSC TARGET REFINEMENT PREP DISPLACED CIV PLAN	JTF FRAGO MEU/ARG TACON JTF SOF SPT TMs TO COAL COORD MSR TRANSFER TO UNOSOM TACAIR/MEU-CASEX PSYOP 72 hr NOTICE DECEPTION PLAN	JOINT/COMBINED TEWT COMMEX AIRSPACE MGT MTG JOINT/COMBINED FIRES COORD MTG MEU DEMO LANDING AT RANGE 6 EXECUTE STOCKPILING VALIDATE CL IV RQMTS TACAIR/MEU-CASEX PSYOP 48 hr NOTICE DECEPTION PLAN	AIR REHEARSAL LASER REHEARSAL COMMEX FIRES REHEARSAL TGT VERIFICATION DISTRO CLASS IV PSYOP 24 hr NOTICE DECEPTION PLAN	JOINT ILLUM REHEARSAL JOINT/COMBINED REHEARSAL TACAIR/MEU-CASEX TACAIR/OH-58D TRNG COMMEX COALITION BACKBRIEFS ATO REVIEW US-COAL ENG TASK ORG OBSTACLE CLR STX/ CLFX PSYOP 1st WARNING DECEPTION PLAN	B/P 2d JOINT/COMBINED REHEARSAL MAINT STANDDOWN INCREASE BASE SEC HALT CONVOYS/ CLOSE LOCs/AIRPORT PSYOP FINAL WARNING CEASE DECEPTION OPS MEDIA DOWN TO UNITS
BDE	BDE WARNORD BACKBRIEF COMJTF DISTRO JOINT CEOI TRANSFER SWORD/ HUNTER SECURITY TO LSC	BDE FRAGO TASK ORGANIZE LDR AERIAL RECON TACAIR/OH-58D TRNG TACAIR/MEU-CASEX ANGLICO ATCH TO BDE MEDIA L/U W/ BDE IIEV DS TO BDE COORD MSR TRANS TO UNOSOM/LSC MECH MOV'T NORTH (DECEPTION PLAN)	JOINT/COMBINED TEWT AM-SANDTABLE PM-WALKTHRU TACAIR/OH-58D TRNG TACAIR/MEU-CASEX COMMEX JOINT/COMBINED FIRES COORD MTG UNIT AERIAL RECONS EXECUTE STOCKPILING MECH MOV'T NORTH (DECEPTION PLAN)	BN BACKBRIEFS VEHICLE TEWT AIR REHEARSAL(OH-58D) FIRES REHEARSAL TGT MTG (BDE) LASER REHEARSAL(LTD) COORD MTG ON POL/ CONTACT PLAN W/ BOF COMMEX MED COORD MTG(BDE) DISTRO CL IV MECH MOV'T SOUTH (DECEPTION PLAN)	JOINT ILLUM REHEARSAL J/C REHEARSAL TACAIR/MEU-CASEX TACAIR/OH-58D TRNG COMMO CHECKS US-COAL ENG TASK ORG OBST CLR STX/CLFX BDE-COAL RECON MIN 3 DOS ON HAND (DECEPTION PLAN)	B/P 2d JOINT/COMBINED REHEARSAL MAINT STANDDOWN INCREASE BASE SEC HALT CONVOYS/ CLOSE LOCs/AIRPORT MEDIA DOWN TO UNITS MOV'T TO TAAs B/P LNO TO ITAL COMMO CHECKS TGT UPDATE INTEL UPDATE
STAFF HHC	BDE WARNORD BACKBRIEF COMJTF DISTRO JOINT CEOI	JTF FRAGO BDE FRAGO TPT ATCH TO 13 MEU TACAIR/MEU-CASEX OBSTACLE ASSESS COORD SUPPLY STOCKPILING DECEPTION PLAN	JOINT/COMBINED TEWT AM-SANDTABLE PM-WALKTHRU COMMEX J/C FIRES COORD MTG TACAIR/MEU-CASEX LNO EXCHANGE AIRSPACE MGT MTG BDE EXECUTION MATRIX DECEPTION PLAN	UNIT BACKBRIEFS VEHICLE TEWT FIRES REHEARSAL TGT MTG (BDE) LASER REHEARSAL COMMEX MED COORD MTG(BDE) DISTRO CL IV TPT (A/C) DS PAKI DECEPTION PLAN	JOINT ILLUM REHEARSAL J/C REHEARSAL TACAIR/OH-58D TRNG TACAIR/MEU-CASEX COMMEX COMMO CHECKS ATO REVIEW US-COAL ENG TASK ORG OBST CLR STX/CLFX BDE-COAL RECON MIN 3 DOS ON HAND	B/P 2d J/C REHEARSAL MAINT STANDDOWN INCREASE BASE SEC CLOSE LOCs MEDIA DOWN TO UNITS MOV'T TO TAAs B/P LNO TO ITAL COMMO CHECKS TGT/INTEL UPDATE
2-14		BDE FRAGO TASK ORG LDR AERIAL RECON	JOINT/COMBINED TEWT AM-SANDTABLE PM-WALKTHRU COMMEX FIRES COORD MTG UNIT AERIAL RECON	UNIT BACKBRIEFS VEHICLE TEWT FIRES REHEARSAL TGT MTG (BDE) LASER REHEARSAL COMMEX MED COORD MTG(BDE)	JOINT/COMBINED REHEARSAL COMMEX COMMO CHECKS OBST CLR STX/CLFX BDE-COAL RECON	B/P 2d J/C REHEARSAL MAINT STANDDOWN INCREASE BASE SEC HALT CONVOYS MEDIA TO BN MOV'T TO TAAs COMMO CHECKS TGT/INTEL UPDATE
2-22	TRANSFER SWORD/ HUNTER SECURITY TO LSC	BDE FRAGO TASK ORG LDR AERIAL RECON COORD MSR TRANSFER TO UNOSOM	JOINT/COMBINED TEWT AM-SANDTABLE PM-WALKTHRU COMMEX FIRES COORD MTG UNIT AERIAL RECON	UNIT BACKBRIEFS VEHICLE TEWT FIRES REHEARSAL TGT MTG (BDE) LASER REHEARSAL COMMEX MED COORD MTG(BDE)	JOINT/COMBINED REHEARSAL COMMEX COMMO CHECKS OBST CLR STX/CLFX BDE-COAL RECON	B/P 2d J/C REHEARSAL MAINT STANDDOWN INCREASE BASE SEC HALT CONVOYS MEDIA TO BN MOV'T TO TAAs COMMO CHECKS TGT/INTEL UPDATE
1-64		BDE FRAGO TASK ORG LDR AERIAL RECON MECH MOV'T NORTH (DECEPTION PLAN)	JOINT/COMBINED TEWT AM-SANDTABLE PM-WALKTHRU COMMEX FIRES COORD MTG UNIT AERIAL RECON MECH MOV'T NORTH (DECEPTION PLAN)	UNIT BACKBRIEFS VEHICLE TEWT FIRES REHEARSAL TGT MTG (BDE) LASER REHEARSAL COMMEX MED COORD MTG(BDE) MECH MOV'T SOUTH (DECEPTION PLAN)	JOINT/COMBINED REHEARSAL COMMEX COMMO CHECKS OBST CLR STX/CLFX BDE-COAL RECON MECH MOV'T SOUTH (DECEPTION PLAN)	B/P 2d J/C REHEARSAL MAINT STANDDOWN INCREASE BASE SEC HALT CONVOYS MEDIA TO BN MOV'T TO TAAs COMMO CHECKS TGT/INTEL UPDATE
2-25		BDE FRAGO LDR AERIAL RECON TACAIR/MEU-CASEX TACAIR/OH-58D TRNG LEAFLET DROP	JOINT/COMBINED TEWT AM-SANDTABLE PM-WALKTHRU COMMEX TACAIR/MEU-CASEX AIRSPACE MGMT MTG FIRES COORD MTG UNIT AERIAL RECON TACAIR/OH-58D TRNG LEAFLET DROP	UNIT BACKBRIEFS AIR REHEARSAL(58D) VEHICLE TEWT FIRES REHEARSAL TGT MTG (BDE) LASER REHEARSAL COMMEX MED COORD MTG(BDE) LEAFLET/LOUDSPKR	JOINT/COMBINED REHEARSAL COMMEX COMMO CHECKS TACAIR/MEU-CASEX OBST CLR STX/CLFX BDE-COAL RECON LEAFLET/LOUDSPKR	B/P 2d J/C REHEARSAL MAINT STANDDOWN INCREASE BASE SEC HALT CONVOYS MEDIA TO BN COMMO CHECKS TGT/INTEL UPDATE LEAFLET/LOUDSPKR
43		OBSTACLE ASSESS	JOINT/COMBINED TEWT AM-SANDTABLE PM-WALKTHRU COMMEX	UNIT BACKBRIEFS VEHICLE TEWT COMMEX DISTRO CL IV MED COORD MTG(BDE)	JOINT/COMBINED REHEARSAL COMMEX COMMO CHECKS OBST CLR STX/CLFX	B/P 2d J/C REHEARSAL ASSUME VB SECURITY MAINT STANDDOWN INCREASE BASE SEC HALT CONVOYS MEDIA TO BN COMMO CHECKS INTEL UPDATE
46		COORD SUPPLY STOCKPILING	JOINT/COMBINED TEWT AM-SANDTABLE PM-WALKTHRU COMMEX EXECUTE STOCKPILING	UNIT BACKBRIEFS VEHICLE TEWT COMMEX DISTRO CL IV MED COORD MTG(BDE)	JOINT/COMBINED REHEARSAL COMMEX COMMO CHECKS B/P SLING OPS MIN 3 DOS ON HAND	B/P 2d J/C REHEARSAL MAINT STANDDOWN INCREASE BASE SEC HALT CONVOYS/ CLOSE LOC COMMO CHECKS B/P SLING OPS INTEL UPDATE

Figure 11.1 Falcon Brigade D-Day timeline

overhead, and OH-58Ds and Cobras would be screening deep over the city a kilometer south of 21 October Road over National Street. There were a lot of moving parts, and fratricide prevention was in the front of everyone's mind.

It was during one of the late-night planning sessions that Ernst and I got into a heated exchange over what was considered deep—referring to the operation's battlespace. We were both getting quite frustrated, and I voiced my opposition by stating, "General, I see the look in your eyes, I hear what your saying, but . . ." Suddenly, he directed everyone under the rank of colonel to leave the room and, when the door was closed, he looked straight at me and pointedly addressed the issue. I quickly became an attentive listener. Despite the uncomfortable encounter, over the coming weeks I would learn a lot from the general.

Montgomery was not enamored with the operation.[3] Although cut off from a dialogue with him, from the few opportunities I had to hear Montgomery speak and provide guidance, I knew he had no intention of retaking 21 October Road or initiating any other offensive action unless the SNA mounted further hostilities. He felt that the operation was unnecessary and risky, so it was eventually scuttled—but it epitomized the disconnect between the two commanders.

Despite the generals' differences, both men agreed on many issues that resulted in a number of highly successful joint and combined exercises. Ernst and his JTF staff superbly planned and executed a number of medical and dental civic action programs. Operation Show Care involved an amphibious landing near the small coastal town of Marka and a simultaneous heliborne landing in the adjacent inland village of Qoryooley (both places about 70 kilometers southwest of Mogadishu), as well as a link-up by the marine forces with the Royal Moroccan Task Force, the sector caretakers. The operation not only provided much needed medical care to the isolated towns, but created immeasurable good will. There were a number of similar operations like Old Port, Kismayo, and campaign Secure Hope. Some were planned and executed, and others, for any number of reasons, were never initiated. Regardless, the planning drill honed the units' staff skills and further fostered cooperation and team play.

Montgomery and Ernst shared a mutual desire for the removal of the marine Humvee from the spot where a mine destroyed it some three months earlier on the morning of 3 October. The charred wreckage had been reduced to a twisted frame, broken springs, and assorted unrecognizable pieces of metal. The Somalis had turned the debris into a monument, including a rather crude plaque, commemorating their success on

Sunday. It conspicuously occupied the center of Via Roma just east of the entrance to the New Port. After Montgomery had suggested its removal, Ernst obliged and directed that we secure the vehicle and dispose of it. Buck Bedard jokingly said one evening, "Let's get that damn thing off the street and drop it in the ocean!" It was apparent that what was left of the Humvee had to go.

A plan was formulated. It would involve a mechanized company-team from TF 1-64. A tank and a couple of Bradleys would rush out the front gate of the New Port and race the 150 meters east on Via Roma to the site of the Humvee remains. Soldiers would secure the area while a team dismounted and attached a cable from a Bradley to the Humvee's frame and quickly retreated with the debris in tow into the security of the New Port. Meanwhile, M1 tanks and Bradleys would overwatch the operation from high ground within the confines of the New Port. AC-130s would be overhead providing both observation and direct fire support, while OH-58Ds would hover a kilometer away keeping a close eye on events. They would also provide the laser spot for Copperhead if it were needed. Additionally, an M113 medical ambulance would be positioned near the entrance of the port to evacuate any causalities that might be sustained.

The young company commander, CPT Kevin Hayslett, who was going to execute the plan had constructed on one of the piers a detailed representation of the New Port and surrounding area using rocks, boxes, and bits of wood. The purpose of this model was to conduct a rehearsal with his key leaders and to use it during his brief-back to his commander, Lieutenant Colonel Clark. The word spread of his briefing, and he soon had more participants than expected. Not only were his battalion commander and S3 on the scene, but General Ernst, the J3, myself, and assorted staff personnel were all present to observe the "rock drill"—a term derived from using rocks arranged on the ground to portray enemy and friendly forces, terrain, and control measures. Its purpose was for discussing and refining the operation, and ensuring that the key leaders had a complete understanding of what was expected. I thought, "Man, all of this attention is a bit much for the young captain!"

But Captain Hayslett was poised and professional as he presented his back-brief, demonstrating his mettle by coping with the presence of the JTF and brigade hierarchy. Once the rock drill was complete and the onlookers satisfied, the mission was set for the following day.

The United Arab Emirates (UAE) troops frequently worked the sector where the Humvee was located, and over the past several months they had established a rapport with many of the neighboring people.

Location of 23mm antiaircraft gun that was attacked by Cobra helicopters first day of command

21 October Rd.

The Pasta Factory—Aideed's weapons storage area

Their commander, a big-boned black officer who spoke the King's English with a touch of arrogance, stopped and asked, "All of this to retrieve the junk on Via Roma?" I responded most assuredly, "Yes!" He said, "Oh, that's no problem. I can get it for you." And off he drove in his brown Jeep Wagoneer with artificial wood trim on the vehicle's side. Bob Clark and I looked at each other thinking, "You don't really suppose?" A short time later the UAE commander returned accompanied by another vehicle. He talked to the guards at the New Port front gate, then darted out the port entrance and sped down Via Roma, only to return minutes later dragging the Humvee remains. I notified JTF headquarters—mission complete!

This was a clear example of taking overwhelming force to the extreme, and conducting a mission that was essentially a towtruck job. But after 3 October no one appeared willing to assume any risk.

The next day I was standing in front of Eric Smith's headquarters at the airfield. He had taken over a partially refurbished two-story building, which TF Ranger had used for its command post. I was waiting to greet Major General Ernst, who was due to arrive at the 2-22d Infantry headquarters to receive a briefing on the battalion's latest force protection measures.

Ernst arrived in his helicopter accompanied by Bedard. As they approached, I came to attention and greeted General Ernst with a salute. It was at that precise moment that I saw in the distance, well beyond Ernst, the airfield, the beach sand dunes, and a quarter-mile out over the ocean, a Black Hawk with the destroyed marine Humvee oscillating beneath the aircraft's fuselage. Ernst greeted me with a "Good morning, Larry." Buck followed by saying, "How are you doing Larry?" I responded, "Fine!" Then Buck asked, "Hey, what did you ever do with the Humvee?" My face must have reflected my concern over the question, because Bedard quickly followed up, "Say, you didn't really drop it into the ocean did you?" Ernst peered at me awaiting my answer. I looked past him at the Humvee dangling over the ocean and replied, "Not yet!" Bedard responded, "Yea, well that's good, accountability and all!" At that very moment, what was left of the Humvee separated from the helicopter and sped toward the ocean a couple of hundred feet below.

The twisted metal appeared to be moving in slow motion, like the old Samsonite luggage commercial in which the durability of a suitcase is demonstrated by its free fall thousands of feet from an airplane to slam into the earth without sustaining damage. As the charred debris rushed toward the ocean, it was the only movement in the distant sky.

I stood staring between Ernst and Bedard as the remains of the vehicle disappeared on the other side of the sand dunes. A professional motion picture director could not have choreographed it any better. We became distracted by Eric Smith's arrival, and much to my good fortune, I never heard about the marine Humvee again.

By January the friction between Montgomery and Ernst was at its peak and you could feel the tension in the air. General Hoar decided to dual-hat Montgomery as both the U.S. forces commander and the JTF commander—a proposal that made sense and certainly supported the principle of unity of command. In mid-January Hoar dispatched a message sending Major General Ernst home. A few weeks later, General Montgomery traded in his blue beret when he relinquished his deputy UNOSOM position.

There were mixed feelings among many of the JTF staff members. They found themselves split between their loyalty to Ernst, who had formed and shaped their headquarters from scratch, and their new leader, who over the past year in Somalia had seen it all and was revered by the coalition leadership. In the customary military way, once Montgomery was at the helm of the JTF, it didn't take long for the staff loyalties to align themselves.[4]

During the remaining months of 1993, the foreign policy debate raged on in the United States. It all seemed to center on the U.S. role as the world's policeman, a posture the American people were reluctant to embrace. But with hostilities subsiding, Somalia slipped from the front of the debate as the Clinton administration steered a collision course much closer to home toward the rogue regime terrorizing Haiti.

Early one morning in Somalia, as I conducted my rounds in the brigade headquarters, I made my way through the troop feeding area. The outside mess facility comprised a few picnic tables on plywood flooring surrounded by a wall of sandbags and covered with tentage and camouflage netting. Located at one end of the dining area was a television set mounted in a makeshift cabinet for the soldiers' viewing pleasure. It served as a link to the outside world, broadcasting Armed Forces Network and CNN programming.

As I glanced in the direction of the TV, a newscast caught my attention. The screen depicted a ship off-loading unarmed UN military observers sporting the customary blue beret onto the docks of Port-au-Prince, Haiti.[5] The ship was the USS *Harlan County*. The news report went on to discuss how the unarmed observers were turned away at the docks by thugs waving pistols and chanting, "We're going to turn this into another Somalia." Confounded by the unexpected resistance, the observers went back on the U.S. warship and steamed out to sea. The report revealed how the United States was threatening to take military action in Haiti, and it portrayed graphic film coverage of the poverty in Haiti and brutality of the repressive regime of self-appointed leader Lt. Gen. Raoul Cedras.

As I paused to view the news report, I shook my head and thought, "At least they can't send us to that hell hole since we're already over here in this one." Ironically, and much to my surprise, our government postponed the nation's military involvement in Haiti for 11 months, when I would find myself, along with the Falcon Brigade, air-assaulting army Lightfighters in olive drab helicopters from a navy aircraft carrier into Port-au-Prince on D-Day, 19 September 1994.

Notes

1. Our OH-58Ds were "vanilla," that is they were for observation and target designation only. They were not armed. The marines flew AH-IT Cobras, which were equipped with the Hellfire missile. They were just weapons platforms, unable to engage autonomously. It was a good marriage for both.

2. The Joint Readiness Training Center moved from Fort Chaffee, Arkansas, to Fort Polk, Louisiana, in 1992.

3. Not only did Major General Montgomery think the operation was unnecessary, but he was disturbed that the plan placed the Pakistanis in a position to "bleed" again, referring to the ambush of 24 Pakistani soldiers on 5 June 1993.

4. As if times were not tough enough, it was during this period that Montgomery, who passionately spoke of his dream to one day own a Winnebago recreational vehicle and travel throughout the United States, was informed by letter from his Colorado Springs hillside neighbor that the neighbor's Winnebago had rolled down the hill and crashed into Montgomery's living room—an ironic twist for Montgomery, who appeared to take the news in stride.

5. The White House, without consulting Secretary of Defense Aspin, drew up plans to send the unarmed observers into Haiti on 11 October 1993. The observer force consisted of 193 Americans and 25 Canadians.

12

THE WITHDRAWAL

This will not be a redeployment. It will be planned and executed
as a withdrawal employing a force sized to resist any threat.
                                    —*Major General Carl Ernst,*
           JTF Somalia Commander (October 1993–January 1994)

On 2 December, Mohammed Farah Aideed was escorted by U.S. security personnel from his compound in the center of Mogadishu to the
airport. To get Aideed to out-of-country talks among rival clan leaders,
Ambassador Oakley placed his air transport at Aideed's disposal. This
came as a surprise to us all and caused anger and disappointment throughout the ranks. Aideed arrived at the airport to stares of disbelief as he was
quickly hustled up the steps of an awaiting army twin-engine C-12 executive aircraft. His destination was Addis Ababa, capital of Ethiopia.

The episode was a blow to troop morale. It just didn't make any
sense, and Senator Hank Brown (Republican-Colorado) later captured
our dismay when he said, "This is one of the most schizophrenic acts
in recent history. It strikes me as strange policy to tell American troops
to hunt him [Aideed] down one day and chauffeur him around the
next." The peace conference proved to be a failure, and Aideed was left
to find his own way home. He took his time, not returning to war-torn
Mogadishu until early February 1994.

Most people back in the United States had forgotten Somalia. The
competing events in Russia and Bosnia and the influx of Haitian
refugees threatening our shores were more than enough to occupy those
interested in foreign affairs. But despite the fading public interest in Somalia, many of our nation's schools enthusiastically corresponded with
the brigade soldiers—an exchange that brought joy and fulfillment to
both the children and soldiers. The student-soldier correspondence was a
product of several church groups, veterans' organizations, and patriotic

citizens who shared a concern for their children's education and the deployed soldier's welfare.

While in Somalia I received a number of supportive notes and letters. One of particular interest was from Clint Eastwood, a conservative who appreciates the military. His note cautioned me to "fly safe over the skies of Mogadishu." The distinguished actor-director and I had met in the late 1970s while I was stationed at Fort Ord, California. We were introduced by a mutual friend, Phil Dacey, in Eastwood's restaurant, the Hogs Breath Inn, in the nearby town of Carmel. Over the years, whenever I made my way back to Carmel, we would share a beer. In addition to enjoying a cold beer, we both liked helicopters.

In 1989 he was learning to fly helicopters, which eventually led to his purchase of a sleek custom-built French Aérospatiale Astar—a beautiful helicopter. One day in the late 1980s, while we were driving back from viewing aircraft at Fritzche Army Airfield at Fort Ord, I asked Eastwood why the movie industry frequently depicted the officer corps as a bunch of incompetent, self-serving jerks eager to enter war. The former Fort Ord soldier smiled as he made it clear that in the minds of some in Hollywood military authority figures, especially officers, as "good guys" didn't sell movies—an opinion he didn't share. At the time I thought that was too bad, but it was now 1993 and after Desert Storm. I could only hope that attitudes had changed.[1]

Back in Somalia my executive officer, Ellis Golson, was due to return to the United States. He was selected to command the 3d Squadron, 17th Cavalry Regiment at Fort Drum. Ellis had the standard precommand courses to attend, along with a 3-month aircraft transition in the OH-58D Kiowa Warrior helicopter—a must because the brigade was scheduled to receive Kiowa Warriors as replacements for the Cobras and the antiquated OH-58A/C Scout aircraft.

To take Golson's place was an older (my age) cavalry officer who was promoted to lieutenant colonel. I had briefly met Raoul Archambault as I passed through Fort Drum, but knew little about him. As the weeks turned into months, though, he gained my admiration and respect. A highly decorated Vietnam War veteran and Somalia returnee, he was a quality officer and genuine human being who would remain as the brigade's "number two" until shortly before I relinquished command. He was the son of a distinguished Rhode Island attorney and former marine who was the recipient of the Navy Cross for heroic action on Iwo Jima during World War II. LTC Archambault preferred to be called "Arch."

Arch possessed the demeanor, intellect, and interpersonal skills necessary to mold the diverse group of soldiers into a responsive team.

He quickly energized the staff as he spearheaded the planning effort for the brigade's withdrawal, and wrote a comprehensive recovery plan for the brigade upon its returned to Fort Drum.

The U.S. forces were not the only ones leaving Somalia. The French and Belgians had announced their withdrawal from Somalia back in September 1993, and the Swedish medical contingent was set to depart in mid-December, but it was the U.S. announcement in October that triggered the exit of three influential donor nations. Germany, Italy, and Turkey all announced in December 1993 that they would start pulling troops out as early as the following January.

The 14th Infantry Golden Dragons relinquished the UNOSOM II ground QRF mission to the Malaysian contingent on 15 December. We retained the heliborne mission and continued to provide backup to the Malaysians with our own ground strike force consisting of M1s, Bradleys, and combat engineer vehicles.

Generals Montgomery and Ernst gave the war-tattered Golden Dragons a warrior's send-off, and then the Dragons climbed the steps of a Tower Air charter airliner and made the 15-hour trek home to snow-covered Fort Drum in time for Christmas. The brave young men received a hero's welcome from cheering family members, friends, and a grateful community. They had seen more killing and fighting than any other unit that served in Somalia. And, unlike their special ops counterparts who had to regroup and get ready for the next crisis ready to happen somewhere around the world, the infantrymen had had to wait an additional 2 months in Somalia before they were relieved of their duties and reunited with their families.

The 14th Infantry's welcome home ceremony was hosted by the chief of staff of the army, GEN Gordon R. Sullivan. SGT Christopher Reid, the soldier who lost his leg and hand in the fight to recover our UH-60 crew members' remains, was on a pass from Walter Reed Medical Center in Washington, D.C., to join in the celebration of his unit's return. Taking advantage of an opportunity, Reid cornered General Sullivan and asked if he would attend his Christmas Eve wedding in the third-floor chapel at Walter Reed. Reid's fiancée, a navy corpsmen, flew all the way from Spain to be with her betrothed during the welcoming celebration. Without hesitation, General Sullivan accepted.

Shortly after the departure of the 14th Infantry, Larry Davis and his 43d Combat Engineers uploaded their rolling stock and construction equipment onto a roll-on roll-off ship and boarded a charter jet to Fort Benning in time to salvage most of the holiday season.

Our Christmas was uneventful. We had the army's usual lavish turkey dinner with all the trimmings, which was a real treat in contrast to our daily diet of the bland T-rations and MREs (meals, ready-to-eat). Our food service sergeant, SSG Otis Griggs, was a first class act: the extra effort by Griggs and his cooks always resulted in a full belly and a smile on the soldier's face. President Clinton would later recognize Sergeant Griggs during a visit to Fort Drum when Griggs was one of a select few who met with the president.

Griggs's culinary repertoire brought Major General Montgomery and Ambassador Bogosian to our headquarters to share the Christmas meal and visit with the soldiers. Prior to our meals being served, I spent the morning and early afternoon visiting our troopers throughout Mogadishu who were on duty. I had done the same for Thanksgiving, but this time there were two notable differences. First, Christmas was sunny and dry with mild temperatures, while Thanksgiving Day was chilly and had seen a steady downpour. Second, during my Christmas visit to many of the sites, I was transported in an M1 tank. Normally I traveled through the outskirts of the city in a Humvee, personally armed with an M16 and escorted by a couple of heavily armed Humvees provided by the 2-14th or 2-22d Infantry. I thought hitching a ride on a tank was a novel way to travel, not to mention secure.

By day's end I concluded that if I were 25 years younger, I would probably be a tanker. Sometime later, I had an opportunity to fire the main gun of the M1 and the Bradley's 25mm Bushmaster. I was impressed with both weapon systems, and how easy it was to acquire a target and make a first-round hit, especially while on the move. There was something special about driving around in that tank.

Lee Gore and his Task Force Raven were also preparing for their return trip home. But TF Raven could not be redeployed without a replacement unit. There was much debate over the best course of action— leave TF Raven in place until the March deadline or replace the unit with another. Aviation was needed in theater through March, and awaiting the redeployment decision was tough for the Raven aviators, who also were fatigued and anxious to go home. The decision to replace TF Raven was made in late November, making Gore's troopers ecstatic. The replacement organization was 4th Battalion, 4th Aviation Regiment from Fort Carson, Colorado, commanded by LTC Keith Stafford.

The 4-4th Aviation's advance party arrived in late December followed by the main body's arrival the first week of January 1994. Each soldier enthusiastically aligned with his outgoing counterpart for a 2-week mission and country orientation. The mission transition was conducted professionally, and occurred without a hitch—just as the two previous aviation battalion reliefs had gone.

The majority of the brigade's equipment departed the theater by ship, but we were still employing the large C-5 transport aircraft to deliver replacements for our battered Black Hawk fleet: new-model UH-60L helicopters delivered directly from Sikorsky's Connecticut plant. The air force loadmasters, respected professionals, have always had the reputation for strict compliance with loading procedures and policies; their interpretation of the regulations are final and uncompromisingly enforced. I had learned early in my army career that regardless of what rank you wore on your collar, if the loadmaster decided it wouldn't be loaded, it wasn't.

During the first weeks of my command in Somalia, I would watch the loadmasters put aside their strict standards and accept almost anything, in any condition, and in any state of cleanliness as they scurried to spend as little time as possible on the ground in Mogadishu. I suspect their compromise was motivated by the real threat of an attack on the airfield and I could hardly blame them—the immense green-gray airplanes were big targets. Later, as hostilities subsided and an uneasy calm fell on Mogadishu, the loadmasters returned to their old ways of doing business, rejecting loads and rightfully demanding observance of standards.

One afternoon, Lee Gore was lamenting about how difficult it was becoming to get the dismantled Black Hawks past the loadmasters. I joked that if the loadmasters become an impediment to getting our older helicopters out, just toss a training artillery simulator within earshot of the loadmaster, and the noise from the explosion would cause the airmen to trip over themselves completing the load. Fortunately Lee didn't take me seriously.

Gore's departure marked a point where I now had all three of my organic battalions (2-25th and 3-25th Aviation along with the 3-17th Cavalry) at Fort Drum, while the brigade headquarters remained in Somalia. LTC Jim Kelley was not only challenged with the double duty of squadron commander and brigade rear-detachment commander, but he, along with the brigade, was struggling with a record winter. Fort Drum was inundated with snow and ice, ultimately receiving over 240 inches of snow for the winter.

One day, Arch called our rear-detachment headquarters via satellite communications to track some logistic issues. During the call, he was advised that it was minus 40 degrees Fahrenheit at Fort Drum. It was a day we were experiencing 105 degrees Fahrenheit at the Mogadishu airfield. Being an old Arizona boy, I concluded that we were getting the better end of the deal.

On 5 January the civilian contractor, Brown and Root of Houston, Texas, assumed responsibility for logistic support to UNOSOM from the U.S.-led UN Logistics Support Command. This was a UN first to have the logistics for a military operation supplied completely by a civilian contractor. BG Larry Lust took off his blue beret as chief of the UN Logistics Support Command to head up the JTF logistics effort.

By mid-January the Falcon Brigade consisted of the headquarters, Smith's TF 2-22d Infantry, Clark's TF 1-64, Stafford's 4-4th Aviation, and Weiss's 46th Support Battalion. During the first week of February, the brigade was further reduced to a strength of 1,384 soldiers augmented by fifty or so marines.

The 24th MEU (Special Operations Capable), commanded by COL Matt Brodrick, relieved the 22d MEU on the waters of the Indian Ocean off shore from Mogadishu. Our withdrawal plan called for a platoon of M109 self-propelled 155mm howitzers to remain at Victory Base, while the remainder of the battery redeployed with TF 1-64. The JTF headquarters had directed Brodrick to temporarily transfer a towed 155mm battery to the Falcon Brigade. The marine cannon-cockers were promptly positioned at the airfield replacing the departing M109s. Having artillery located on both flanks of Mogadishu provided complete coverage of the city. The gun tubes' locations in relation to our predetermined targets, like militia command and control, assembly areas, and weapons caches, were especially critical for the laser-designating OH-58Ds. From their predesignated airborne battle positions, the helicopters had to remain close enough to the gun-target line to ensure that the seeker on the Copperhead precision munition captured the helicopter's laser energy.

With the ever increasing threat of an attack on one of the large 747 or DC10 charter aircraft, Montgomery decided to ferry the remaining U.S. troops out of Mogadishu. A 1950s-vintage Greek-flagged cruise liner, *Mediterranean Sky*, was contracted to sail the troops from Mogadishu to Mombasa. From Mombasa they would travel by commercial aircraft back to the United States. A second ship, the U.S. training ship *Empire State* was deployed to the area as a backup. In early February, the first to sail on *Mediterranean Sky* were members of TF 1-64 along with soldiers from the 46th Support Battalion. Bob Clark and Jack Weiss joined their troopers on board the luxury liner and steamed toward Kenya, the first leg of their well-deserved journey home.

The brigade's 1,384 troopers included Eric Smith's 2-22d Infantry TF, which was augmented with two armor-mechanized company-teams (13 M1s, 12 M2A2s, and 3 ACEs); 4-4th Aviation; A Company, 224th

Maintenance Battalion; and the U.S. Marine artillery battery. The brigade headquarters was relocated from the embassy compound to a newly constructed temporary headquarters building at the airfield, and 2-22d Infantry TF occupied defensive positions at the airfield and the New Port. The JTF headquarters followed suit by moving to a new headquarters complex near the beach, which was protected by high sand dunes and the security of the airfield. We had circled the wagons awaiting the arrival of March.

I usually fenced a couple of hours on Sunday afternoon to relax and bask in the warm African sun. It was the only event that came close to routine, other than my nightly dose of malaria prophylaxis. I had a small private area where I could enjoy a nonalcoholic O'Doul's beer and listen to Jimmy Buffet on my headset. I would run away from Somalia listening to songs like "Margaritaville" and "Cheeseburger in Paradise."

In mid-January the clans of war-torn Mogadishu reached a peace agreement and promised to punish, under harsh Islamic laws, anyone who violated it. Although clan elders from both Aideed's Habr Gidr and Ali Mahdi's Abgal clans were present during the meeting, the conspicuous absence of the two powerful warlords placed in question the ability to enforce any peace in Mogadishu. It was not until late February that Aideed and Ali Mahdi agreed to stop fighting each other and begin talks on a transitional government—discussions that never led to anything substantive. Somalia was slowly returning to the way it was before UN intervention.

Our combat units were training less because the reduced force left few soldiers to do anything but carry out essential tasks. The combat forces, unlike their combat support and combat service support counterparts, whose wartime capabilities are enhanced during humanitarian and peacekeeping operations, struggled to maintain their fighting edge. Combat support and service support forces are able to practice the same tasks they are expected to perform in war or peace: water purification, distribution of supplies, administration, and the like.

Although our combat forces assumed a sedentary posture the final 45 days, the JTF remained actively engaged in an aggressive civil affairs operation. The civil affairs soldiers, under the watchful eye of the combat troops, continued to provide humanitarian assistance by distributing food, water, medical supplies, cots, and school supplies to over thirty schools, twenty orphanages, and several hospitals and clinics. They also implemented several medical, dental, and veterinary civil action programs. Additionally, the JTF initiated civil action projects that included building repairs, well enhancement, and drainage improvement.

I gained an appreciation for the civil affairs soldiers. They proved to be a combat multiplier by winning the trust and confidence of the Somali people, but then, as now, it was essential that their efforts were fully integrated into the overall plan. I had occasion to experience these well-meaning soldiers getting so enamored of what they were doing and the people they were trying to help that they soon found themselves needing help.

Late one afternoon we had to launch observation and attack helicopters to search for an overdue civil affairs team, led by the brigade S5, which was visiting a clan elder some 20 miles north of Mogadishu. The S5's intentions were good, but he had no business being that far from the city. It was not part of our plan, and turned out to be an unsanctioned mission that involved clansmen of little political consequence. This visit did not support the brigade's or the JTF's civil affairs objectives. All this had resulted in a couple of tense hours, but the team arrived safely back at our compound. After that episode no civil affairs mission was conducted without my personal approval.

There was little hostile activity by the clans in Mogadishu either directed at us or at each other. In early February, a marine-escorted convoy with two U.S. diplomats came under fire from two snipers in the center of the city. The special security detachment of marines, which was not part of UNOSOM, immediately responded with automatic weapons and grenade launchers. The unfortunate outcome was the death of eight civilians. Aideed, knowing that U.S. involvement was near its end, instructed his followers to remain calm and not to retaliate. He condemned the killings and proclaimed that "the excuses the Americans are giving for killing our people is nonsense and baseless."

The attack on the diplomats was followed early one morning by a large bomb detonated next to a security wall constructed from sea-land containers stacked three high at the New Port. The blast woke the city up and demonstrated the vulnerability of the UN security around the airport and port facilities. The explosion blew a section of nine containers into an area that had previously been occupied by coalition soldiers readying for redeployment, strewing the area with shredded metal and debris. The motive for the explosion was never determined, but it was thought to be labor related.

The United Nations employed a large number of the local populace, whose jobs ranged from unskilled construction work to clerical help. Additionally, many of the local businesses and support operations like the port had increased their employment to meet the growing needs of the UN presence. But as the UN force was downsized, so was the need for labor. The random shootings and disturbances from disgruntled unemployed workers became increasingly a concern.

When the UN World Food Program decided to lay off eight of fourteen Somali employees in Beledweyne, they armed themselves with grenades and held the Algerian program director hostage. A few weeks later the Somali director of the International Medical Corps was threatened with death by his laid-off driver, and a British aid worker for the World Food Program was kidnapped. The Somalis did not understand the reductions, and they responded in the manner they were accustomed to—with violence.

The SNA for the most part remained passive. Its members sponsored weekly rallies at a grandstand adjacent to Via Lenin, disseminated their propaganda through local media, and continued with their subtle intimidation of Somali workers and UN employees. Since they were not directly participating in armed hostilities, their heavy weapons, including their technicals, were kept under wraps. (Before international involvement in Somalia, whoever had the biggest gun ruled, and Aideed and his followers were well armed and placed to pick up where they had left off before U.S. and UN intervention.)

Periodically, one of our sniper teams armed with Barrett .50-caliber or M24 7.62mm sniper rifles would observe and engage a militiaman driving a technical or carrying a crew-served weapon.[2] These snipers were lethal, and they proved a superb deterrent against the movement and transport of militia weapons near our compounds. With a single shot they could reach out and touch a belligerent at 1,000 meters, and they did so frequently. Each of the U.S. fortifications had a complement of trained snipers, a mix of Special Forces, marines, and soldiers resident to Falcon Brigade units.

Our heliborne snipers also proved extremely effective. Equipped with the Barrett, the sniper flights were usually in concert with our Eyes over Mogadishu night missions. The sniper aircraft (UH-60) would trail the lead helicopter by about a half-mile. Although the aircraft were completely blacked out, if the lead helicopter attracted ground fire, the sniper aircraft would observe, acquire, and engage the target with the aid of night-vision accessories. Typically, the helos carried two teams of snipers and spotters equipped with a hand-held laser designator. The Special Forces snipers would sit on wooden benches in the troop compartment with their feet braced against cargo straps and their rifles slung from the ceiling. Airborne snipers were only employed for a couple of months; we eventually ceased operation because of concerns for the teams' safety if the aircraft experienced a hard landing.

In early January the number of sniper engagements increased markedly. One of the engagements may have resulted in the death of a pregnant Somali woman who was an innocent bystander several yards behind the intended target. Though never substantiated, the unfortunate incident drew an intense news media inquiry about our use of sniper teams. The Defense Department promptly provided the following news release:

> Over the last couple of days, there have been news reports of incidents involving US snipers. Under the Rules of Engagements, it is permissible for our forces to engage Somalis with crew served weapons, RPGs or machine guns, as possession of these weapons demonstrates hostile intent. Our forces also have the ability to take any necessary actions to defend themselves.
>
> The loss of life of the Somali woman was indeed tragic. We regret any loss of life in Somalia. In the incident, US forces engaged a Somali armed with a machine gun, in accordance with the ROE. Two shots were fired at a legitimate and confirmed target. The first shot missed, the second hit the intended target. A command inquiry could not state conclusively that a US fired round did or did not strike the Somali woman.[3]

Although I am a proponent of the employment of snipers, I believe that most people feel there is something unclean—unsporting or not chivalrous—about their use. Some see sniping as a dishonorable method of prosecuting war and expect more from our military. The alleged killing of the young Somali woman only reinforced the skeptics' view and illustrated how a misplaced round can instantly result in human tragedy.

Though of little comfort to a victims' family, provisions for reimbursing surviving relatives through a claims process have been set up by our government. The U.S. Foreign Claims Act provides the authority to pay or deny claims that arise out of conflict or war. In Somalia neither our government nor the United Nations was under any legal obligation to pay compensation for incidental damage, including loss of life, incurred during a combat operation. Although no claimant came forward on behalf of the pregnant woman, because she met her death during a combat operation there was no legal obligation to offer compensation. If her death had come from being struck by a military vehicle on a routine supply run, her heirs would have received payment (we unfortunately had these experiences, and the families were promptly compensated).

We were under the jurisdiction of the judge advocate, Headquarters 9th Air Force, Shaw Air Force Base, South Carolina. The 9th Air Force is Central Command's air force component command. Every Wednesday, the brigade's Judge Advocate General (JAG) officer, who was appointed by the Foreign Claims Commission, would entertain claims at the front gate to the embassy compound. He worked diligently to ensure that the claims would comport with local customs while maintaining fairness in arriving at a decision. It was not an easy task, and during the brigade's time in Somalia, we were blessed with two extremely competent JAG officers.

In awarding a claim, the JAG officer had to determine whether the death or injury was incidental to a combat operation. If the claimant had a legitimate petition, then the next step was to determine the sex of the casualty. The maximum allowable payment for the accidental death of a male was 100 camels, or $10,000, and for a female, 50 camels, or $5,000. Age and health were factors. The heirs of a young boy would receive less than those of a young working-age male, as would the heirs of a child-bearing woman receive more than those of an old woman. The disparity in payment between the sexes mirrored the Somali culture, and any deviation was a delicate matter.

Cultural peculiarities also challenged the intelligence community. The in-country intelligence apparatus worked hard to keep a finger on the pulse of the various clan operations and intentions. The source most relied upon was human intelligence (HUMINT), yet it was the least dependable because of the Somalis' propensity to embellish. At the national level, the HUMINT resources consisted of the Joint Operations Support Element made up of the U.S. intelligence agencies and the U.S. Liaison Office (USLO), which was our diplomatic presence in Somalia. At the theater and JTF level there were counterintelligence teams made up of army and marines, air force Office of Special Investigations Teams (OSI), special operations forces, and the civil affairs teams.

Imagery assets were the most abundant intelligence resource. Secondary imagery and overhead imagery comprised the national level resources. Theater and JTF intelligence assets included the navy's tactical airborne reconnaissance pod system (TARPS) slung under low-flying jet aircraft; a specially modified navy P3 Orion patrol plane; a single-engine superquiet airplane with a real-time downlink to JTF HQ; the Pioneer unmanned aerial vehicle with a downlink to JTF HQ; the Night Hawk ground FLIR system; and hand-held aerial and ground still and video cameras.

A detachment from the National Security Agency gathered signal intelligence (SIGINT) and emitter intelligence. SIGINT was probably the most reliable source of intelligence, although what you heard may not have represented the truth. The Somali militiamen always seemed to outdo one another with their exaggerations. It didn't matter if they were submitting a report to a superior or having a casual conversation with a crony—it was as if embellishment was embedded in the culture. Of course, many of the militia spent a great deal of time whacked out on their favorite weed, which would account for some of their erratic behavior and exaggeration.

The brigade headquarters soldiers were anxious to make the trip home. Many had been almost 8 months in Somalia, the longest stay of any Americans but for those few assigned to UNOSOM II headquarters. We had a solid plan for a brigade headquarters relief in place by Matt Brodrick's 24th MEU headquarters, which conducted a 2-day overlap with our troopers that culminated in mission assumption on 28 February 1994. The remaining army elements, including an aviation detachment from 4-4th Aviation, fell under 2-22d Infantry TF and reported to Brodrick. Lieutenant Colonel Smith and his outfit remained in country 3 weeks after the Falcon Brigade's departure before they loaded onto *Mediterranean Sky* for their trip to Mombasa.

Along with packing the sea-land containers for shipment and cleaning the seemingly endless number of wheeled and tracked vehicles traveling through the New Port wash racks, the helicopters had to be flown to dockside and "prepped" for shipment by sea. The aircraft required minor dismantling, and then they were overlaid with a protective covering ("shrink wrap") to stave off the corrosive effects of the lengthy ocean journey. The plastic coating, affixed in large strips and stuck on by heat gun, was applied by a Maryland National Guard outfit activated expressly for this purpose. To protect the guardsmen from the periodic Somali sniper or stray bullets, we constructed a large U-shaped barrier of several sea-land containers stacked two high on the edge of the pier. The guardsmen were quick in their work, and before long all our equipment was loaded and heading out to the open ocean.

The brigade headquarters strength was reflected in seventy-three personnel, enough to conveniently fit what was left of our organization into the troop compartment of a C-5 transport. The first day of March saw the sun rise over the Indian Ocean as it had everyday for the past 8 months that the brigade had occupied the sands of Somalia, but this day was different. You could feel the excitement in the air and see the anticipation on the faces of the soldiers. In the early hours we hefted our rucksacks onto our backs and grabbed our kit bags, then marched to the old Ranger hangar that had been converted into a staging area for departing troops. We formed a single line and went through customs, then into a sterile area to await our time for getting on the giant iron bird.

Major General Montgomery hosted a fitting farewell and delivered inspiring remarks that touched each of the soldiers. The brigade headquarters had spent 8 of Montgomery's 13 months in Somalia, and elements of the 10th Mountain Division had been with him through the entire ordeal. It was an emotional farewell for everyone.

With the brigade's colors firmly in the hands of Command Sergeant Major Brown and the Headquarters Company guidon flapping in the breeze, the last remaining soldiers of the 10th Aviation Brigade headquarters marched in single file toward the boarding steps of the aircraft. Minutes later we were on our way.

As the plane raced down the runway we were all entertaining thoughts of what had been and what was to be. I wanted to believe what we did would have a lasting effect and would make things better. It's important to feel that what you are doing has purpose, especially when human life is at stake or, more troubling, when life has been lost. I had struggled with the realities of Somalia and our involvement everyday as I carried the message of the importance of our presence to the soldiers. I not only wanted to believe, I needed to believe. But in my heart I knew our efforts were in vain. I knew that in a matter of months these people would be suffering again. And so I abandoned those thoughts and turned to the pleasantries of going home to my fiancée and my children. I didn't want to deal with Somalia anymore.

I could hardly wait until we were away from Mogadishu and high enough to out distance any surface threat. Arch, John Bendyk, Dwight Brown, and I occupied seats in the front crew cabin of the aircraft. We were on our way home, with a brief stop in Cairo for a plane change, a fuel stop in Rota, Spain, and then nonstop across the Atlantic Ocean to Griffis Air Force Base, New York. About 3 hours into the first leg of the flight, the air force captain pilot in command (PIC) approached me and said there might be a fuel consumption problem. He would recalculate, but he thought we might have to go somewhere else for fuel. We were over Sudan and peering out of the aircraft from 30,000 feet; I saw only hundreds of miles of *nothing*. I thought, "God! I can't even escape Somalia without an incident." I found it odd that fuel was a problem, but I was in no position to dispute the young captain's projections. After the PIC made a number of hurried calls, he settled on Luxor, Egypt, to replenish his fuel supply.

Luxor, ruled 1,300 years before Christ by the pharaoh Tutank-hamen, is on the Nile in the south central part of the country. Its large military-civilian airport plays host to many commercial aircraft that transport thousands of tourists to the sacred Valley of the Kings. But on this day there was no activity.

As the huge military transport approached the Egyptian airfield, the airport personnel became anxious: it was apparent that the Luxor airport authorities didn't know what to make of the situation. Here was this oversized camouflaged military plane landing and occupying most of their parking apron, and then there was a full complement of armed, desert-camouflaged U.S. soldiers off-loading. When we disembarked from the aircraft, we were quickly herded to a patch of desert 100 me-ters from the C-5 where we stood under the watchful eye of two very nervous Egyptian security police until the refueling was complete.

The aircrew huddled near the front troop door of the aircraft. The copilot, also a captain, was even younger looking than the PIC, as were a number of NCOs in the crew. There was an air force colonel on board, who had kept pretty much to himself during the flight and read a book until we experienced the fuel crisis. That seemed to energize him. It turned out that he was conducting an evaluation of the aircrew, which I suppose the young captains failed.

Once we were airborne, the remainder of the journey was pleas-antly uneventful. The return of the headquarters to Fort Drum marked the end of 15 months of brigade participation in Somalia. The 10th Aviation Brigade had been instrumental in UNITAF and UNOSOM II operations, and the outfit's performance had earned the unit a secure place in military history.

Notes

1. Six years later I was contacted by Tom Rooker, a member of Eastwood's production team at Malpaso Studios in Burbank, California. I had known Tom for a number of years. Clint was preparing to shoot a new movie entitled "Space Cow-boys" and wanted a military advisor on the set to assist him and his directors. East-wood had asked Tom if I had retired from the service and would be available for the four months of filming. I was pleasantly surprised and flattered by the offer, but I was still on active duty and had to decline. I settled for a visit to the movie set to view the filming a few months later.

2. Each time there was a report of sniper activity, General Montgomery would receive nervous calls from the CENTCOM commander in chief inquiring if we (U.S. forces) were being too forceful. Montgomery consistently responded that "we take no chances."

3. Defense Department news release, Office of the Assistant Secretary of De-fense—Public Affairs, 11 January 1994.

13

OUTCOME

No command, no commander was better served. Our forces
were magnificent. They weathered every storm, served their
country with honor, and gave Somalia the chance to rebuild.
—*Major General Thomas Montgomery,*
Commander, U.S. Forces Somalia (May 1993–March 1994)

The marines returned to their ships on March 25 after the last army
troops had departed Somali soil—and after one last tragic event for
the U.S. forces. Earlier in the month, eight airmen had been killed
when their AC-130H Spectre gunship crashed into the ocean 200 yards
off the coast near Malindi, Kenya, en route to support operations in
Somalia.

But despite the Americans' departure, the United Nations continued operations with the 20,000 remaining UNOSOM troops. The U.S.
presence was reduced to a few troops in logistical and supply jobs at
the UN headquarters, and some forty personnel assigned to the USLO
being secured by fifty-plus marines.

Between 4 May 1993 and 25 March 1994, the United Nation's experience with the use of chapter VII in peace enforcement operations
proved difficult and costly. Sixty-eight UN peacekeepers died and 262
were wounded in action, making this the bloodiest peacekeeping operation since the Congo crisis three decades earlier.[1] During the same period the United States experienced twenty-six killed in action, two nonbattle deaths, and 157 wounded in action. Earlier, during UNITAF
operations between 9 December 1992 and 4 May 1993, the U.S. losses
were four killed in action, four nonbattle deaths, and fifteen wounded
in action. Total U.S. service member casualties in Somalia amounted to
thirty-six killed and 172 wounded, and it cost the American taxpayers
in excess of $3 billion.[2]

Major General Montgomery's parting remarks captured the reality and the challenge both the United States and United Nations faced when conducting UN Charter chapter VII operations when he said: "We have a lot of work to do with the UN in terms of the UN being able to do a Chapter VII mission in the future and to do it more efficiently and better than we did here."

The conditions in Somalia continued to deteriorate. The United Nation's military forces maintained a "hunkered-down" mentality, while its political influence diminished to a point of irrelevance. By summer the technicals were back on the streets of Mogadishu, while banditry, looting, and clan skirmishes became the norm in the outlands. Aideed and the SNA were up to their old tricks again, reflecting the attitudes displayed a year earlier.[3] Mid-September marked the departure of USLO in Somalia, and for a short time a small number of personnel from the office monitored conditions in Somalia from Nairobi.

Concluding that the international community could no longer facilitate a peace and rebuild Somalia's political, legal, and law enforcement infrastructure, the United Nations announced it would withdraw all forces by March 1995. The United Nations looked to the United States for military support during the crucial withdrawal period from the war-torn region. President Clinton obliged by dispatching an MEU as part of a seven-nation combined task force to oversee the extraction of the last remaining UN forces. Not only did the United States feel an obligation to assist the United Nations departure from Somalia, but it was in our interest to ensure that equipment like the M60 main battle tanks and Cobra attack helicopters we had provided to the Pakistanis did not fall into Somali hands.

As we departed there was no famine in Somalia. The outskirts of Mogadishu showed some semblance of normality with agricultural production on the rise and security provided by improvised deals between local clans and factions. Despite these encouraging developments, Mogadishu returned to routine armed encounters between the rival followers of Aideed and Ali Mahdi.

Mohammed Siad Barre, the man who had ruled the impoverished African country for more than 20 years, died on 2 January 1995, in exile in Lagos, Nigeria. He was 80 years old.

In May 1996, Mohammed Farah Aideed was fatally wounded in a shoot-out with rival clansmen. He died in a hail of gunfire—the way he met his death was nothing more than an extension of the way he lived his life. Aideed was a violent man, yet I derived no satisfaction from his death, nor did I feel any remorse as I read the report of the fatal

*The author (second from left) and
CSM Dwight Brown (far right) pose with clan elders north of Mogadishu*

action in a brief *Washington Post* newspaper article occupying a single column on the bottom at page 17.

Ironically, in the summer of 1996 Aideed's third son, Hussein Mohammed Aideed, returned to Mogadishu from the United States where he had lived since he was 14. In his early 30s, the former part-time Orange County, California, government employee and ex-marine reservist, who had participated in UNITAF as an interpreter, became the self-proclaimed president of Somalia. He has the full support of the SNA and the Habr Gidr clansmen, which makes his proclamation reality in the confines of his piece of Mogadishu.

On 16 October 1996, Hussein Aideed, Ali Mahdi, and Osman Atto signed a cease-fire agreement—another pact in a long list of agreements. Fighting broke out less than a month later, resulting in 135 dead and 900 wounded over a 5-day period, and illustrating the fruit of Hussein's gains and the failure of the last mediation effort by Kenya's President Daniel arap Moi.

On 29 May 1997, Hussein Aideed and Ali Mahdi Mohammed announced from Cairo yet another cease-fire agreement after meeting with Egyptian President Hosni Mubarak, Egypt having taken up where Kenya left off, in another effort to broker a peace between the warring factions. This meeting led to still another in Cairo during December 1997, where the parties agreed to hold a January 1999 national reconciliation conference for all of the factions of the war-torn territory. Meanwhile, in August 1998 Aideed held unilateral talks with Ethiopian Prime Minister Meles Zenawi, with the intent of forging friendlier relations with the bordering nation—a country with a long history of war with the Somali. Despite the rhetoric and long list of meetings by the clansmen, Somalia and its people are no further along than the day we departed the rocky shores of that East African land.

The brief 3-year period when the international community intervened provided hope and expectations of a better way of life to a desperate people. We did make a difference and we did make things better for the Somalis. Unfortunately, it was the Somali people themselves who were unwilling or unable to take advantage of the world's attention. John Hirsch and Robert Oakley best capture the Somalis' missed opportunity in their book, *Somalia and Operation Restore Hope:* "The Somalis had been given every opportunity and assistance to resolve their difference and start rebuilding their country but had instead turned the other way, back toward violent struggle for personal, political and factional advantage.[4]

Although the United Nations may have overreached its charter and its capabilities when the Security Council approved resolution 814 and chose chapter VII as the vehicle to force the rebuilding of a nation, the Somalia experience should not inhibit our nation's involvement in future peacekeeping operations. The Somalia episode must act as a constant reminder that a clear concise policy with a measurable end-state is imperative before we commit our treasure to an operation—a criterion that may well be out of reach of the United Nations.

Notes

1. John L. Hirsch and Robert B. Oakley, *Somalia and Operation Restore Hope: Reflections on Peacemaking and Peacekeeping* (Washington, D.C.: United States Institute of Peace, 1995), p. 145.
2. Thomas Montgomery, *U.S. Forces Somalia,* briefing slide, 18 May 1994.
3. Hirsch and Oakley, *Somalia and Operation Restore Hope,* p. 146.
4. Ibid., p. 146.

PART 2

Preparation and Conduct of Military Operations in Haiti, September 1994–March 1995

We hoped for a peace dividend. We ended up with a mailbox full of unexpected, unwanted bills—Somalia, Bosnia, more trouble with Iraq.

—*General Gordon R. Sullivan,*
Chief of Staff of the Army (1991–1995)

The nature of modern warfare demands that we fight as a joint team. This was important yesterday, it is essential today, and it will be even more imperative tomorrow.

—*General John M. Shalikashvili,*
Chairman, Joint Chiefs of Staff (1993-1997)

**Aboard the USS *Dwight D. Eisenhower,*
14 September 1994**

You couldn't help being impressed by the display of joint military might and the heightened activity surrounding the departure of the nuclear air-craft carrier USS *Eisenhower* from its homeport in Norfolk, Virginia. As the senior army commander aboard, I was suffused with pride as I stood on a crowded catwalk atop the ship's superstructure, six stories above the aircraft-landing surface, and gazed down on the fleet of fifty-one olive drab Army helicopters arrayed across the 4.5-acre flight deck. Two thousand 10th Mountain Lightfighters occupied the hangar bays below, anxiously awaiting their fate. Forty-five days earlier, no soldiers or sailors on board had imagined that they would play a part in such a bold, innovative approach to U.S. force projection.

It was 10:30 A.M. and the sky was clear and blue, accented by a gentle sea breeze. The entire circumference of *Eisenhower*'s flight deck was lined with alternating soldiers and sailors, as the seamens' loved ones gathered on the dock to bid them farewell. Family members were waving banners and American flags, while television news helicopters circled overhead and the harbor's fireboat spouted streams of water from its many nozzles. Regardless of which direction you looked there was activity, fashioning a sense of importance on a grand scale.

We were on our way to Haiti. As the harbor tugs strained to maneuver the mammoth 95,000-ton *Eisenhower* in the direction of the open sea, my thoughts began to digress as I reminisced about how we arrived at this historic juncture in U.S. military history.

14

FORT DRUM,
NEW YORK, APRIL 1994

Readiness is . . . our first responsibility in providing for the common defense. Readiness is the key to deterrence and if required,
to fighting and winning.
—*General John A. Wickham, Jr.,*
Chief of Staff of the Army (1983–1987)

It didn't take long after our return from Somalia for the brigade to
resume the rigors of life in the 10th Mountain Division. Our cohorts
quickly forgot what we had experienced and where we had been, but then
many of them had been down the same road well before us. After a 2-
week leave for the brigade headquarters personnel, it was back to business. I was never one to rest on my laurels and I encouraged my subordi-
nates not to do so either. The brigade had accomplished everything that
was asked, and it was time to move on. Even if one were so inclined to
indulge in past successes, the division's fast-paced schedule did not afford
the luxury.

The cavalry squadron, along with a robust support slice from the
brigade headquarters, was deploying to the Joint Readiness Training
Center a month after our return, the attack battalion was scheduled for
a gunnery exercise in early May, and the assault battalion was repairing its war-battered UH-60 fleet.

The brigade's recovery from Somalia was calculated and methodical. Lieutenant Colonel Archambault and the staff had developed a
sound plan with measurable milestones to return the brigade to fighting
trim. It was a 5-month recover-refit-retrain program. The division
and installation staffs were in full support—crucial for the plan's success. Every day large flatbed trucks were arriving with dismantled
Black Hawks and Cobras, and a seemingly endless number of sea-land
containers.

The brigade had logged 27,000 flight hours in Somalia, and the readiness of our aircraft fleet was well below standard. Two-thirds of our Black Hawk aircraft (twenty-three) were either in or scheduled for a complete rebuild program. The Cobra fleet wasn't in much better shape. A third of the attack helicopters was undergoing extensive maintenance: the salt-laden coastal air in Somalia had corroded virtually every aircraft part. The rebuild program, called the Somalia Aircraft Recovery Program (SARP), involved refurbishing the airframe and its components from top to bottom. For the Black Hawk, the process cost on average $750,000 per aircraft and took about 179 days to complete. The contractor's being limited by space and labor resulted in no more than six aircraft in the program at any given time. We were fortunate to have the SARP maintenance facility collocated with our operations at Wheeler-Sack Army Airfield, although a few aircraft were rebuilt at Hunter Army Airfield, Georgia. To the credit of the contractor, the finished product was like a new helicopter.

My return to Fort Drum in upstate New York presented some unexpected challenges. Because I had raced through Fort Drum on my way to Somalia, I had not had the opportunity to develop the essential relationships, with either the division command group or staff, that a brigade commander would have normally obtained after 6 months of command. Although the division leadership and staff had done yeoman's work to support the brigade's every need while deployed in Somalia, upon my return to Fort Drum I found myself starting from scratch in an effort to establish my credibility. In Somalia my connection with the division was through COL Evan Gaddis, the division chief of staff. Gaddis was responsive to the brigade's needs and proved to be a friend in court. I knew names on the division staff, but few faces, and I knew fewer of the installation personnel. It was as if I had just arrived on station to assume command of the brigade.

Although I wore the 10th Mountain patch on my shoulder, Major General Ernst and Major General Montgomery wrote my initial command fitness report. I was concerned that my 6-month absence from the 10th might in some way call into question my loyalty. Fortunately this was not an issue, for I was quickly absorbed into the 10th Mountain team.

The brigade had received its share of recognition for its exploits in Somalia. The Army Aviation Association of America bestowed its coveted Aviation Unit of the Year Award, and the Daedalians, a group with its origins in World War I, presented the brigade their prestigious Brigadier General Carl I. Hutton Memorial Award for safety.

Awards and trophies were nice, but times in the brigade were tough. Equipment readiness was not our only problem; the upcoming months were burdened with change and challenge. Because of our extended stay in Somalia, the entire brigade had a number of soldiers who had been kept well beyond their normal tour in order to maintain a degree of continuity throughout the deployment. It was now time to let those soldiers go. The personnel system had no mercy: we experienced a loss of over 35 percent of the brigade in less than 60 days.

In early May, LTC Lee Gore relinquished command to LTC Bill Driver, and June saw the passing of the yellow and gold cavalry squadron colors from Jim Kelley to Ellis Golson. As is the army way, capable leaders are replaced with equally able officers.

The brigade was about to embark upon a major transformation. We were turning in the few remaining UH-1 Huey helicopters and replacing them with additional UH-60s, and we were programmed to replace all of the AH-1 Cobras and OH-58A/C Kiowa helicopters with the modern OH-58D Kiowa Warrior. The force modernization effort would occur over 16 months, commencing with 3-17th Cavalry, followed by 2-25th Aviation. When complete, the brigade would fly and maintain two airframes instead of four. The benefits were obvious: fewer parts, tools, test equipment, people, and training requirements. It made a lot of sense, and I had championed the concept from its inception, actively promoting its acceptance. I had even written an article for a military journal describing a similar force structure equipped with the Kiowa Warrior and the Black Hawk. But it was practical experience that caused me to recognize the flaw in the new organization and my shortsightedness.

The absence of the OH-58A/C left a void in the light utility helicopter mission for the brigade. I wouldn't comprehend the magnitude of the problem for another year, but I was quick to realize that we were institutionally restricting our capability and limiting aviation's strength—flexibility.

The $979 per flight hour Kiowa Warrior is not a troop carrier. It is a two-pilot aircraft with an aft compartment crammed with electronic processors, denying even the pilots a suitable place to store personal gear. Left with only the Black Hawk to transport soldiers and supplies, the customary, run-of-the-mill missions that required one or two passengers would defer to the UH-60. At $1,626/flight hour compared to $293/hour for an OH-58A/C, a Black Hawk's routine flights would become costly.[1] Necessities like transporting the chaplain or making a mail run were either going to cost more or be denied. It was a case of the aviation community placing procurement and force modernization funding in the glamorous missions of attack and cavalry and air assault, and neglecting the mundane daily administration/utility missions required in peace and war—an issue that still remains unresolved.

With the snow melting, the cold northern New York spring gave way to the long, warm sunny days of summer. We were beginning to get our replacements, and, with the exception of our UH-60 fleet, the equipment we had not turned in was up to Department of Army standards.

Lieutenant Colonel Archambault vigorously labored the staff through a series of exercises, and the battalion commanders were aggressively training and prepping their units. The three battalions were on separate and distinct vectors. The cavalry squadron was standing down awaiting receipt of the OH-58D, the attack battalion was maintaining the status quo until its turn to draw down in preparation for the Kiowa Warrior, and the assault battalion was getting stronger each day with the arrival of new people and airframes.

An OH-58D Kiowa Warrior firing a Hellfire missile

Although I felt the first 6 months of my command could not be equaled, I knew that the challenges presented by force modernization would be great and would present a different dimension to brigade command. With the exception of the light utility issue, the brigade restructure and reequipping would result in an organization better able to support the 10th Mountain Division Lightfighters anytime, day or night. I concluded that I would spend the remaining months of my command managing force modernization.

Note

1. Based on FY1999, Department of the Army, average flying hour cost for specific airframes.

15

THE ALERT

Like it or not, most of you will find yourselves in a place you never heard of, doing things you never wanted to do.
—*General John Shalikashvili*, Chairman, Joint Chiefs of Staff (1993–1997), addressing U.S. troops, spring 1994

I returned from California on a Sunday evening, 31 July 1994, to my quarters at Fort Drum after a 2-week holiday with my children, Brian, David, and Laura. I had no sooner walked through the door than my telephone rang. It was COL Jim Campbell, my next-door neighbor and the division's chief of staff. Campbell, who had replaced Colonel Gaddis, said Major General Meade wanted a meeting first thing in the morning with all of the major subordinate commanders. He couldn't divulge the subject, but said it was extremely important.

The next morning all of the colonel-level commanders, along with the division and installation staff principals, gathered in the division emergency operation center (EOC). Major General Meade and his two assistant division commanders, BG George Close, who had replaced Gile, and COL Theodore (Ted) Purdom entered the basement war room.

The previous Friday, Meade had been summoned to Atlantic Command (ACOM) headquarters in Norfolk, Virginia. There, he was briefed by the ACOM plans officer on Operation Restore Democracy (later changed to Uphold Democracy), a plan involving a forced entry into Haiti. Although it was a plan known to few, after the October 1993 *Harlan County* incident in Port-au-Prince, Joint Task Force (JTF) 180 had been established using the XVIII Airborne Corps headquarters as the nucleus for the task force headquarters.

Under the direction of LTG Hugh Shelton, commander of XVIII Airborne Corps, the corps had been planning and rehearsing variations of the invasion plan for the previous 10 months. The draft plan was completed in February 1994, and it had been worked and reworked countless times. During his visit, Meade was charged with forming Joint Task Force 190 and developing an alternative plan for operations in Haiti. Meade's plan was to be executed in a relatively permissive, uncertain environment.

We were not aware of JTF-180 or its planning effort when Meade stepped in front of the assembled officers and commenced briefing us on what he had been asked to do. Details were sketchy and he wasn't sure of the extent of our involvement, but two bits of information leaped to the front: we were to be prepared to act within the next 30 to 45 days and to expect a permissive or semi-permissive environment. We all shared glances thinking, "What was semi-permissive?" Meade went on to say that he was on tap to provide his initial concept brief to the commander in chief, U.S. Atlantic Command (CINCACOM), Adm. Paul Miller, on Wednesday, 3 August.

I had been in command of the brigade for 10 of my scheduled 24 months, and I saw my rather mundane plan to manage the brigade's force modernization effort for the remainder of my tenure dissipate before my eyes. The one thing proving to be a certainty in the 10th Mountain Division was uncertainty! It was the sign of the times.

The Haiti planning and preparation would proceed on a need-to-know basis, making the cancellation of some soldiers' summer leave difficult without a credible explanation. The few troopers whose liberty was disrupted early on were good sports, suspecting that something was up. Neither they nor I realized just how big it would turn out to be.

I attended a series of meetings and briefing throughout the following 2 days. My initial concern was our aircraft availability, especially the Black Hawks. Although the assault battalion was regaining its readiness, only nineteen of its thirty-two UH-60s were mission capable. We expected three more from the SARP program over the next 2 weeks, bringing the total to twenty-two available assault helicopters.

Major General Meade mentioned the possible use of an aircraft carrier, but no one was sure if we would be supported by a fleet aircraft carrier, an amphibious assault ship capable of transporting helicopters and Harrier jump jets, or, for that matter, any seaworthy platform at all. The command group had little confidence in the use of a carrier, and I shared their skepticism.

If army helicopters were going to launch from a ship, we were well behind the power curve in training and qualifying our aviators in navy deck-landing procedures. From my command experience in the 25th Infantry Division in Hawaii, where we routinely performed deck landings, it was a resource-intensive proposition. Such specialized training required ground school, a ship or floating platform with the standard Navy markings, and a qualified navy or army instructor pilot to certify each aviator. Additionally, there was a need for over-water survival training, as well as the procurement of all the necessary equipment to keep a downed crew member alive in the water in the event of a mishap. The training task would be formidable.

In my heart of hearts, I felt the navy would never allow the decks of a fleet aircraft carrier to be cleared of its life blood, naval air, and replace it with army aviation and muddy-booted Lightfighters. Nor would the marines condone the use of one of the navy's amphibious assault ships for the task. I was confident the carrier business was a dead issue.

I met with my battalion commanders and selected staff members to brief them on what I knew. With Arch at the helm, we stood up our own crisis-action team composed of a few chosen officers and NCOs. I was blessed with a staff teeming with Somalia veterans who knew what it took to move the brigade and understood the challenges presented. All the principals had served in their staff capacities throughout the Somalia deployment with the exception of the S3. John Bendyk had been promoted and transferred a couple of months earlier, and replaced by MAJ Steve Semmens. As Lee Gore's S3 and then his executive officer during combat operations, Steve was more than qualified for the job. An extremely bright officer, he possessed a solid background in assault and attack helicopter operations. Semmens was surrounded by a number of energetic company-grade and noncommissioned officers who enthusiastically did his bidding.

There was much to be done, but the cloak of secrecy limited our actions. We anxiously awaited General Meade's return from ACOM headquarters.

16

HAITI

Nightmare republic.
—*Graham Greene,* author of *Getting to Know the General*

This would not be the United States' first intervention into Haitian affairs, nor the first time our military would set foot on Haitian soil. President Woodrow Wilson had dispatched the marines to Haiti in 1915, ostensibly for humanitarian intervention under the Monroe Doctrine. Many Haitians believed the foreign presence was merely a means to protect U.S. investments and to establish a base to protect the approaches to the Panama Canal. During the marines' occupation, a new constitution was introduced in 1918 that permitted foreigners to own land. The new constitutional proviso, coupled with the marine presence until 1934, assured our country a firm political and financial position in Haiti.

Haiti is situated some 750 miles southeast of Miami, Florida. It is approximately the size of the state of Maryland and shares the Caribbean island of Hispaniola with the Dominican Republic. Relative to the area it occupies, Haiti (from an Arawak Indian word for mountains) is more mountainous than Switzerland; the highest peak, Chaîne-de-la-Selle, reaches 9,000 feet above sea level. Inhabiting the western third of the isle, Haitian society represents two cultural traditions, Dahomean African and French. But long before the French and Africans arrived, what is known today as Haiti was discovered by Christopher Columbus during his first voyage in 1492. He claimed the land for Spain and upon his departure he left forty-two Spaniards behind to establish a permanent colony and construct a fort near what is today Cap-Haïtien. By the time Columbus returned to the colony the next year, the Spanish colony and its populace had been destroyed by the isle's inhabitants, the Arawak Indians. This did not discourage the Spanish

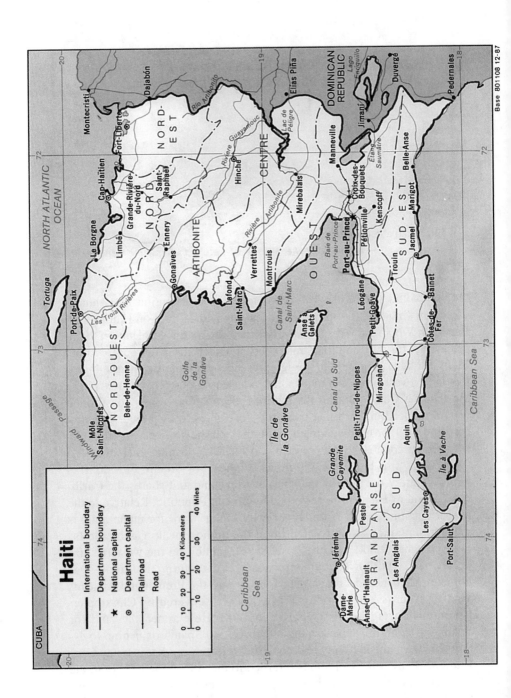

Base B01108 12-87

156

from colonizing their newly discovered land—a consequence that led to the demise of the island inhabitants.

The 300,000 Arawak Indians succumbed to infectious diseases so rapidly after contact with the Europeans that they left no appreciable influence on the racial composition or the culture of the present-day population. Within 50 years after the discovery of the Arawaks, the native Indians numbered fewer than 500.

The Spanish introduced African slaves in 1512 to work the gold mines and fill the labor void left by the eradication of the Arawaks. In 1625, the French gained a foothold in Haiti by occupying an old French pirate base on a small island off the northern shore of Haiti called Tortuga or Tortue. The French in 1697 gained formal control of Haiti through the Treaty of Ryswick, and the ensuing 100 years saw Haiti become the world's wealthiest colony. Today's Haitian population is composed almost entirely of the descendants of slaves imported from west central Africa in the seventeenth and eighteenth centuries.

During a major slave rebellion that started in 1791, some 100,000 slaves either murdered or forced the European settlers to flee. The result is the present-day culture based largely on African traditions, modified by some European influences. Ninety-five percent of the Haitian population comprises blacks, and the remaining 5 percent are mulattos and Europeans, making Haiti more ethnically homogeneous than most countries in Latin America and the Caribbean.[1]

Haiti gained its independence from France in 1804. Today, Haitians draw an immense pride from their country's being the second oldest republic in the Western Hemisphere. Yet Haiti is fundamentally a two-class society with the mulatto elite as the upper class and the blacks composing the lower class. A small middle class began to surface in the 1920s, with a limited number of blacks achieving political and commercial success.

The country's colorful past has been plagued with political turmoil and a history of repression and terror. In 190 years of independence Haiti has experienced twenty-one constitutions and forty-one heads of state. Most Haitian heads of state were military men, and few lived out their terms in office. Nine declared themselves heads of state for life, twenty-nine were assassinated or overthrown, and in the nineteenth century only one president left office alive.

One of the more notorious leaders was François Duvalier, known to the world as Papa Doc. A physician turned politician, in 1957 he was elected in a plebiscite. Duvalier was a black man, and a student of voodoo, who ruled with an iron fist and gained popularity with his promise to end the mulatto domination by placing the economic power into the hands of the black masses. Papa Doc, along with his secret police, the dreaded *ton-tons macoutes,* spread fear and repression throughout the country. In 1971 the ruthless dictator, who had been elected president for life, died leaving his 19-year-old son, Jean-Claude, to succeed him.

Jean-Claude, known as Baby Doc, and inheriting the mantle of his father's notoriety, ruled for 14 years. During the final months of his regime he clearly had lost control of the country and was faced with a rebellious people, so a hasty clandestine departure became his only option. In the early morning hours of 7 February 1986, an unmarked U.S. C-141 transport aircraft arrived at 2 A.M. at the Port-au-Prince airport to whisk Baby Doc, his wife, and their entourage of twenty-three to exile in Talloires, France. It was the final chapter of the Duvalier dynasty. Haiti had suffered 29 years of deprivation, repression, and state terrorism under the Duvaliers.

The replacement regime was headed by Lt. Gen. Henri Namphy with the collaboration of two other military members and two civilians. The new provisional government was entitled the National Council of Government. Although the interim government led to a new constitution in 1987, the country would not see the first openly and fairly elected president until late 1990.

In December of that year a populist priest, Father Jean-Bertrand Aristide, sponsored by the Lavalas Party, was elected president of Haiti. Aristide was a black Haitian who had the overwhelming support of the impoverished masses. Depending upon whom you speak to, Aristide has been described as prickly, vacillating, and whiny, or smart, charismatic, and spellbinding. Regardless, the popular leader took office on 7 February 1991 and commenced with sweeping reforms and the arrest of dozens of Duvalierists. During his initial months in office, the soft-spoken priest earned a reputation as an anti-American demagogue who threatened private enterprise and condoned violence against his political opponents. He enjoyed lukewarm support from the U.S. government, and in his own country Aristide eventually lost what little support he had from the Haitian middle class and wealthy when he suggested that the minimum wage be increased from $3 to $5 a day.

On September 1991, Police Chief Lt. Col. Joseph-Michel François and officers of the Haitian army overthrew Aristide's government, after only 7 months in office. François led the coup, but then relinquished the reins of government to Lt. Gen. Raoul Cedras, leader of the armed forces. Aristide fled first to Caracas, Venezuela, and then to the United

States. His departure was followed by thousands of refugees taking to the high seas in search of sanctuary in the United States.

Cedras, a mulatto, had the support of the police and the military, or Force Armée d'Haïti (FAd'H); the right-wing political organization known as the Front for the Advancement of and Progress of Haiti (FRAPH); and the *attachés,* who were a mafia-type criminal element with ties to FRAPH and the military. Cedras in turn gave his support to Supreme Court president Emile Jonaissant, who assumed the de facto provisional presidency of Haiti. As is Haiti's history, the triumvirate running the country spread intimidation and terror throughout the destitute nation.

Years of repression have resulted in a country of abject poverty. Haiti has the lowest annual per capita income in the Western Hemisphere and is essentially a nation of sick people. The Pan-American Health Organization, a branch of the World Health Organization, released a study in 1991 stating that one in ten pregnant women in Haiti is infected with the AIDS. About 10 percent of the population suffers from tuberculosis, syphilis, gonorrhea, viral hepatitis, and typhoid fever. Malaria and acute diarrheal disease are endemic.

President Clinton was first confronted by the Haiti problem even before his inauguration: the U.S. Coast Guard had estimated that as many as 200,000 Haitians were readying to flee by boat. Clinton, concerned about the political implication of these refugees arriving on the shores of Florida, announced that outgoing President Bush's repatriation policy (direct return) would remain in effect. He stated that once he took office, he would pursue negotiations and stiffer sanctions, but after the October 1993 USS *Harlan County* fiasco discussions within the administration regarding military intervention began to surface.

Since June 1993 Haiti had been under a UN fuel and arms embargo, and had all its assets abroad frozen. Nothing seemed to have much of an affect on the military junta, when suddenly in July 1993 the United Nations and the Organization of American States (OAS) brokered the Governors' Island Accord. The agreement called for Aristide's return from exile, the departure of the military junta, and the lifting of international trade sanctions. It appeared that a peaceful, orderly transition of power was in place. But Cedras continued to stonewall the efforts of the United Nations, and it wasn't long before the world realized that he had no intention of relinquishing his hold on Haiti.

With U.S.-Haiti policy making little headway, the Congressional Black Caucus began pressuring the administration for more action, and in April 1994 black activist Randall Robinson, head of the lobbying group TransAfrica, condemned the U.S. direct-return policy as racist. He staged a much-publicized hunger strike to protest the policy—a performance that had an apparent effect on the president's thinking.

In July the military junta expelled the UN human-rights monitors. This action aided the United States in gathering support for passage of UN Security Council resolution 940 authorizing the use of force to restore Aristide. Under an expanded UN embargo, the last commercial aircraft left Haiti on 30 July, virtually closing the country to the outside world. Military involvement was almost assured when, during the final week of August, Cedras ignored the UN special envoy sent to facilitate a last-ditch effort at mediation. The blatant rejection of the envoy by the junta was exacerbated by the brutal killing of long-time Aristide associate and ally Jean-Marie Vincent. It was now not a matter of if the U.S. would intervene militarily, but when.

Note

1. Robert J. Tata, *Haiti—Land of Poverty* (Washington, D.C.: University Press of America, 1982), p. 20.

17

THE PLANS

Make no little plans; they have no magic to stir men's blood.
—*Daniel H. Burnham,* Planner

The 10th Mountain Division's concept involved air-assaulting an infantry brigade or a portion of a brigade into Port-au-Prince in order to secure the commercial airfield and the port facility. Follow-on forces would arrive by strategic air and ship after the two ports of entry were secure. Port-au-Prince was determined to be the center of gravity for the entire operation, but the northern coastal city of Cap-Haïtien was also deemed essential. The marines were signed up to secure the northern port city.

The operation plan specified seven essential elements for mission success:

- Deploy quickly and execute rapid entry of forces
- Control the center of gravity: Port-au-Prince (and Cap-Haïtien in the north)
- Control the countryside
- Return President Aristide
- Maintain the initiative and momentum
- Stand up Haitian Public Security Force
- Ensure unity of effort

In response to the division's plan, the brigade staff developed several courses of action. One was to equip the Black Hawks with the extended-range fuel tanks and self-deploy the UH-60s 1,700 miles along the eastern seaboard to Guantanamo Naval Base, Cuba. Guantanamo (GTMO) was proposed as the initial staging base (ISB) because of its facilities and proximity to Haiti. The OH-58A/C and Cobra aircraft would be transported by air force strategic airlift (C5-C141) from Griffiss Air Force Base, New York, to GTMO (pronounced *get-mo*) for link-up. We considered the small island of Great Inagua north of Haiti as an ISB, but we discarded its use because it lacked the infrastructure GTMO offered. (Little did we know that the mosquito-infested island of Great Inagua was destined to be someone else's ISB.) We also investigated the naval base at Roosevelt Roads, Puerto Rico, as a brigade ISB, but the distance from the objective area and the necessity to overfly the Dominican Republic made it an unsuitable course of action. As the JTF plan matured, Roosevelt Roads was designated for transloading infantry forces from strategic transport to tactical airlift.

With the extended-range tanks, the Black Hawks would skim the surface of the 150 miles of open water that lie between Cuba and Haiti, deposit the troops on the objectives, and return without refueling. This course of action limited the number of troops and equipment that could be transported, extended the length of time the aircraft were airborne, and meant the Cobra gunship escort would arrive at the objective area needing fuel. The AH-1, devoid of any ordnance, did not have the fuel capacity to make the initial flight and arrive on the objective with any loitering time, much less burdening the helicopter with its combat load. We would need AH-64 Apaches with external fuel tanks, or we would have to establish a forward area rearm and refuel point (FARRP) somewhere in or near Haiti. If we employed AH-1s, the plan would require CH-47 Chinook helicopters loaded with Cobra ordnance and aviation fuel. Chinooks with internal fuel bladders are called Fat Cows, and this course of action would not work without them. We would also require additional Chinooks or Black Hawks to transport more troops in order to arrive on the objectives with adequate combat power.

Tactically, we knew it was imperative that we exploit army aviation's strength of night operations. Regardless of which course of action was chosen, conducting an early-hour insertion into Port-au-Prince was in order. Accepting some risk, we first needed to establish a FARRP on the western-most edge of the island of Gonave. The Cobras would relocate to the FARRP prior to the Black Hawks' departure from the ISB. Once armed and refueled, the Cobras, following an H-hour sequence, would link up with and accompany the Black Hawks to the objectives.[1]

This would require precise timing involving extensive over-water night-vision goggle (NVG) flight; a challenging environment because of the lack of a definitive horizon, impaired depth perception, and other phenomena associated with NVG over-water flight. Of special concern for the single-engine Cobras pilots was power train failure.

I remembered the discomfort of flying over the open ocean in Hawaii during daylight hours in a single-engine helicopter, and the character-building 90-mile legs using NVGs between the islands of Oahu and Kauai. This would not be an easy task for our pilots and would require a great deal of training to ensure that the aviator was confident. We determined that extended low-level NVG flights over upstate New York and Lake Ontario would work toward this goal.

Another course of action we explored was loading an amphibious assault ship at GTMO and steaming to the coast near Port-au-Prince. Army helicopter blades can be folded, but it is a maintenance-intensive procedure that requires a test flight once they are reconfigured for flight. Therefore, folding blades was not a practical option. Without the compact placement of the UH-60s on the amphib's deck, we would be unable to airlift a credible infantry force in the initial assault. Although sailing up to the shores near the city would afford us the luxury of a quick turnaround, we would not be able to initially mass sufficient combat power. At one point we considered employing two of the navy's helo assault platforms.

Our final course of action involved a fleet aircraft carrier. I was convinced it wouldn't happen, but General Meade asked us to consider its use. We possessed marine and joint publications on various helicopter-suitable ships, but we found nothing on an aircraft carrier; nor did we have anyone who understood the nuances of a big-deck carrier operation. Our first step was to find out how much deck space would be available. We scurried to find ship dimensions, only to discover that no two aircraft carriers are alike.

While the brigade crisis-actions team diligently worked to develop the options, LTCs Russ Forshag and Bill Driver wasted no time as they collaborated to overcome the training challenge. Russ was from southeastern Louisiana and had commanded the 3d Helicopter Assault Battalion (Knighthawks), 25th Aviation Regiment, for 21 months. He was a Somalia veteran who possessed a keen understanding of the assault helicopter mission, having taken his battalion from UH-1s to the Black Hawks early in his command. Russ would prove invaluable in the coming days and weeks. Bill Driver, the son of an army officer, was new to command, but proved to be a quick study. He was a superb trainer who was eager to build his team.

Under the guise of joint training, Russ had coordinated with the post engineers to paint on the airfield taxiways a number of navy shipboard helicopter landing pads to the dimensions and specifications found on a ship. A similar technique had been used in 1942 by LTC

Jimmy Doolittle when he painted the flight deck dimensions of an aircraft carrier on an army air forces airfield during his preparation for launching B-25 Mitchell medium bombers from the USS *Hornet* to attack the Japanese mainland. Forshag figured start with single-spot landing sites, and once that was mastered an aviator could easily progress to multispot, large-deck vessels. He was right. From the navy's perspective, once an aviator completed ground school and the required number of landings and takeoffs to qualify on a ship with a single helicopter landing spot, the aviator was qualified to land on any ship—single- or multispot. But if the aviator first qualified on a big-deck ship like an amphibious assault ship, he was not qualified to land on anything smaller. I later discovered that everything that has to do with a ship and its operation is at the discretion of the ship's captain— a very powerful man.

Major General Meade and his planners returned to Fort Drum late on Wednesday, and I was promptly summoned to the EOC. Admiral Miller had approved Meade's concept and stated that he and the chairman of the Joint Chiefs had discussed the 10th Mountain being ready by 1 September. We had a little more than 3 weeks. The plan called for a joint operation into Haiti with a MEU assaulting from the north and occupying the city of Cap Haïtien, and a 10th Mountain brigade combat team air-assaulting from a navy aircraft carrier into Port-au-Prince. Once the Port-au-Prince airfield and the port facility were secure, 10th Mountain follow-on forces would arrive. At some point after the marines had secured Cap Haïtien, a second 10th Mountain brigade combat team would relieve them. Additionally, Special Forces troops were to be a major participant, playing a big part in winning the hearts and minds of the people.

There were myriad details that had to be worked out, and a great deal of training that had to be accomplished in a very short time, but General Meade and his planners had developed a solid plan. Spearheading the planning effort was the talented G3, Tom Miller. A promotable lieutenant colonel, Miller would be promoted to colonel to perform his duties as JTF-190's J3.

Meade selected COL Andy Berdy to lead the combat brigade team from the carrier for this historic army first. Berdy, a 101st Airborne (Air Assault) Division veteran of Desert Storm, knew how to plan, train, and execute air-assault operations. As the commander of the 10th Mountain's 1st Infantry Brigade, Andy had worked hard to train his soldiers in the rigors of air-assault operations and was the likely choice to lead the Lightfighters into the heart of Port-au-Prince. He would have two of his infantry battalions, 2-22d Infantry and 1-87th Infantry, accompany him on the carrier, while his third battalion, 1-22d Infantry, would follow on from Griffiss Air Force Base via strategic air once the Port-au-Prince International Airport was secure.

Also ready at Griffiss would be COL Jim Dubik, commander of the 2d Combat Brigade Team. Dubik is known throughout the army for his visionary thinking and his operational and strategic concepts; his writings had stirred both controversy and praise during a time the army was plotting its future for the twenty-first century. Jim's intellect, skillful leadership, and independent thinking were the right mix for the challenges that lay ahead in northern Haiti.

The plan was still soft, plagued with uncertainties and unknowns, but we had to remain proactive. We did not have the luxury to wait for protracted decisionmaking and bureaucratic impediments. There just wasn't any time. I had assured General Meade that the aviation brigade would be ready by 1 September, and now I was having my doubts.

Note

1. "A successful air assault operation is a sequence of actions carefully planned and precisely executed. The basis for timing is the moment when the first aircraft in the first lift of the operation is to touch down on the landing zone. It is referred to as H-Hour. The H-Hour in air assault operation is equivalent to the attack time in a mission order." *Air Assault Operations,* Department of the Army Field Manual 90-4.

18

PREPARATION

Prepare your units to go to war. No mission or requirement precedes this.

—*General Edward C. Meyer,*
Chief of Staff of the Army (1979–1983)

On Monday, 8 August, all the major subordinate commanders presented their training plans to the commanding general. The completion date for the mission training was 31 August. The infantry brigades focused on small-unit tactics and techniques culminating with a day/night, company combined live-fire exercise involving all of the organic weapon systems of the division. The rules of engagement stated that supporting fires had to be direct and observed. This excluded the division's artillery and mortars from the actual operation, but their use was incorporated into the training. In Haiti, the troopers on the ground would have to rely on the lethal AC-130s and attack helicopters for their fire support. The live-fire exercises would include the notional play of the AC-130, for each company commander had an opportunity to incorporate the gunship platform into his planning and simulate its employment. All of the division's eighteen rifle companies were provided the same training opportunity.

Although the 3d Squadron, 17th Cavalry was submerged in force modernization with the Kiowa Warrior and would not deploy, I decided to submit Alpha Troop, the squadron's ground troop, to the same live-fire training program as the division's rifle companies. CPT Robert Finnegan and his Alpha troopers would accompany us to Haiti and play a critical role in our success.

The division's entire plan hinged on a trained and ready aviation force able to launch from a navy carrier. Without the ship-qualified aviators and properly equipped helicopters, the operation wouldn't happen. After a thorough mission analysis, we provided JTF headquarters with our force requirements. We needed a second Black Hawk company, a Chinook company, and either Apaches or Kiowa Warriors to ensure nighttime weapons' pinpoint accuracy. Our preference for attack aviation was the Apache with its extended range and inherent survivability. Having commanded the outfit that ran the Apache through the rigors of its initial operational test in the early 1980s (coupled with the helicopter's success during Desert Storm), I knew the twin-engine Apache was well suited for the mission. The plan involved staging a company of UH-60s, attack aircraft, and medevac aircraft on the aircraft carrier, while the CH-47s and second Black Hawk company would launch from GTMO and link up with the carrier force in Port-au-Prince.

The brigade was pressing hard. We had the helo-ship operations manuals for the ground school, freshly painted landing spots, plenty of helicopters, and a bunch of enthusiastic aviators. All we needed were a floating platform or ship and the navy's blessing. Steve Semmens coordinated with the Second Fleet Headquarters in Norfolk for a couple of their navy instructor pilots to be dispatched to the North Country to validate our training.

The two naval aviators were quick to certify the ground school and then spent the remaining time flying with our pilots. They were impressed and complimented the work that Forshag, Driver, and the brigade's instructor and safety pilots had accomplished. It was a monumental task, because we were confronted with training in excess of 120 aviators for both day and night deck qualifications. At times it appeared as if we didn't have enough time in a 24-hour period. Although confronted with a new set of visual cues associated with shipboard operations, the army aviator's real challenge was assimilating the navy jargon. Terms like *port beam* and *starboard bow,* traffic patterns like Charlie, Delta, and Alpha, and ship-to-pilot and pilot-to-ship signals became second nature to the army pilots.

A crucial piece of hardware was still missing. A floating platform, essential for the final phase of deck qualification training, still had not been identified. We directed our request to ACOM headquarters, even suggesting the use of a coast guard ship in the Great Lakes region. I raised this concern daily with JTF HQ, but to no avail. As the days passed we were still without a platform.

There was no shortage of mandatory training. Along with the deck landing training, we were mounting the wings and extended-range fuel tanks on all our Black Hawks. This was a time-consuming task, as was the associated training for the aviators. Because of a fatal accident in Germany a couple of years earlier involving a UH-60 equipped with extended-range tanks, there was explicit guidance on training in their use and employing them. Every pilot was required to perform a couple of flight hours with the tanks mounted. This training was consuming more aircraft flight hours and more time—both precious commodities.

Every crew member had to undergo water survival training. We commandeered one of the indoor pools on post and commenced with the most basic tasks of water survival and drownproofing, eventually graduating to the more complex tasks of using the helicopter emergency egress device (HEED).[1] We capped our training by requiring the crew members to free themselves from the confines of a "dunker" and climb to the safety of a one-man life raft. Someone located a portable dunker at the Brooklyn Coast Guard Station. The borrowed tubular contraption, referred to as the shallow water egress trainer or SWET chair, places a fully outfitted aviator in a harness surrounded by an array of 2- and 3-inch tubing. The device is inverted in the pool and the crew member soon finds himself or herself upside down in the water. The challenge is to get unlatched and swim free of the dunker. This sounds easy enough, but some soldiers became disoriented and found this a difficult task. Firing their personal weapons at the range provided a more familiar challenge for the aviation soldiers.

As with our infantry counterparts, live fire was essential to our readiness. We conducted day and night attack helicopter gunnery and door gunnery for our UH-60 crews. Just as with the 20mm cannon of the Cobra, we equipped the Black Hawk M60 machine guns with the AIM-1 laser, making our gunners deadly accurate at night. Our live fire was not limited to the aircrews; we requalified all our soldiers in their personal and crew-served weapons. We were training 7 days a week as the frustration over competing for range resources increased with each day.

The division was struggling with the force package while dealing with the challenges of setting up the JTF headquarters. With the 10th Mountain headquarters as the nucleus, the JTF headquarters was formed between 9 and 11 August with soldiers, sailors, airmen, marines, and special operators arriving from their parent commands that spanned the globe. Once formed, JTF-190 set out to refine the plan as it essentially became a living document.

Admiral Miller visited Fort Drum on 11 August to review the progress. The post was a hive of activity. I attended several briefings at JTF headquarters, where the timeline was discussed, modified, and discussed again. Force requirements were also high on the agenda, and I was hoping to hear about additional helicopters and a floating platform to complete our deck qualifications—but still no indication.

Because of the tight security we were required to maintain, Arch had chosen the brigade conference room as our planning and meeting space. The walls were overlaid with aeronautical maps of the East Coast and the Caribbean, large-scale maps of Haiti and Port-au-Prince, and butcher-paper charts depicting calculations and priorities of work. There was a long, dark wooden executive table that extended down the center of the room. Its surface was cluttered with stacks of manuals, scribbled notes, scraps of paper, and reference materials.

We inundated JTF headquarters with requests for information. There were so many unanswered questions and so little time. On Friday afternoon, 12 August, we received one answer we had been anxiously anticipating: the fleet carrier USS *Theodore Roosevelt* would be available for our training. The flight deck would be cleared of its fixed-wing fleet and be awaiting our arrival somewhere off the coast of Virginia on Sunday, 15 August. I had hoped that we would receive a little more than 24 hours' notice and a more definitive location, but we were elated to have a ship identified. With a fleet carrier at our disposal, I was beginning to feel anything was possible.

We were still installing the aircraft plumbing for the extended-range fuel tanks on many of the Black Hawks, and attaching Kevlar ballistic blankets to the troop compartment floors to provide some protection from small arms for the Lightfighters. We were also in the middle of equipping the entire fleet with the satellite-based global positioning system. With the modifications ongoing, there were few airframes to send to *Roosevelt*.

We required enough aircraft, including maintenance backup of each type, to qualify the aviators. We would simply trade out the pilots while the aircraft remained running or "hot seat" the crews. Seventeen hours after notification, Forshag, Driver, and sixteen aircraft crammed with aviators departed Fort Drum at 8 A.M. to travel 600-plus miles to Fort Eustis, Virginia. The crew members would remain overnight at Fort Eustis, then depart the next day for the open ocean in search of *Roosevelt*. With the aid of an initial heading, periodic radar vectors, and clear skies, the army aviators intercepted the carrier some 100 miles off the East Coast. After initial radio contact with "Mother," the call sign used by the navy to describe a parent vessel, the helicopters were hurried to their temporary home.

It didn't take a rocket scientist to figure something was up, and it didn't take the local media long to determine that the procession of helicopters departing Fort Drum early Saturday morning were destined for a navy carrier. It was too large an operation to conceal. Our public affairs office was quick to put the media's suspicions to rest, enthusiastically promoting a joint training exercise with the navy. Fort Drum's own newspaper ran an article on the event the following week, highlighting the arduous training and the unique environment. Our trip to *Roosevelt* never reached the media beyond Drum's immediate area.

I was tethered to a number of daily JTF planning sessions and meetings. On Monday, 16 August, I broke away and flew by commercial air to Norfolk, Virginia, where I climbed aboard a Black Hawk for a 90-minute journey to *Roosevelt*. It was difficult to grasp how something so big could appear so tiny in the open ocean, but from afar small and insignificant looking she was. Seeing the small dot on the horizon made me realize that ships, even with *Roosevelt*'s displacement, might not be as easy to detect on the high seas as some would like you to believe.

As we approached the carrier, the gray steel mass of the floating city became more and more immense, finally dwarfing everything flying or floating near her space. When equipped as part of a carrier battle group, the *Roosevelt* is home to 5,300 sailors and over ninety combat aircraft. The ship's sheer size represents our navy's strength and lethality.

Navy Capt. Ronald L. Christenson, *Roosevelt*'s commanding officer, was a helo pilot, and his crew welcomed the army contingent with open arms. The aviators began their training immediately, and it continued 24 hours a day until all the pilots were qualified. It was quite the sight to observe the army aviators receiving their briefings in ready rooms normally occupied by naval aviators. Each battalion had its own ready room on 03 level, one of the carrier's horizontal levels or decks. The ship's hangar bays are considered 01 level, with everything above that called a level (the flight deck is 04 level and the captain's bridge is 09 level). All levels below the hangar bays are decks (1st deck, 2d deck, down to the 7th deck that is just above the bilge pumps).

At night the ready rooms were illuminated with red lighting as were the crew chiefs' work areas and corridors. The red glow preserved the soldiers' night vision; otherwise it would take 30 minutes for their eyes to fully adapt to the night. The sight of aviators and crew chiefs conducting their trade under red lighting is common to the army aviation crew member, but with the goggles attached to their helmets and the ship's hatches, narrow passageways, and low ceilings as a backdrop, the below-deck operation took on the appearance of a low-budget sci-fi movie—though there was nothing low-budget about this operation.

For us to conduct our night operations, Captain Christenson had to black out the carrier. We were riding 95,000 tons of steel plunging into the pitch-black night twelve stories above the waterline, charging around the Atlantic Ocean with minimal lighting: an incredible feeling—almost as if we were part of the vast dark sea that surrounded us. Standing on the flight deck in the darkness without the aid of NVGs subordinated your sense of sight to those of touch and sound. You could feel and hear the machines' presence, but the helos were nearly invisible to the naked eye. The wind generated by the helicopters caused you to walk leaning into the rotor wash to counter the force, while the whine of the turbine engines and roar of the rotor blades penetrated your hearing protection and vibrated your inner ear.

There were 2- to 4-foot seas as everything was conducted deliberately and to standard, soldiers and sailors working as one. The sailors who work the flight deck wear colored vests, which identify the duties they perform. The color coding makes it easy to identify who is who in the flurry of activity between men and machines that characterize flight deck operations—although the effectiveness of the colors is diminished under blackout conditions. Yellow shirts direct movement of aircraft; white shirts handle safety-related jobs; green shirts hook aircraft to catapults and handle arresting wires; purple shirts fuel aircraft; brown shirts, the plane captains, watch over individual aircraft; blue shirts chock and chain aircraft into position, drive tractors, and pull aircraft; red shirts handle all weapons and ammunition; and silver shirts handle aircraft crashes and fires. As guests of *Roosevelt*'s sailors, we quickly learned that everything on a carrier has its place and every action is deliberate.

Roosevelt's flight deck is the length of about three football fields placed end to end with a large tower-like structure, the island, located on the center starboard of the flight deck. My first visit to the island and the home of the AirBoss, Cmdr. Terry L. Tippin, provided me an opportunity to view the heart of the air operations at work. The heart and soul of the operation comes in the form of an experienced naval aviator with the rank of commander. It became apparent to me that next to the skipper, the AirBoss must be the most revered and feared man for the aviators on the ship. If he says it flies, it flies. If he says it doesn't, then it doesn't. He is assisted by the MiniBoss, an experienced lieutenant commander. The AirBoss is responsible for all of the air operations in, on, and around the carrier, and if this rated sailor is worth his salt, his iron-fisted rule results in smooth-flowing air ops.

As I stood in the control tower my first night and watched Tippin

An AH-1F Cobra on board USS Roosevelt

bark instructions to my aviators, I couldn't help notice his aircraft status board: a long, thin piece of Plexiglas that lists the aircrafts' tail numbers and pilots' names and reflects a graphic representation showing whether an aircraft is airborne or has landed. Two things immediately caught my attention: all the tail numbers and pilots were army—a first since army aviators flew their P-40 Warhawks from the deck of USS *Chenango* in November 1942 in support of Operation Torch, the invasion of Morocco; and second, the navy still required a young seaman to write the information on the transparent board with a grease pencil—backwards.[2] I'm sure there is a good reason for this antiquated procedure, but for the likes of me I sure couldn't figure it out. I thought, "Hey, this is the information age!" I discovered several more peculiarities in navy carrier operations.

The navy uses JP5 fuel in its aircraft because of its low flash point, and will not allow an aircraft on their ships loaded with any other grade of jet fuel. Our standard fuel at the time was JP4, therefore we made arrangements to refuel with JP5 prior to our arrival on *Roosevelt*'s deck. Additionally, we discovered that army aircraft mooring chains are not compatible with the hooks mounted in the ship's deck, requiring a makeshift application for *Roosevelt* and a follow-on request for navy chains for our future ops. Despite these disparities, it didn't affect our ability to train.

Our instructor pilots were real pros, and, once again, the expertise of Somalia veteran Dave Coates was exploited to ensure success. Coates was on assignment orders to Korea, but he had volunteered to deploy to *Roosevelt* and assist with the training until his departure—a mark of his dedication and professionalism.

For 4 days and nights, the army aviators had exclusive use of the flight deck. The 24-hour-a-day operation resulted in more than 1,200 deck landings, with 600 of them occurring at night using NVGs. Additionally mechanics, armament, and other support personnel trained with their navy counterparts. It was a rewarding experience for everyone involved and both services learned a new way to conduct business.

Service parochialism was left behind at the home station. Mission success was paramount. The support and camaraderie between the navy and army were commendable, and the attitude of both soldier and sailor, regardless of rank, was one of mutual respect and cooperation.

Although at times when listening to the enthusiastic service members, you might conclude they were on different ships. Navy AMCS (AW) Frank M. Brennan, maintenance control and flight deck coordinator, said, "Its fun having them [army] out . . . They do things a lot different. The flight deck's having quite a time converting." SSG Ronald R. Breton, 3-25th platoon sergeant, said, "We're working with a different style of operating, but it's amazing how many things are the same."[3] Despite the different perspectives, the mission was a success and we were ready to conduct operations from a ship.

The return trip to Fort Drum was uneventful, other than a noise complaint about the helicopters in central Virginia brought about by flying close to the heavily forested terrain in order to avoid a low cloud ceiling and limited visibility. Once home, we were still confronted with plenty of unanswered questions and a great deal of training that needed to be accomplished. While keeping Berdy's ground plan in the forefront, one of the issues we struggled with was how would we position our aircraft on deck to arm our attack aircraft and efficiently load the soldiers, depart, return, refuel, and repeat the process several times? Additionally, we had no idea how many helicopters we could safely place on the ship's deck.

These questions and several more led to the construction of a 10-foot-long scale drawing on butcher paper replicating the surface area of an aircraft carrier's flight deck. We spread the ship's schematic over the length of the conference room table. Semmens's soldiers then constructed scale templates of UH-60, OH-58, and AH-1 helicopters, depicting the Kiowas and the Cobras as narrow cutouts with their two rotor blades aligned with the fuselage, while the four-bladed Black Hawk was represented as a circle with a tail. As was expected, the Black Hawks occupied much of the deck space. Rumors from the JTF headquarters suggested the mission platform would be USS *America,* so we adapted her dimensions. We were also eager to take a close look at her.

Lieutenant Colonel Archambault led a team of three down to Norfolk to affect direct liaison with the command of *America.* Navy Capt. Ralph R. Suggs commanded the conventionally powered carrier. His ship has the largest flight deck (4.57 acres) of the navy's carriers. Arch discovered upon his arrival that special operation liaison teams from Fort Bragg, North Carolina, and Fort Campbell, Kentucky, were also on board. He notified me upon his return about the special operators, and we both agreed that the operation was much broader in scope than we realized. By this time we knew we would launch from a navy carrier, although we had yet to receive a formal operations order—and we would not receive one.

Our liaison team was able to determine what the ship offered. Of particular interest was its organic maintenance capability, storage capacity, and the services provided. Later, as I became familiar with a carrier's maintenance and shop capability, I concluded that the navy technicians could probably build anything they chose. All in all, the army folks were impressed: we joked that the navy could construct a helicopter from scratch if they possessed the blueprints. The shops, materials, and expertise the ship maintains are like those routinely found at our depots.

Shortly after Arch returned, we received a troop commander from 4th Squadron, 2d Cavalry (Air Cavalry), XVIII Airborne Corps, Fort Bragg. The regimental cavalry squadron had aviators flying from the stern of navy frigates skirting Haitian waters. The pilots were equipped with OH-58D Warriors, and they were on the lookout for nighttime violators of the embargo and any unusual activity along the coastline. The Warriors' limited numbers, coupled with their superb nighttime surveillance capability, had led to the command restricting their operation to the hours of darkness. It had also facilitated the concealment of the clandestine operation.

The arrival of the 4-2d cavalrymen at Fort Drum meant we would be augmented with an eight-aircraft troop. With the OH-58Ds already operating in theater, we planned for their link-up prior to our launch from the carrier.

The second Black Hawk company did not materialize. Corps made a decision to place an 82d's Airborne Aviation Brigade Black Hawk company at our disposal once it was directed by the JTF commander. I suspected we would not receive an outfit from the 82d—they had better things to do. I called on the STU-III secure telephone to COL Gene LaCoste, commander of the 82d Aviation Brigade, and asked him about his unit and its support to us. I knew Gene only as a fellow commander, and he was well respected. He asked me if I was "read-on," a term used if you had the authority to know the information. I responded that I was read-on to my outfit's mission, and one of his companies was supposed to be part of it. I was not sure what else I needed to be read-on about. LaCoste went on to say that he really couldn't discuss anything with me because I wasn't read-on to his mission.

We said our good-byes and that was the end of our conversation. I never spoke to Gene again until well after my return from Haiti some 6 months later. It was a first-hand look at how compartmentalization prevents a free flow of information—shades of my experience in Somalia. We went on to request direct coordination, but didn't receive approval until a couple of weeks before D-Day. Corps aviation did dispatch two UH-60 crews to Fort Drum to be liaison and participate in our rehearsal. One of the pilots was 1LT Jeffrey Shelton, son of the corps commander. I had known Lieutenant General Shelton, a 6-foot-5-inch North Carolinian, when he was a major in the infantry brigade I was assigned to in the 25th Infantry Division some 20 years earlier, and when his son Jeff was a toddler. With young Shelton's arrival at Fort Drum I suddenly was feeling old.

It was at this time that we were informed that something less than a full-up Chinook helicopter battalion would support us. The unit would be the Medium Lift Battalion, 159th Aviation Regiment, XVIII Airborne Corps. I was delighted to hear that a former executive officer of mine when I had commanded an attack battalion, LTC Al Page, was commanding the outfit. Page was a solid citizen, and I was also pleased that we would have another battalion headquarters available. Page dispatched an aircraft and crew to Fort Drum for liaison and to participate in our rehearsal.

On 29 August, the JTF's major subordinate commanders were on the calendar for a back brief to Major General Meade. The general had directed that a World War II–era gymnasium located on Fort Drum's old post be converted into a secure briefing area. It was a good idea. A

The terrain board in a converted gymnasium
used for planning and back briefs during Operation Uphold Democracy

large-scale terrain map of Port-au-Prince and vicinity, which occupied
half of the gym's basketball court, was the vehicle for our briefings.
Enlarged hanging maps of Port-au-Prince, Cap-Haïtien, and Haiti complemented the floor diagram. Bleachers arrayed on one side of the gym
were oriented toward the large area map and provided the ideal place
to seat and address the entire command and staff team.

Following General Meade's approval of our plan we were set for a
rehearsal. Meade directed two rehearsals, 29 and 30 August. The 30 August rehearsal would be for record. Wheeler-Sack Army Airfield would
replicate Port-au-Prince International Airport with a tent positioned on
the northeast side of the active runway simulating a Haitian police compound. A large open field adjacent to the airfield with an arrangement of
tents and engineer tape on it would represent the port facility and fuel
storage area. A Fort Drum air assault strip (a dirt airstrip carved out of
the forest) served as USS *America,* while a training field near the main

cantonment area of Drum was used by the two Chinooks from 2-159th as the tiny island of Great Inagua. Under the XVIII Airborne Corps invasion plan, the 2-159th would stage from Great Inagua. Our plan called for 2-159th to join up with us once Port-au-Prince International Airport was secure.

An AC-130 circled above the objective area, while the division civil affairs officer orchestrated a number of soldiers to represent civilians on the battlefield, Haitian military, and paramilitary. These U.S. soldiers dressed in civilian attire waved banners and signs and yelled pro- and anti-American slogans as they role-played the intelligence communities' projected reaction by Haitian civilians and military to our arrival. The soldier-actors proved an effective tool, but ensuring that our Lightfighters arrived on the objective according to our planned timeline presented another challenge.

Flying the distance between carrier and objective was not practical, so we duplicated the helos' flight time from *America* by extending the ground time at the point of departure, then flying the last few minutes to round out the calculated flight period.

Early in the planning, Andy Berdy and I advocated removal of the nylon web seats from the Black Hawks. Although General Meade had the authority to direct the seat removal, he opposed doing so for safety concerns. The UH-60 carries eleven combat troops with the seats affixed. Without the seats, the aircraft can carry anywhere between fifteen to twenty troops, depending on how the soldiers are equipped, but there is an inherent risk when the seats are not installed. If the aircraft were to experience a hard landing or crash, the soldiers would be without the shock absorption provided by the seats. On the other hand, by removing them, combat power can quickly be massed on the objective. This was an important variable because, with the reduced number of aircraft at our disposal, we needed to haul more soldiers per airframe.

Meade had not decided whether we would proceed on D-Day with or without seats, but Andy and I shared the concern for rehearsing as if we were planning to execute. The precedence for training without seats had been established in both the special operations community and the 101st Air Assault Division. But, despite the precedent, the commanding general remained firm with his decision.

General Meade is a staunch disciplinarian, always keeping an eye on the welfare of his soldiers. This was probably never more evident than in his relentless campaign to ferret out soldiers in the division who were nonswimmers and provide them the resources to learn the lifesaving skill. One would assume that swimming is a requisite skill for a soldier, but it is not. To Meade's credit, he initiated the vital swimming program shortly after he assumed command. Although challenging for the subordinate commanders to give up the soldiers and the time, it was one of the most worthwhile programs I had observed. The new swimmers became "born again" soldiers flaunting a newfound confidence. The two rehearsals at the airfield accomplished the same results for the entire joint task force.

Although much was simulated, the rehearsals synchronized the battlefield operating systems and instilled a feeling of confidence throughout the force. Everyone involved shared in the success, but special recognition had to go to my operations officer, Steve Semmens, and Berdy's operations officer, Jeff Baughman, who jointly planned the air assault. The division's operation plan had been evolving throughout the month of August, and, with the rehearsals concluded, it was complete and blessed by the commanding general.

The brigade was set to go. MAJ Richard Everson, the brigade logistician, was once again conducting his logistics "magic." He had the support piece ready—everything from supplies packaged and uploaded to securing M4 carbines for the aircrews. I attribute his experience and personal involvement in the planning, redeployment, and recovery from Somalia as an essential ingredient in the brigade's ability to respond to the Haiti operation. Additionally Rick, along with the other Somalia veterans, was intuitively able to determine what really was needed and what wasn't. It only made sense, they had been through this drill just 5 months earlier.

The 10th Mountain Lightfighters were ready! The entire division had been conducting operations 24 hours a day since early August. The commanding general, sensitive to the soldiers' sacrifices, declared the 3-day Labor Day weekend as nontraining days. He encouraged the troops to spend time with their loved ones and families. I took a break and escaped to Boston for the Labor Day weekend, where I had an opportunity to meet up with my wife-to-be, Cathy Privat.

While in Boston, I was introduced by a mutual acquaintance to the then Senate Majority Leader, Bob Dole. This took place in a hotel lobby, and I was introduced as a brigade commander in the 10th Mountain Division. Dole had been an officer in the 10th Mountain during World War II when he had sustained serious wounds, the most apparent being his impaired right hand. I had to believe that the senator knew of President Clinton's intentions in Haiti and that he had probably been briefed on the plan. But if Dole was privy to the 10th Mountain's part in the Haiti operation, he sure didn't let on. After initial pleasantries, our conversation turned to more parochial issues much closer to home. He was very concerned that the army's Fort Riley in his home state of Kansas might succumb to the base-closing initiative. He expressed his opinion that Riley had served the army well over the years and he figured it would continue to do so. He asked me whether Fort Drum was going to make the list of closures and was the community rallying around the military post. I gave him an enthusiastic yes, and explained there was a concerted effort to retain the installation on the rolls. I told him I felt Drum would survive, but that I was confident not at the expense of Riley. He nodded with approval.

What I didn't say to the senator was that I couldn't arrive at a good reason to support an army post smack in the middle of the harsh winter weather environment characteristic of northern New York. Despite some of the finest people I have ever met who make up the surrounding community and citizen support unsurpassed in my military career, the extreme winters severely inhibited training. Most Fort Drum units aggressively sought ways to go south during the winter months to accomplish mission-essential battle drills.

Senator Dole and I wished each other good luck and parted company. I enjoyed the brief exchange, but we both had more pressing matters to attend to. I wanted to spend time with Cathy, and I was looking forward to forgetting all about the army and the challenges facing the brigade, at least for a few hours.

Notes

1. HEED is a miniature scuba tank designed to provide the crew member a few additional minutes to escape from a submerged aircraft.

2. John Gordon IV, "Joint Power Projection: Operation Torch," *Joint Force Quarterly* 4 (Spring 1994), p. 60–67.

3. "Army Fliers Conquer Flight Deck," *Rough Rider* 8, no. 49 (16 August 1994).

19

THE GO-AHEAD

Confidence is the cornerstone of success in battle: each soldier's belief in his own competence, his trust in that of other members of his unit, and their collective pride, cohesion, and effectiveness.
—*Field Manual 100-5, Operations,*
Department of the Army, July 1976

Upon my return to Fort Drum the pace didn't miss a beat as the troops began reviewing a number of publications on Haitian culture, language, and traditions, as well as familiarizing themselves with the rules of engagement, which were refined daily. Railroad cars by the dozen began arriving on post, and vehicles and their loads were checked and rechecked.

We were in September and it still wasn't clear who the enemy was; Lieutenant General Cedras and his FAd'H and militia forces, the FRAPH party members, *attachés,* or all of the above. If we entered a permissive environment, then there would be no enemy—maybe? On the other hand, if we met resistance, would it be the ill-equipped military, the uniformed police, or the paramilitary *attachés* with their BMWs and Uzis? There was no Haitian air force or navy to speak of, and the poorly trained Haitian army numbered less than 1,000 soldiers armed with a few mortars, large-caliber machine guns, and howitzers, and six V-150 light APCs. The ragtag 2,000–3,000-man militia was armed with World War II–vintage rifles and suffered from dysfunctional leadership, while the police possessed only sidearms. We knew the capabilities of all the potential hostile organizations in Haiti, but which group(s) would be adversaries was not ascertained until hours before our launch. Even at that point, the who and the when remained problematical.

The mission was still not public, but the level of activity at our isolated fort near the Canadian border concealed little about the division's

intentions. The 10th Mountain was going somewhere and the surrounding Fort Drum community knew it. Tuning into the nightly news
told the rest of the story.

The frustration over the situation in Haiti within the Clinton administration was reaching its peak. Between the XVIII Airborne Corps
plan and ours, the invasion force was well in excess of 20,000 troops.
The administration had reached a point where even the nay-sayers were
on board. The media bombarded the American people with news of an
impending invasion of Haiti. The television news shows had commen-
taries by one expert after another, each speculating on the how, when,
and where the attack would occur. Adding to the media frenzy was the
daily violence occurring in Haiti—events the electronic media felt
compelled to pipe into American households nightly.

Back in July I had agreed to an Army Aviation Association of
America–sponsored golf day for the brigade on Friday, 9 September.
Having canceled everything that was on the calendar for August, and
feeling confident that the brigade was ready if called, I told the soldiers
to go ahead and plan the event. Lieutenant Colonel Archambault had
recently taken up golf, and, like most bitten by the golf bug, had become an avid player. Arch and about forty officers and enlisted soldiers
from the brigade kicked off their tournament early that Friday. I didn't
participate. I'm a poor player and I felt my presence was needed back
at the headquarters. My intuition was right.

Arch didn't get past the first hole before he was summoned to the
clubhouse to receive my call informing him we were about to receive
the order to move out. The tournament was postponed for 9 months.

COL Tom Miller received an execute order late Thursday night,
and to his delight noted that it directed the JTF to do preciously what
had been planned and rehearsed. At 2 A.M. Friday, Miller went to General Meade's quarters to inform him that the order was received and the
mission was a go.

Later in the day, I received a verbal order to deploy the brigade to
Norfolk to occupy the nuclear aircraft carrier USS *Dwight D. Eisenhower.* This was the first time that *Eisenhower* had been mentioned,
and I was beginning to wonder if there were more aircraft carriers in
our future. After all, this was the third mentioned in as many weeks.

Eisenhower was at sea, and she had been ordered to clear the decks
of her fixed-wing fleet and head for Norfolk, Virginia. The carrier
would arrive at her home port on Sunday and was on orders to sail for
Haitian waters the following Wednesday morning, 14 September, with
or without us. We had 5 days.

Late Saturday afternoon *Eisenhower*'s executive officer, Capt. Leo Enwright Jr., accompanied by several of the ship's key department heads, arrived at Fort Drum. We gathered that evening in our conference room where we discussed our concept of operation and what we were planning to bring aboard to support the operation. Enwright articulated his skipper's intent, and his shipmates brought much needed information about the carrier's on-board capabilities, procedures, and limitations. Both groups huddled over the 10-foot drawing of the carrier deck, and everyone had his say on the pros and cons of aircraft placement. They were willing partners, eager to participate considering they had been notified of the mission less than 24 hours earlier.

It was crucial to establish a liaison on board *Eisenhower* as soon as possible. Once again, I relied on Lieutenant Colonel Archambault and his team. That evening, I directed our liaison team to depart early the next morning to return with Enwright in preparation for our arrival.

Arch and his team of five officers, armed with the butcher paper schematic, helo templates, and the gear they would need for the next several months, flew to Norfolk Naval Air Station where they boarded a navy C-2 Greyhound twin-engine aircraft. Observing the army officers in battle dress uniforms (BDUs) carrying their rucksacks and weapons, the air station personnel paused and stared curiously. For the army aviators, the completion of the hour-long flight to *Eisenhower* resulted in their first shipboard "arrested" landing.

Sending Arch and his team early paid big dividends. Not only was he able to express my intent to the ship's captain, but the team's advance work meant that upon the main body's arrival there would be few unanswered questions. Additionally, Arch was able to identify our troops' sleeping and work areas.

Eisenhower's captain was Alan M. Gemmill, a naval aviator, and he ran a tight ship. He and his crew welcomed the army aviators as the two service teams quickly went to work solving the challenges confronting the joint force and arriving at the correct mix of aircraft to be placed on the deck for the assault. This was all predicated on getting as many as possible of Berdy's Lightfighters on the ground in the initial helicopter assault (Figure 19.1).

Up to this point there had been no JTF/division or brigade combat team involvement in carrier operations as we began occupation of the flattop. As with *Roosevelt,* all of the coordination had been initiated and conducted by the aviation brigade. I can only assume it reflected the commanding general's confidence in the brigade. But army command and control aboard ship was never addressed, which resulted in

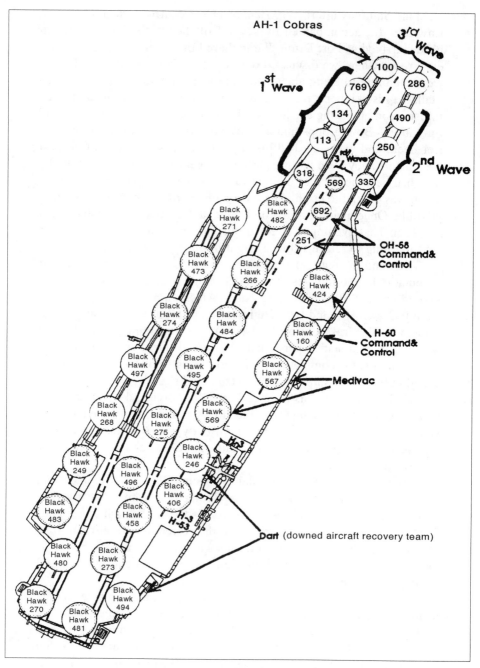

Figure 19.1 Aircraft Configuration on Board USS Eisenhower

some confusion early in the voyage. The first nonaviation brigade personnel to set foot on *Eisenhower* arrived 3 days after our assembly on the ship. By that time, we not only had implemented our operations center and were well on our way to establishing a routine, but we had established rapport with the captain and his crew.

Gemmill wanted his staff to interact with only one army counterpart, not staff representatives from the various tenant army units. That made sense, so I decided it would be my staff until Brigadier General Close arrived with his team. Close was in charge of TF Mountain, our senior headquarters, but neither he nor his key players were expected to arrive for several more days. Close dispatched an advance team led by a captain along with the brigade combat team soldiers. But Close's team was not properly staffed or senior enough to be effective. The team tried to exert its influence, but that just wasn't practical and led to a frustrated TF Mountain advance element.

Most of the brigade's equipment, like the division's, was transported 300-plus miles by rail and convoy to the port of Bayonne, New Jersey, awaiting transshipment to Haiti. Major Everson led our logistics effort. Our priority was to get everything we needed to Norfolk prior to *Eisenhower*'s departure. To complicate matters, we had been challenged all along with exactly what we could take. If we were to place it on the carrier, it would have to be airlifted by a helicopter. There would be no exceptions. Russ Forshag said it best: "You bring it, you sling it." Although the navy would have one CH-53 Sea Stallion for heavy lift, and once in country the CH-47s would join us, the workhorse would be the Black Hawk. A purposeful decision was made that everything placed on *Eisenhower* would be within weight and configuration for external lift by a UH-60.

Making *Eisenhower* combat ready with the army forces required the assembly of soldiers, supplies, and equipment from several different locations. It commenced with the brigade self-deploying forty-eight aircraft directly to the ship. Additionally, three UH-60V helicopters from Fort Bragg's 57th Medevac Company linked up with the aviation team at Norfolk.[1] Five navy helicopters that provided search and rescue (SAR) and a heavy-lift capability augmented the fifty-one army helicopters.

Simultaneously, shop sets, kits, and other equipment were shipped by commercial transport to the port facility, while twenty-five Humvees were convoyed from Fort Drum to Norfolk. A contingent from the Army Component Headquarters (TF Mountain), Berdy's headquarters accompanied by his two battalions of infantrymen, and the division support command forward element were deployed by charter air. Pallets of ammunition, ranging from 2.75-inch rockets to 9mm rounds, were shipped from depots to the carrier, destined for her magazine.

The flight from Fort Drum to Norfolk was routine. The forty-eight helicopters were broken into a series of flights with 30-minute separation so that we wouldn't congest either the refueling stops or the airways if we were forced to file instrument flight rules. I enjoyed piloting for a change.[2] I had logged plenty of time in Somalia occupying the back seat of a UH-60, and I knew there would be plenty more back seat time in store for me in Haiti.

The flight of helicopters cruised at 1,000 feet above the Chesapeake Bay paralleling the coastline. The blue water, unlimited visibility, and golden rays penetrating a thin layer of scattered clouds that glistened on the waters surface created a tranquil visual imagine. All the crew members were full of anticipation, and many wondered if this was the calm before the storm.

As we approached the Hampton Roads bridge and tunnel, I could see three large aircraft carriers docked parallel to one another. With the exception of the one in the middle, with a few helicopters, their decks were clear. The close proximity of the three carriers gave the appearance you could jump from one to another. It was a collection of billions of dollars and a fourth of the navy's major instrument for force projection. The sight was impressive. The carriers made all the other ships, the dock cranes, and the multistory buildings near their mooring appear small and insignificant by comparison.

Assembled in the waters of the harbor were USS *America, Eisenhower,* and *Roosevelt. America,* with its uncharacteristic black superstructure, had a half-dozen Humvees on her bow covered by canvas. If the intent was to conceal the wheeled cargo, it failed. The vehicles were exposed halfway up their sides, and I could only assume that the army-green shipment would soon be joined by its special operations owners. Sure enough, under the cloak of darkness, the ship was later loaded with Rangers and sailed toward open ocean to rendezvous with the Rangers' helicopters.

After landing on the *Eisenhower,* I disembarked from the helo and was accorded the traditional greeting afforded a senior commanding officer. A total of eight sailors in two facing rows, representing various departments of carrier operations and commonly referred to as sideboys, formed a corridor as a boatswain piped me aboard with the trilling of his whistle. At the end of the human corridor Captain Gemmill met me. After a hearty handshake and a brief exchange of courtesies, we retired to his quarters where we discussed how we would conduct business on *Eisenhower*. In the course of our conversation, I discovered that we shared the same undergraduate alma mater, the University of Arizona. There was no significance to our common education other than we were two boys who had spent a few years in the late 1960s in the Southwestern desert and were about to embark on a historic journey.

Personnel, equipment, and supplies continued to arrive at dockside 24 hours a day as the floodlights on the dock and in the hangar bays turned night into day. The large open bays took on the appearance of a freight warehouse.

I occupied the commander, air group quarters and was quite pleased with the size and luxury afforded me. The large living room proved useful for my meetings with the commanders and staff. There were a number of administrative actions that still needed to be accomplished, but under Arch's supervision things were quickly falling into place.

The miles of gray-painted crisscrossing corridors and narrow hatchways throughout the carrier caused more than one soldier to become disoriented. The conscientious sailors always came to the rescue, taking the soldiers by the hand and leading them to their destination. I speak from experience. Our soldiers were not only learning to navigate the metal maze, but they were adapting to the navy jargon—referring to the latrine as the "head" and a door as a "hatch."

I discovered that on a ship you couldn't escape the captain's voice. When he wants to talk to you, he does. Unlike my service, which has formations or assembles soldiers in the post theater to address an issue, the ship's skipper just presses his push-to-talk switch on the ship's public address system. Regardless of whether the sailor is eating lunch or taking a shower, the captain's voice reaches every rivet in the ship's hull. I found it a very effective way to pass the word. On occasion, I followed Captain Gemmill's morning address to talk to the soldiers and express my appreciation to his crew.

Early Tuesday morning the ship's public information officer knocked on my quarter's hatch. He said that the press would interview Captain Gemmill and me in 30 minutes. The interviews would be conducted separately, but would be a live feed to CNN's morning news. The CNN interview would be followed by affiliates of ABC, NBC, CBS, and a couple of independent networks that would air delayed broadcasts. The public information officer hastily briefed me on reporters' personalities (who was friendly and who was not). It was all happening very fast.

I respect the power of the press, and my thoughts reached back to my first encounter with the television media. It was 1979 and I was flying

Black Hawks on USS Eisenhower's deck

lead in a flight of two AH-1G Cobra gunships in the skies over Fort Hunter-Liggett, California, when I received an urgent call over the radio, "Jaguar 03 this is Jaguar 06." It was my company commander, CPT Richard Diamond, directing me to a set of map grid coordinates where a group of television reporters were assembled. He and the division commander, MG Philip R. Feir, were collocated with the reporters, and he asked if I would climb to altitude and dive on the gathering below. This would be a treat, because with the advent of nap-of-the-earth flying we had rarely gotten above a few hundred feet and certainly not to make a diving attack. Diving fire had gone out with the Vietnam War and was only to be resurrected in Somalia. I took the aircraft up to a couple of thousand feet and executed a maneuver called a wing-over. I was flying front seat, and although not the best seat to conduct the maneuver, I had been taught by some of the finest warrant officer gun-pilots in the business.

I came screaming out of the sky simulating a gun-run on the group below, followed by a steep climb to a near-zero airspeed, pedal turn, and the execution of a return to target—all of which were characteristic of the Vietnam era. After a couple of diving gun-runs followed by an equal number of return to targets, Diamond directed me to land in a field next to the TV journalists. I knew this meant an interview and that all three of the major networks were present (CNN was still years away). I could see it clearly: mom, dad, grandparents—hell, everyone would see me next to my high-speed lethal fighting machine. It would be my turn at Andy Warhol's 15 minutes of fame, and I was about to get my quarter of an hour in the limelight.

As we approached the grassy field to land, I passed the flight controls to the backseater, CPT Tom Wills, to prepare for my exit. After the helicopter was on the ground and the engine was reduced to flight idle, the entourage of reporters began to descend upon us. As they worked their way through the tall dry grass I couldn't help but notice a stunningly tall, shapely blonde reporter leading the pack. I was a bachelor with an eye for a beautiful woman, and she had my attention. I quickly placed my hand palm out signaling them to hold their position. The rotor blade had not stopped going around and I didn't want anyone to get hit. Additionally, I wanted to exert my authority so that they knew I was in charge.

We just received approval to wear the new one-piece flight suit that the other services were issued, and I was one of the lucky few who wasn't wearing the baggy brownish green two-piece ensemble—a uniform I would later regret being discontinued, because it was practical and comfortable.

I slid my tinted helmet visor up and secured the helmet on a hook affixed to the top of the cramped cockpit. I twisted the small mirror intended for making eye-to-eye contact with the backseater while in flight, and adjusted it so I could fluff up my hair and position my aviator sunglasses. After all, this had the potential for national television coverage.

The Cobra's fuselage is only 39 inches at its widest point, the engine air intakes. Therefore, the canopy is like that of a jet fighter—long sleek Plexiglas that wraps around both aviators' heads. Later Cobra models had canopies that were squared off, disrupting the sleek snake-like appearance. The canopy door exposes one side of the canopy for egress and is hinged near the centerline of the canopy. There is a division between pilots allowing the front seat door to swing up and open to the left side, while the backseat canopy door opens up and to the right. The curved canopy doors lock into place at approximately a 90-degree angle from the fuselage by a mechanical strut creating a gull-wing appearance when viewed from the front.

As the reporters approached, I reached up and grabbed the leather handgrip, then pulled myself out of the confined cockpit and extended my left leg to a foothold protruding from the exterior fuselage. As I released my grip and shifted weight to reach the step, my survival vest snagged on the canopy door latch at the nape of my neck. I found myself dangling from the canopy door. The door strut bowed under the weight and my frantic movements as I attempted to regain a foothold. My sunglasses were hanging off my face secured by one ear and my boots were thumping the fuselage as I kicked in a desperate attempt to locate a footing. Finally, I was able to secure a firm hold and reach around behind my back and unhook my vest from the entanglement. I jumped down alongside the aircraft, attempting to reposition my sunglasses and regain my composure only to have a microphone stuck in my face by the young blonde journalist. With all the network cameras filming away she asked, "Captain, do you always get out of these helicopters in that manner? Seems like a lot of work to me!" What could I say? At that point all I wanted to do was run and hide. The best I could hope for was a local report, and since the entire division was in the field maybe no one I knew would view it . . . and as far as I know, no one did.

Here I was years later, and this time it was the whole world that would be watching. I knew there were some things I could screw up, but this wasn't one of them. This time I stood with my feet planted firmly on the pier in the shadow of *Eisenhower*. The interviews went fine. I stressed our preparedness and the cooperation between the services. At one point, I corrected the CNN reporter when he pointed to the deck of the carrier and referred to the Black Hawks as Apaches. To the television viewers it was irrelevant, but upon my return to *Eisenhower,* the Black Hawk pilots went out of their way to thank me for setting the record straight. They had been watching the report on the monitors throughout the ship. I conducted interviews with the media for 2 days right up to the time the ship pulled away from the dock. I soon learned that the aviators weren't the only ones scrutinizing my every word.

Major General Meade, Admiral Miller, and Defense Secretary William Perry would later tell me that they approved of my TV performance. I could only imagine what would have happened if the interviews had not been favorably received by my leadership. What and how I spoke carried as much weight as how we were going to conduct the operation.

We had loaded equipment and supplies up to the last minute. Now it was time to cast off. Once clear of the pier, *Eisenhower* steamed for the mouth of the harbor. As I stood on the superstructure, the sea breeze caressed my face while the soldiers and sailors manned the rails.

Note

1. Walking the carrier deck one day I noticed that painted on the nose of one of the Medevac UH-60Vs was a bayonet superimposed over a 7th Infantry Division patch. The 7th had been inactivated months earlier and this was an aircraft transferred to the 57th. I told the crew to paint it over before the day was through. They did, but not before someone took a photo—a photograph that conspicuously graces the main entrance to the Pentagon and gives the impression that the operation involved 7th Division forces.

2. My copilot was CWO Robert L. Yates, Jr. Bob was a standardization instructor pilot who I frequently flew with, and over the months came to like. He was professional and appeared to be an all-around good guy. Much to my shock and dismay, Yates turned out to be a monster in sheep's clothing. In September 2000, he confessed to the brutal murders of eleven women and a young couple in Washington state between 1975 and 1998.

20

SETTING SAIL

Jointness means nothing more than teamwork.
—*General Colin L. Powell,*
Chairman, Joint Chiefs of Staff (1989–1993)

As *Eisenhower* made its way toward the open ocean, the soldiers and sailors enthusiastically attacked the tasks at hand. The significance of combining the power projection capability of a navy aircraft carrier and the quick-strike and staying power of an army helicopter air assault force was about to be demonstrated.

It was on Wednesday, 14 September, and Major General Meade was hosting a briefing to Admiral Miller and his staff in the converted gym the following day at Fort Drum. I needed to be there, but Meade directed me to stay on board the *Eisenhower* until the Secretary of Defense William Perry had completed his visit. While in Norfolk I had greeted and escorted Secretary of the Army Togo West, Chief of Staff of the Army Gordon Sullivan, and several other DOD officials of lesser stature. Their presence reinforced the importance of the mission and "pumped" the soldiers and sailors. But this time the carrier's visitors would arrive while we were on our way.

Before Secretary Perry's arrival, Captain Gemmill had initiated a battle drill requiring a 100-percent accountability of the 5,000-plus soldiers and sailors on board. An essential exercise, it ensures that everyone is where he or she is supposed to be during a crisis, and, of equal importance, it is a quick way to identify a sailor overboard. The navy has this drill down pat, but we had a way to go. After a few iterations, we established our battle stations and refined our accountability procedures. After a couple of hours of steaming time, Secretary Perry, accompanied by Admiral Miller, arrived via helicopter provided by the executive fleet.

Perry and Miller addressed the servicemen and women, and praised their groundbreaking mission and their spirit of cooperation. Earlier on the admiral's bridge, Perry, Miller, Gemmill, and I had scanned the deck activity. When responding to a question from Perry on the difficulty to prepare for this mission, I had told him it was challenging but that the innovation by individual soldiers and sailors made the difference. I went on to say that by nature the army and navy are flexible enough to respond in a like manner in the future. After all, from a dead start we arrived at this point in 45 days. With the enthusiasm of a baseball player who just hit a home run, Admiral Miller placed his hand on my shoulder and exclaimed, "You see Dr. Perry, we're on the threshold of a new way of doing business." Miller had advocated for sometime the combining of army and marine forces on navy carriers, much to the disapproval of many in the navy hierarchy. He had previously pioneered the concept of adaptive joint force package trials by removing a portion of the carrier's air wing and replacing it with small contingents of marines or army Special Forces.

Miller had made his point, and the secretary's visit proved inspirational for the soldiers and sailors. With Perry and Miller on their way back to Washington, I quickly boarded a navy helo for a flight back to Norfolk. I left Bill Driver in charge in my absence. The ship had seven army lieutenant colonels aboard, and Bill was the senior commander. Lieutenant Colonel Archambault and the brigade staff would conduct the interface with the ship's staff.

Upon my arrival at Norfolk I boarded a navy C-12, a small executive-style airplane, for the journey north to Fort Drum. I arrived at Drum late but in enough time to sleep in my own bed one last time. The next morning, the JTF leadership presented their plan to Admiral Miller and his accompanying staff. General Meade commenced with opening remarks followed by COL Tom Miller presenting an overall concept. Then each of the commanders, employing a 5-foot-long white pointer with a red tip, walked the terrain to explain how his piece of the operation worked. It was an impressive presentation, and when complete, all the questions were answered and all of the loose ends tied up. We were ready. Admiral Miller gave us a thumbs up.

Brigadier General Close, CSM Jesse Laye (10th Mountain Division command sergeant major), Colonel Berdy, a number of other soldiers from the 10th Mountain, and I boarded a navy reserve C-130 for a flight to Nassau, Bahamas. We spent a sleepless night in an isolated lounge of the airport, stretched out on couches, chairs, and the floor awaiting our transportation for the next leg of the journey. Early the following morning, an H-3 and CH-53 from *Eisenhower* arrived to transport us on a 2-hour flight over the Atlantic to the carrier. I had been away from the ship for 38 hours and the pace of the activity had not missed a beat: everyone was moving with purpose.

Plans were refined and rehearsed, since everything from moving large numbers of troops up and down the aircraft elevators to issuing ammunition had to be exercised. Employing a three-dimensional simulation called TOP SCENE (Tactical Operational Scene), the army aviators sat in front of a computer monitor with an aircraft flight control stick and practiced their flight routes over the city and their ingress and egress at the objective. The movie-like rendering of real-world terrain was a marriage between an advanced program that converts high-altitude, high-resolution satellite imagery with National Imagery and Mapping Agency digital terrain data. The result is realistic scenes with all of the topography and man-made structures in a given geographical area. It is all viewed from the cockpit of the aircraft, with little left to the imagination.

At this point the only aviation at our disposal was what we had on board the carrier. If we were to lead the assault into Port-au-Prince, the Chinooks and Kiowa Warriors would join up later. If we became a follow-on force, we would probably inherit the aircraft in country. We had to plan as though those promised aircraft did not exist.

The third day at sea brought a full rehearsal. Ammunition was uploaded on the Cobras and Black Hawks, soldiers entered the aircraft, and the initial sling loads (Humvees) were positioned. Andy Berdy and I were still troubled because we were rehearsing with the seats in the UH-60s, but our hands were tied.

When launch hour arrived, the OH-58 and AH-1 scout/weapons teams departed, followed shortly by the assault aircraft. A command-and-control UH-60 was airborne, as were the Medevac and SAR aircraft, while Black Hawks jockeyed over the stern for position above the sling loads.

This huge floating city, with an armory, a bakery, a carpentry shop, a hospital, a laundry, a library, fire stations, a print shop, a post office, and its own radio and television stations, moved effortlessly through the Atlantic waters. Capped by an airfield bustling with activity, *Eisenhower* has a crew, including its air wing, of 5,000, but has accommodations for 6,287 and carries provisions for 3 months at sea. The army aviators began referring to the ship among themselves as the "MAAF," for mobile army airfield. Although not fitting for such a prestigious combatant, the soldiers' naming meant no disrespect.

USS Eisenhower *somewhere in the Atlantic Ocean*

The aircraft made several turns, flying routes over the Atlantic Ocean southeast of the United States until all systems and procedures were tested, including rapid "hot" refueling. The carrier could refuel seven UH-60s in a couple of minutes, and could pump so much fuel so fast that I was concerned that the pressure would burst the small 71-gallon OH-58 fuel bladder.

Aiding in our preparations were army aviation and troop command personnel and contractors led by LTC Joe Planchak. They worked together around the clock in the hangar bay to calibrate and test each of the three Cobra weapon systems. The efforts of these civilian-soldiers, coupled with those of aviation brigade and *Eisenhower* maintenance personnel, produced extremely high aircraft availability rates. We would commence the operation with 100-percent availability—every aircraft was mission ready.

As the preparations continued, I took the opportunity to return in a small way some of the skipper's hospitality. Since Mark Gemmill was an aviator, I offered him an opportunity to fly and shoot the Cobra. He didn't hesitate—and the skipper proved to be a credible "stick."

The hangar bays were filled with row after row of Lightfighters' rucksacks neatly aligned with one another. The gear was positioned by order of departure, and, as *Eisenhower* slashed through the Atlantic waters, the soldiers continued at a feverish pace with their training. Two hundred soldiers at a time would form up on the large aircraft elevators and rise to the carrier deck in a matter of seconds. A portion of the ship's deck was used by the infantry to practice their actions upon landing and rehearse their civil disturbance and crowd control formations.

Eisenhower has two nuclear reactors that can supply power without refueling for 18 years, while its four engines are capable of delivering speeds in excess of 30 knots. At those speeds the moored helicopters had to be constantly checked for blade security. Add a 10- or 20-knot headwind and the aircraft rotor blades would be flapping in 50-knot winds—a condition which left unattended to could easily lead to blade or component damage. This was an unintended consequence and it required constant vigilance. The high winds also presented a challenge when shutting down an aircraft, because unlike navy helicopters, army helos are not equipped with rotor brakes to stop the blades from turning: the rotor blades just wind down, gradually running out of inertia.

Once, after making a steep pentacle approach in a helicopter onto a rugged hilltop in the mountains of Korea, I had shut the aircraft engine off to wait for a passenger. The winds off the nose of the helicopter were so strong that the rotor blades continued to turn for my entire 30-minute wait, never stopping as I restarted the engine for my departure.

We monitored the deck winds with portable communications. When I boarded *Eisenhower,* I was provided a radio for communication throughout the ship. This is common practice for navy key and essential personnel. I asked the captain to notify me if the bow winds exceeded 45 knots so that we could intensify our scrutiny of the helos. As a precaution, the soldiers and sailors constantly walked the deck to ensure the aircrafts' moorings remained secure.

I found myself making many trips to the captain's bridge to peer down on the flight deck and count helicopters. I became obsessed with counting the aircraft—it was as if I would shut my eyes and discover one missing. It was during one of these accountability sessions that I noticed the name of the ship stenciled in small flat-black letters on the tail boom of one of the Black Hawks. Upon closer examination, I discovered that all our aircraft were labeled with the ship's name. Under the cloak of darkness *Eisenhower*'s sailors had launched a painting campaign. There was not an army helicopter untouched. It was professionally done, and the dark paint used was so subdued that you had to strain to discern the name from the dark olive drab fuselage paint. I decided to let it remain. After all, it was done in the spirit of team play. But all of this did little to ease my paranoia and drive to personally account for each helicopter, a condition that plagued me throughout our deployment in Haiti. Later, while on shore, I looked forward to my early evening stroll through our assembly area, which inevitably resulted in a walk down the flightline counting helicopters. I would then match my total to the units' flight schedules. But that compulsive behavior occurred much later, for on *Eisenhower* my obsession for accountability was just in its formative stage.

21

THE COUNTDOWN

In Haiti we have a case in which what is right is clear.
—*President Bill Clinton*

A s *Eisenhower* approached the Caribbean waters negotiations were at an impasse. In a last-ditch effort Clinton had called upon the peacemaker Jimmy Carter. The former president, along with Senator Sam Nunn (Democrat-Georgia) and retired General Colin Powell, was dispatched on 17 September to Haiti on behalf of President Clinton in an attempt to broker a peace. Carter was selected because he had had an on-and-off dialogue with Raoul Cedras for several weeks. Nunn was selected because he was regarded as the premier arbiter on military matters, and Powell for his prestige and bipartisan popularity. The high-profile trio went right to work initiating discussions with the Haitian leaders.

On 18 September, Lieutenant General Shelton (JTF-180 commander) and Major General Meade (JTF-190 commander) arrived on USS *Mount Whitney*, the command-and-control ship and commander, Second Fleet flagship, while *Eisenhower* passed by Cuba and entered the waters near Haiti.

Paratroopers of the 82d Airborne Division, along with their air force transports, were at Pope Air Force Base, North Carolina, set for an airborne drop into the Port-au-Prince area, while their and the XVIII Airborne Corps aviation relocated north of Haiti to Great Inagua. Special operations aircraft from Task Force 160 along with 2,000 Rangers and 1st Special Forces Group soldiers were afloat on *America* off Port-au-Prince, while the 2d Battalion/2d Marines, which constituted the MEU, floated in the waters off Cap-Haïtien. The armada was complete with a floating hospital, USS *Comfort*. The formidable force, under the control of JTF-180 headquarters, was poised to execute their plan—an invasion designed to quickly neutralize any Haitian resistance. The

10th Mountain brigade commanders were never briefed on the details of this plan nor on the extent of our involvement.

Back on 2 September, Admiral Miller had directed JTF-180 and JTF-190 to develop merged time-phase force deployment data (TPFDD) to be able to execute both plans and retain flexibility. A merged plan was quickly developed. It was good thinking, because it afforded the National Command Authority the option to change the level of applied force at the last minute—and time was quickly running out.

It was nearing 1 P.M. on Sunday, 18 September, and Gen. John Shalikashvili, chairman of the Joint Chiefs of Staff, advised President Clinton that the 82d Airborne would have to begin its loading sequence if the operation was to proceed as planned. Clinton gave the go-ahead. The wheels were in motion, and concern began to rise about the fate of the Carter-led negotiating team for every passing minute reduced their margin of safety.

At 5 P.M., as negotiations were going on with Cedras and Jonaissant, a Haitian general rushed into the room and announced that the 82d Airborne had just left Fort Bragg. He charged that the negotiations were a trick to keep the leadership isolated and in one spot. Although the outburst resulted in some very tense moments, the arbitration moved forward, and by 6 P.M., Carter notified President Clinton that an agreement was close. Clinton advised Carter that he had 30 minutes before he would order him out of Haiti.[1] It was not long after that Cedras and his cronies accepted the United States terms, and Jonaissant signed the agreement.

At 8 P.M., with the paratroopers in the air and just hours before H-Hour, President Clinton canceled the invasion and recalled the aircraft. An hour later, at 9 P.M., Lieutenant General Shelton ordered the execution of a modified version of the merged plan—an excellent example of the flexibility provided to the political leadership by the military's approach of adaptive planning.

For those of us on board *Eisenhower*, it was a night of tension and multiple changes. At my level, the execution of the corps' plan the 10th Mountain's plan, the merged plan, or a variant simply boiled down to were we going first or second? All afternoon we oscillated between leading the assault on Haiti the following day or conducting an air movement into Haiti on Tuesday or Wednesday as the follow-on force. With every call from *Mount Whitney* came a new be-prepared order and with every order came a slight variant to the rules of engagement (ROE).

Leaders at all levels were diligently working with their soldiers to ensure that each one thoroughly understood the ROE. We had issued multiple personal ROE cards, each colored coded. Our vehicle for explaining and ensuring an understanding of the ROE was a series of vignettes produced by the 10th Mountain's Judge Advocate General's office. These situational examples allowed the soldier to think through his actions well before he was confronted with an actual situation. Vignettes had proved extremely effective in Somalia, but this time it was more complex. One minute you are going in shooting and the next you aren't—or are you? With white, yellow, and blue cards the potential for confusion was great. One soldier remarked, "If we postpone the operation another day, we might end up with enough for a complete deck of playing cards."

The ROE weren't our only last-minute concern. Because of the efficient fueling capability on board *Eisenhower* and the close proximity of the carrier to our objectives, we opted to drop the extended-range fuel tanks from the Black Hawks, except those on the C2 and Medevac aircraft, both of which required a long loitering time. Aviation ammunition was brought to the flight deck via the magazine elevators, and the Lightfighters were issued their ammunition and rations as they commenced their last-minute precombat checks.

Anticipation and anxiety were mounting. Army and navy chaplains circulated among the soldiers providing reassurance and discussing loved ones and home and offering prayers. It was still unknown who or what we would be confronted by once on the objectives, but we had to plan for the worst—combat. Although we had a number of Somalia and Desert Storm veterans, the majority of the soldiers had not experienced combat.

Port-au-Prince is a city of 1 million people. Like most third-world capitals, the rural migration to the ruling city had resulted in a population that exceeded its infrastructure. A once beautiful harbor city centered around the presidential palace and port facility, its French colonial architecture had long since succumbed to neglect and the abuse of time. The city's beauty was marred by the encroachment of the seemingly endless corrugated tin shanties, which created acres of suburban slums. With a failed power generation and distribution system, the city had taken on the appearance of Mogadishu by night.

Under the cover of darkness, Gemmill sailed *Eisenhower* into the Haitian waters known as the Canal-du-Sud, which is a stretch of ocean between the island of Gonâve and the mountainous southern peninsula of Haiti. In the early morning hours of Monday, 19 September, Brigadier General Close received word that we would commence the operation at 0930 hours, H-Hour, on 19 September, D-Day. We established a launch hour from *Eisenhower* at 0900 hours.

We made a last-minute plea to General Meade for the removal of the UH-60 troop seats. He gave the OK. We could now transport seventeen Lightfighters per Black Hawk instead of eleven. Although great news, it meant that all the aircraft loads had to be reconfigured along with modification of the air movement table. The delayed decision prompted the UH-60 crew chiefs to chant a cadence, "Seats in—seats out, tanks on—tanks off, sleeves up—sleeves down," as they diligently labored to accomplish the task.

As the morning sun crested the summit of the 8,900-foot Massif-de-la-Selle mountains of Haiti, the soldiers and sailors aboard the carrier could see the faint outline of land on either side of the ship. It would not be long now, as the ship's crew and her lethal human cargo conducted their final checks.

Major General Meade transferred from *Mount Whitney* to *Eisenhower* and was provided a briefing by the commanders and Task Force Mountain staff on our preparations and timeline. Upon completion of the briefing, General Meade made his way to the forward ready room housing Bill Driver and his Cobra pilots. Because they would lead the air assault to the objective, he wanted to be sure they understood the ROE. As they gathered around the general, he methodically took them through a vignette, something he was a master at doing. Ironically, it was one of Driver's Cobras that test-fired a 20mm cannon an hour later en route to the objective, resulting in a flurry of activity and an inquiry from the commanding general.

By 8:30 A.M. the deck of *Eisenhower* was covered from one end to the other with spinning rotor blades. The whining turbine engines and the roar of the whirling helicopter blades slicing through the air was deafening. Looking down from above onto the flight deck, the olive drab airframes blended into the dark color of the ship's deck as if the aircraft and deck were one.

The huge 65-ton starboard aircraft elevator surfaced flush with the deck carrying 200 combat-ready Lightfighters. The navy deck handlers sporting white vests safely led the infantry past the turning blades to their designated aircraft. Within minutes the second elevator load arrived. I walked out on the deck and peered up at the ship's superstructure. Below the large gold naval aviator wings painted on the front of the tower was a 5-foot colored stencil of a 10th Mountain Division patch—a fitting token of an historic operation.

I tossed my gear on the floor of the UH-60 equipped with the command-and-control console as I joined Andy Berdy facing the fixed map display and collection of radios located in the center of the troop compartment. We had a full aircraft, loaded with our operations officers and Andy's fire support officer and intelligence officer. Two minutes prior to our aircraft's departure the UH-60 side door slid open. It was General Meade's aide, CPT Drew Meyerowich of Somalia fame. He said the commanding general wanted to see me "right away!" I unbuckled and exited the aircraft.

I approached Meade at the base of the tower. He asked me which aircraft I was in. As I pointed to it he stated he would fly with me. He went on to say I needed to find space for his aide, interpreter, political advisor, Douglas K. Watson, and Command Sergeant Major Laye. The wind turbulence on the deck from the helicopters was nothing compared to the personal turbulence this was causing. I was upset as I scurried around like a misplaced crew chief trying to find a seat for the general's retinue. Jesse Laye, a soldiers' soldier, could see my frustration and abruptly relieved me of finding him a seat. He jumped into one of the cramped lead aircraft. I looked at Mr. Watson and pointed to a helicopter. He was unceremoniously stuffed into one of the troop carriers to share floor space with the Lightfighters. Meyerowich and the interpreter joined Meade in the command-and-control Black Hawk. Ironically, the two sat on the floor, while General Meade occupied the seat between Berdy and me.

Note

1. "A Man with a Mission," *Newsweek,* 3 October 1994, p. 33.

22

THE ASSAULT, 19 SEPTEMBER 1994

Your time is up.
—*President Bill Clinton*, nationally televised address,
18 September, referring to the military junta controlling Haiti

Once airborne, Major General Meade informed me that he did not want any of the aircraft to cross the Port-au-Prince runway threshold before 9:30 A.M. I told him that could not be, because we had planned and briefed for the Cobras to pass over the airfied 60 seconds before H-Hour. It was critical that we adhere to the H-Hour sequence because everything was predicated on the tires of the lead assault UH-60 touching down at precisely 9:30, but Meade remained adamant about not crossing the threshold before 9:30. I contacted both Bill Driver, Dragon 06, and Russ Forshag, Knighthawk 06, directing them to adjust to the change. You could hear the frustration in their voices as they responded with "Wilco" (short for will comply). The two commanders adjusted the airspeed of their flights to meet the new time. Months later, General Meade let me know that the adjustment in time had been directed from above. CNN had been broadcasting all morning that 9:30 A.M. was the invasion time, so I could only conclude that we obliged the media.

An AC-130 was flying several thousand feet overhead, and the weapons operators employing the aircraft's enhanced optics reported everything they observed and were ready to provide pinpoint fires if necessary. The 10,000-foot active runway had some minor obstructions, and although the operators observed a great deal of activity around the terminal complex, the police barracks at the east end of the airfield appeared idle. There was no apparent organized threat from uniformed forces.

A special operations EC-130 jammed packed with electronic gear was orbiting off Port-au-Prince, broadcasting on open radio and television frequencies appeals in Creole for calm as the U.S. force was about to descend on the Haitian capital. Additionally an army four-engine airplane, painted to look like a commercial aircraft, flew above Cap-Haïtien observing activities in the port city and along the shoreline, while instantaneously beaming the images back to the marine commander aboard his command-and-control ship.[1] It was a well-orchestrated effort with all the parts synchronized.

At 9:30 A.M. on Monday, 19 September, Driver and his Cobras, at 100 feet above the ground, bolted across the west end of the Port-au-Prince main runway and quickly circled the airfield perimeter looking for any hostile intent. His gunships took up mutually supporting overwatch positions near the airport. A minute behind the attack aircraft was Forshag and his lead flight of Black Hawks loaded with 2-22d infantrymen, commanded by LTC James Terry and destined for the police barracks and the terminal.

The assault aircraft inserted the Lightfighters just as rehearsed, first placing the soldiers near the police barracks and then directly in front of the passenger terminal. The apron near the terminal was clut-

Infantry boarding UH-60s on the flight deck

tered with derelict aircraft, vintage 1930s DC-3 transports, which contrasted with the UH-60 helicopters.

The troopers hit the tarmac, heaving their rucksacks to the ground and taking up prone fighting positions behind them. The Black Hawks departed as quickly as they arrived, leaving bits of grass and debris churning in the air. After the rotor wash and turbulence subsided the young warriors fanned out—only to be confronted by microphones and cameras of an inquisitive press and Haitians waving pro-American banners. The entire operation was watched by the world via CNN. Even the soldiers and sailors aboard *Eisenhower* who had launched the aircraft minutes earlier could for once see a side of the operation they usually just heard about.

Although pleasantly surprised by our reception, this did not reduce the need for alert soldiers with force protection fore most in their minds. Our analysis had concluded that the most likely threat to U.S. forces would be drive-by shootings, tossed grenades, or sniper fire, and the Haitians were also apt to use Molotov cocktails. All of this caused much apprehension.

The infantrymen continued to stream across from the carrier into the airfield perimeter. Simultaneously, Black Hawks hovered over the ship's fantail and hooked up to the awaiting Humvees, quickly slinging them to the west end of the airport. Meeting no armed resistance, the operation became a continuous shuttle of troops and equipment from *Eisenhower* to the objective areas.

It was during the air movement of the Lightfighters that a serious flaw in our plan that placed our soldiers at risk became obvious. We had gone into the operation knowing we would be unable to provide every soldier a set of waterwings (a life preserver). Therefore, it was decided that as the troops arrived on their objective, a soldier in each aircraft that was part of the assault would gather the waterwings and pass them to the next arriving aircraft. The floatation devices would be taken back to the carrier and reissued to the awaiting troops.

During our preparations, we had managed to round up just over 400 sets of waterwings—the army's total available inventory. That number, although far from optimal, enabled the aircraft to return to the ship, pick up Lightfighters already equipped with the floatation devices, and drop off those waterwings just retrieved from the infantry ashore. We expected to stay two aircraft turns ahead, so that there would be no interference with the troops next up for the airlift to shore.

The plan began to unravel from the beginning; the last thing a soldier wants or needs to deal with once on the ground is gathering or turning in equipment. As the aircraft returned to the carrier, the numbers of flotation devices recovered became fewer and fewer. After a couple of iterations we ran out of waterwings. It was a poor plan based on an unrealistic assumption and was abandoned halfway through the operation. We defaulted to an earlier plan to equip each aircraft with enough floatation devices to cover the passenger load, just as the navy and marines do. It satisfied the requirement, but with seventeen troops crammed into an aircraft cargo compartment, it would have been extremely difficult for a trooper in trouble to retrieve a life preserver.

Our time in the Black Hawk with General Meade was short. We dropped him off after the first lift of Black Hawks landed at Port-au-Prince airfield, while Berdy and I remained airborne throughout the air assault—in excess of 5 hours. General Meade joined Lieutenant General Shelton, who had just landed in his own army helicopter from *Mount Whitney*. Protected by only a few soldiers, both generals jumped into a vehicle along with U.S. Ambassador William L. Swing and drove to Cedras's headquarters. This would be the first of many meetings the trio would have with the deposed leader. Meeting every other day, Cedras and the three U.S. officials met right up to the night of 12 October, when the Haitian general left the country.

The skies above Cedras's headquarters and Port-au-Prince were buzzing with helicopters. The aircraft congestion was reduced by flight-following with *Eisenhower*'s tower and maintaining contact with an air force AWACS plane controlling the upper airspace. Although there was plenty of aircraft maneuver room above the city, Port-au-Prince is bordered on the north and south by two rugged mountain ranges that form natural barriers.

The city of 2 million residents living in an endless maze of narrow streets and alleys is located on the western coast at the base of the Plaine Cul-de-Sac, a wide valley that divides the central region of Haiti from its southern region. The chaotic capital creeps up into the foothills of the steep Massif-de-la-Selle mountains to the south and is in the shadow of an equally rugged mountain range on the north. All of this would make for a formidable challenge if we had to take the city by force.

An hour after our forces had touched down on the airfield, lead elements of the 1-87th Infantry commanded by LTC Ed Sullivan were airlifted from the carrier into the port facility without incident, and by 11:00 A.M., the first follow-on forces aboard strategic air began arriving at the international airport. An hour after the port was secure, the roll-on, roll-off ship *Callaghan,* which had sailed from Bayonne only 4 days earlier, docked and began to unload the division's equipment. Twenty-four hours later, *Callaghan* was steaming north to Bayonne for another load.

By the days' end the U.S. force had secured the Port-au-Prince airport, the port facility and adjacent petroleum storage area, the port at Cap-Haïtien, and communications and government buildings in both Port-au-Prince and Cap-Haïtien.

I positioned Bill Driver and a portion of his attack battalion and Finnegan's cavalry troop, augmented with a refueling, maintenance, and air traffic control (ATC) team, forward to Port-au-Prince airfield to provide responsive fire support to Berdy. As night fell, we opted to terminate air movement operations until the following morning, and we recovered the remainder of the aircraft to *Eisenhower.* The aviators had a productive first day's work, transporting 1,622 Lightfighters and fifty-five sling loads in 225 sorties from *Eisenhower.*

The first elements of JTF-190 were on the ground, too. JTF-180, under Shelton's command from *Mount Whitney,* would continue to command the entire joint operation area, while Meade and JTF-190 would command the land forces, minus the marines in the north, from ashore.

Port-au-Prince remained calm that night: the jubilant supporters were reserved in their celebration. The city was concealed in darkness, showing only a few scattered pockets of light for the privileged few with access to portable generators. This would be the first of many nights on which the soldiers of the 10th Mountain would hear the pounding of the drums and incessant chanting associated with the practice of voodoo.

Roman Catholicism is the official religion of Haiti, but the majority of Haitians also believe in and practice some aspects of voodoo.[2] An informal religion, voodoo has no established theology, scriptures, or clergy. The fundamental elements are music, dance, magical invocation, and rites and cults focusing on the dead. There is a distinction made between *voudun* and *vaudun. Voudun* is considered black magic or the evil branch of voodoo, while *vaudun* is considered white magic or the good branch. Soldiers had been warned by their information handbooks of possible suicide attacks or other seemingly irrational actions by Haitians who might be under the influence of voodoo spells. The caution resulted in many young American imaginations working overtime the first night on Haitian soil.

After a good night's sleep and a full belly of navy chow, we commenced D-Day+1 with the air operations. Once again the deck of *Eisenhower* was bustling, and along with the AirBoss, we relied upon MAJ Scott Zegler to keep things on schedule. Scott Zegler was Russ Forshag's operations officer and he not only became the AirBoss's right-hand man throughout the operation, but his expertise and calm demeanor resolved many misunderstandings in the tension-filled control tower.

Although support troops needed to be relocated to the ground, this day would be devoted almost entirely to sling-load operations. There was much to be off-loaded, and although Captain Gemmill and his crew were generous hosts, they were eager to retrieve their air wing and get on with navy business. We didn't want to overstay our welcome.

Every available open space, outside of the airport active and approach, was littered with equipment and supplies brought from the carrier. We were dropping the loads and recovering the slings faster than the soldiers on the ground could organize the cargo, yet sling availability quickly became a concern. We weren't retrieving enough slings to support the cargo that still had to be transported. Zegler dispatched his assistant, LT Steve Osterholzer, to remedy this problem. Once at the airfield, Osterholzer realized the magnitude of his task: equipment with slings attached was scattered over acres. He made a beeline for an air force officer engaged in off-loading the C-141s and C-5s to ask for some help in gathering the much needed slings. The flight suit–clad air force officer turned out to be a brigadier general spearheading the airlift operations at Port-au-Prince airport. Sympathetic to the young army officer's predicament, the general directed a group of airmen armed with a forklift to help out. Aided by the airmen, Osterholzer quickly accomplished his mission, and what could have been a show stopper for the operation became manageable. But we did experience some problems that quickly gained attention.

The Black Hawk crew chiefs had a bad habit of hanging out the door-gunner's window as the aircraft slowed for its approach. The crew chief is responsible for clearing those portions of the aircraft the pilot is unable to see, but much of this extending from the aircraft portal was considered the cool thing to do. With the external stores (wings) attached, the crew chief was able to lean even farther out by grasping the wing support. On this day, there was an incident that got everyone's attention and reinforced the importance of following the rules.

Sling-load operations required the crew chief to go to the rear of the Black Hawk troop compartment, attach his nylon security harness

A UH-60 Black Hawk preparing to
sling-load a humvee from the USS Eisenhower's fantail

and retaining strap (a monkey harness) into a floor-mounted D-ring, and then go to his hands and knees to observe the cargo hook and appended load. The load is viewed through a small trapdoor in the center floor. From this point the crew chief is able to report the load status to the pilots and, if necessary, initiate a manual release.

During sling-load operations when returning to retrieve another load, the written procedure requires the crew chief to strap himself into one of the troop seats along the back wall, while still retaining his connection by the monkey harness. Crew chief Ronald Bordner was participating in sling-load operation, and as his aircraft was returning to the ship to pick up another load, he did not return to his seat. Instead, with the aircraft doors open, he decided to hang his head over the edge of the troop compartment to look at the ocean below. A strong crosswind gust blew into the compartment, shifting the aircraft and tossing him out of the helicopter. Bordner was not missed until minutes later when the pilots went down their prelanding checklist for landing on the carrier. The checklist words "crew, passengers and mission equipment" require a response from a crew chief. The intercom was silent. Bordner was dangling 200 feet above the ocean and 5 feet below the left wheel of the aircraft attached only by his nylon monkey harness.

Seeing the stretched security harness leading from the D-ring across the floor and out the side of the helicopter, the pilot quickly reduced his forward airspeed to near zero, bringing his aircraft to a hover. The AirBoss, observing everything from his perch atop the superstructure, immediately placed all operations on hold and cleared the flight deck. Although this appeared to be a simple matter of hovering over the ship's deck and dropping Bordner off, there was concern that the strap wouldn't hold for the quarter-mile journey or that Bordner would become tangled in the landing gear. Worse yet, he might be crushed by the wheel during an attempt to deposit him on the ship. Bordner hung limp under the helo as he slowly oscillated. After several very tense minutes, the embarrassed crew chief arrived over the flight deck under the aircraft, and the pilot cautiously lowered Bordner to the deck. The latter hastily pulled his quick-release to escape the grasp of the helicopter.

I saw this mishap with my own eyes and can only imagine the many near-accidents or foul-ups to which I was not privy. One was the loss of a UH-60's basic load of machine gun ammunition into the ocean when the crew made a steep turn in a holding pattern while waiting to land on *Eisenhower.* The boxes of ammunition slid across the cargo floor and out the open doorway right into ocean.

Back on Haitian soil, Finnegan positioned his cavalry troopers along the southeastern perimeter of the airfield. Driver occupied a taxiway, apron, and rundown group of buildings that had once housed a portion of the Haitian air force. We had selected the complex during our planning at Fort Drum using overhead photography and pictures taken from ground level. It placed the aviation force far enough out of the airport's main airflow and airline terminal operations, while providing us facilities to billet our troops and maintain our aircraft. In a matter of days, I discovered that some people preferred our removal from the Port-au-Prince airport entirely.

By the end of the second day, we had slung 350,000 pounds of cargo and equipment in 112 sorties and had transported 408 troops. Forshag and his assault pilots recovered to the carrier for a final night. I collocated the brigade headquarters with Driver at Port-au-Prince International Airport. I went from the luxury of previous air-conditioned quarters and *Eisenhower*'s endless cuisine to a filthy, windowless structure and MREs to sustain my strength. I was quite accustomed to the hardships of field life (although compared to the infantryman who had to lie on the ground to rest, I had it pretty good). I had spent my formative years in the army as an infantryman, so dirty hair, no showers, and living with the body odor of myself and my comrades was part of being a soldier.

Furthermore, I had been raised in the Arizona desert, so high temperatures alone had never troubled me. But Haiti and its sweltering heat was different: you couldn't escape it and there wasn't any protection from the tropical humidity. These conditions sucked out your energy; this was exacerbated by the weight of the 3.2-pound Kevlar helmet, armored protective vest, and the thick cotton BDU worn with its sleeves down. It made for a good weight-reducing program: as one lieutenant joked, "'Jenny Craig' on the cheap!" There were no air-conditioned buildings, nor fans to circulate the air. And unlike Somalia where the sea breeze dried your skin and cooled your brow, the air in Haiti was stagnant and thick with moisture.

At night it was worse. I would stretch out under the mosquito netting in my boxer shorts, every inch of my body coated with each day's grimy perspiration. My underarms stuck to the side of my body, the sweat ran down between my legs to leave a sticky film. My hair, though cropped short, was coated in greasy oil, and my scalp was caked with the day's grit and grime. All of this was made worse by the mosquitoes buzzing around the netting looking for an opportunity to feast. I was miserable. It was finally on day five that I experienced my first full bath—a trickle of water from a canvas bag suspended from a pole brought great pleasure. Up to that point, I had relied upon the best field personal hygiene invention ever, Baby Wipes! The troops received their first good cleaning as they bathed in the water runoff gushing from the building downspouts during a tropical rain.

Personal discomforts aside, our concern was still force protection and personal security. We were exposed to a roadway, which skirted the perimeter of the airfield, and houses that lined the road. Finnegan was aggressively patrolling the neighborhoods adjacent to our location on the airfield, and his troopers made sure that no one got any ideas. A couple of times we did observe Haitians videotaping our activities, but we were unable to catch those suspicious characters. Such episodes reinforced my desire to eliminate any direct observation quickly.

On the morning of day three I flew back to *Eisenhower* to ensure that we left the ship as we had found her and to convey my thanks to Mark Gemmill. While I was talking with Russ Forshag in the compartment we used for our operations center, I noticed on one of the television monitors that a helicopter a quarter-mile off the port was very low over the water and that its rotor wash was kicking up a great deal of water. This bothered me because the salt spray, once sucked in, would rapidly corrode the engines and components. That I was able to view this at first hand was because the television image was the work of a group of sailors whose sole function was to videotape activities on the ship. This is PLAT (pilot landing assistant television), and the navy does this for safety assessment, to facilitate learning, and as a sort of blow-by-blow picture log.

Just as my eye caught the low-flying aircraft, so did the PLAT operator. As he zoomed in on the aircraft I couldn't figure why one of the Black Hawks was so low over the water. When the image became clearer, I saw that it was *Eisenhower*'s CH-53 Sea Stallion, which had just taken off into the wind from the carrier's bow. As the aircraft turned downwind, it had begun to sink—descending below the plane of the flight deck toward the water below. The aircraft had gone beyond its operational limits. With its high gross weight (loaded internally with ammunition), slow airspeed, and downwind condition the flat-gray helo was slowly settling toward the ocean.

As the pilot applied more power, the six fully articulated rotor blades coned upward. I had never seen blades bowed upward like that before—almost like fingers extending from an outreached hand. The pilot was pulling all of the available "collective," the control lever that governs the vertical movement of a helicopter. The increased power and pitch in the blades aggravated the condition by creating turbulent air ("dirty" air) around the main rotor blades, and the result was even less lift. The huge Sikorsky helicopter began to rotate slowly as the pilot started to lose his directional control because the same air condition was negating his tail rotor's effectiveness.

All eyes were on the helicopter as the mishap unfolded in what seemed slow motion. The aircraft rotated on the surface of the water; then as if in one last lunge for freedom from the ocean's grasp, it lifted in the air about 20 feet, still spinning slowly clockwise and spouting streams of water. Again, the blades coned and the rotating helicopter began to settle back into the water. This time, as it touched the water's surface, it stopped rotating and appeared to pause on the ocean's surface as water splashed into it through the open cargo doors. Now the blades were coned so much that I thought they were going to fly off. Suddenly, the pilot jettisoned the two 250-gallon fuel tanks attached to the fuselage, and like a rocket, the helicopter shot straight up in the air about 50 feet. The pilot nosed the aircraft forward, gaining airspeed while "beelining" to the security of *Eisenhower*'s deck.

I don't know who that pilot was, but I had to believe that he soiled his trousers. This was a hair-raising experience to watch, and I could only imagine what was going through the helicopter crew's mind—but to the pilot's credit, he managed to maintain control throughout the ordeal. As for the helicopter, it must have had everything from its nose to its tail overtorqued, which meant a complete rebuild. At least it wasn't on the bottom of the ocean with its crew.

Captain Gemmill had much on his mind at this point, so I made my good-bye brief. Russ Forshag transloaded the ammunition from the crippled Sea Stallion to a couple of Black Hawks, and we bade farewell to *Eisenhower* and her crew. It was the end to a historic operation as Gemmill and his crew readied for the return of their air wing.

On my trip back to the airport I stopped by the port facility, and it was there that General Meade landed next to my helicopter. He ran over to me and said, "Hey Larry, I'm sorry I never get by to see you and your guys. The fact is I don't have time to do anything but deal with pressing problems. And you and your team are doing great!" It was good to receive kudos from the boss.

Notes

1. The army aircraft flew from one of the Providenciales Islands located north of Haiti and part of the British Caicos Islands chain. The arrival of the unmarked plane on the small Caribbean island prompted a local commercial air operator to challenge the crew and insist that there wasn't enough business for another commercial operation. His fears were quickly put to rest.

2. *Haiti Information Handbook* (Washington, D.C.: Department of Defense, August 1994), pp. 2–12.

23

THE OCCUPATION

Every action needs a certain time to be completed.
— *Clausewitz*

By the end of the third day, the entire brigade with corps attachments was consolidated on the southeast end of the Port-au-Prince airfield. The 4-2d Cavalry OH-58D Kiowa Warriors never were attached, and the Black Hawk company from the 82d Airborne Division had never left Great Inagua. Driver and Forshag's aviators had accomplished it alone. By the end of the third day Forshag's Knighthawks had transported forty-four sling loads and airlifted 170 soldiers, and for the period of $2^1/_2$ days their total was 211 external loads and 2,200 troops transported in 539 sorties.

With the arrival of the 1st Battalion, 159th Aviation Regiment—the Gunslingers, so named because they sling artillery around the battlefield—and C2 Black Hawks from Great Inagua, we had a little over eighty aircraft and 1,100 soldiers jammed into about 40 acres of airport area. Field sanitation became a major challenge as we constructed several latrines throughout the area. We had multiple teams trained and equipped to deal with the problem, but the sheer volume of human waste required frequent closure and relocating of the sites. The unglamorous subject of portable toilets and waste reclamation trucks became a JTF priority. The aviation brigade was not the only unit confronted with a disposal problem: waste retrieval truck availability became a nightly item briefed at the commanding general's evening updates.

Along with LTC Al Page and his 1-159th came two additional CH-47s and a couple of UH-60s from the 101st Air Assault Division. The Fort Campbell team was earmarked for fighting fires in the city. The Chinooks arrived equipped with two huge Canadian-built 500- and 1,000-gallon water buckets affectionately called Sims and Bambi, while the UH-60 crews were trained as spotters for the big helicopters or any fire-fighting aircraft that might be employed. It was a unique mission, and one we fortunately did not have to execute. If we had met resistance during the initial assault, there was a good chance the ensuing combat would have ignited an uncontrollable fire in Port-au-Prince. The sprawling slums, crammed with shanties constructed of wood, cardboard, and tin, were pushed up against the upscale neighborhoods of the city. The makeshift dwellings shared common walls and were separated by narrow disjointed alleyways riddled with potholes, restricting passage to nothing larger than bicycles and small carts—all of which made for an explosive situation of potential firestorm proportions. Fire retardant from above would be the only solution.

But fires weren't on the minds of the Haitian people. Businessmen, police, and cronies of Cedras were bracing themselves for reprisals, a predictable backlash from the impoverished who had been oppressed for years.

The combined JTF-180 became a multinational force with missions to establish a stable and secure environment, assist in restoration of democracy to Haiti, and ensure the prompt return of President Aristide. With this in mind, Colonel Berdy's brigade aggressively conducted patrols in Port-au-Prince and the surrounding area. Berdy's Lightfighters ferreted out weapons caches while maintaining a visible U.S. presence. The XVIII Airborne Corps 16th Military Police (MP) Brigade commanded by COL Mike Sullivan arrived shortly after D-Day and immediately occupied the Haitian police stations scattered throughout the sprawling city. Sullivan's MPs patrolled sectors and established a number of checkpoints in search of weapons and "wanted" belligerents. Things were relatively quiet, with no organized resistance or threatening activity. Our threat assessment was beginning to shift toward disgruntled police personnel and the criminal element.

My security concerns focused on our assembly area at the airport. A 4-foot-high chainlink fence with a couple of strands of barbed wire was all that stood between curious Haitian onlookers and the cavalrymen of Alpha Troop. If we were going to remain on the airfield, we needed more force protection: I wanted to eliminate direct observation as well as any direct fire that may have been intended for us. I believed in the adage of out of sight, out of mind, and I knew just the way to do it, but I needed some help.

On day four I got the help I was looking for. I ran into an old acquaintance, COL Dan Labin. Dan and I had served together as battalion commanders in Hawaii. Much to my delight his current command encompassed the mayorship of the port's operations. I expressed my desire to surround the brigade's encampment with stacked sea-land containers, and asked if he had any he wanted to part with and a rough terrain container/cargo handler to position them. I didn't expect many, but to my good fortune Labin needed to dispose of a few hundred derelict containers cluttering the dock. He was desperate to make room for the hundreds of supplies arriving by ship each day.

So over the following 2 weeks, the containers were brought to the airfield at night and during the day were placed end to end under the watchful eye of the cavalry security force. Near the troop sleeping areas and the dining facility the wall was two containers high; the added height along with restricted activity near the barrier ensured troop safety.

It may seem that we were constructing a fortress, but it was my intention to provide a protected environment for our soldiers and I pledged that we were not going to allow any penetration of our perimeter by belligerents, or thieves, a promise I kept. The only thing that would cause us to move would be indirect fire (and I knew that a few 60mm mortars were unaccounted for by the Haitian army).

My attitude toward force protection, and that of many of my fellow conventional force commanders, was the target of much criticism from the Special Forces and NGO communities, centering on the intimidating appearance of the conventional soldiers, outfitted as they were in full battle gear with weapons at the ready. The critics charged that our communicating that we would not drop our guard caused otherwise sympathetic Haitians to keep their distance and not share information or offer assistance. I believe the criticism is valid, but the action was prudent for the large combat force. Our mission was to provide a safe and secure environment and displaying well-disciplined, unapproachable soldiers suited me just fine. We hadn't known what to expect when we arrived and we weren't taking any chances. If a different behavior was required, then it was time to bring in a follow-on force. The Special Forces teams by structure and training were much more flexible and proved extremely effective in executing their piece of the mission.

The U.S. force expanded operations on 21 September when Task Force Raleigh, commanded by BG Dick Potter and made up of the 3d Special Forces Group, started deployment throughout the countryside. The Special Forces operated from three main forward operating bases. In teams of six to eight, these soldiers not only ranged the country but also did everything from repairing water pumps to providing medical support to the sick. There is little doubt that their appearance in the outlying provinces made the difference in winning and losing the people's support, and stands as one of the underpinnings for the success of Operation Uphold Democracy. From the aviation brigade's perspective, it meant we would be required to support the Special Forces teams permanently stationed at their twenty-seven isolated outposts, all of which required resupply every few days. These resupply missions became a prime consumer of flight hours.

On 24 September, the 2d Brigade was deployed from Griffiss Air Force Base on strategic airlift to Roosevelt Roads, Puerto Rico, where it was transloaded into C-130s. Cap-Haïtien runways could handle neither C-141s nor C-5s, so the durable Hercules troop carrier finished the job. COL Jim Dubik and his Lightfighters conducted a relief in place with the marines the following day and quickly commenced to fan out into the countryside.

To provide the planned responsive aviation support to the 2d Brigade, I directed Bill Driver and an aviation task force built around his headquarters to relocate 85 miles north to a small airfield on the outskirts of Cap-Haïtien. His force consisted of an attack helicopter company, a Black Hawk platoon, a Medevac section, and an ATC component. The Chinook's large carrying capacity made Driver's task easier. He preferred the isolation and serenity of the northern city over the hustle and congestion of Port-au-Prince, and didn't miss the price of being near the flagpole—that is, the meetings, briefings, and constant scrutiny. Like Dubik, Bill was pretty much his own boss and he thoroughly enjoyed his independence.

High above the part of Haiti that was the 2d Brigade's sector stands one of the engineering marvels of the New World—the Citadelle. When I would fly north to Cap-Haïtien, the flight path would take me directly past the massive structure. On its perch atop the rocky mountain it often looked like a stone ship jutting through the clouds. It was of French design and it matched any castle I had seen in my years of travel throughout the world.

The Citadelle, on the 3,000-foot mountain peak of Laferrière, was built at the beginning of the nineteenth century by the self-proclaimed emperor Henri Christophe as an impregnable bastion for the fight against an eventual attempt by the French to reconquer Haiti. The work began in 1805 and was still in progress at the time of the his death in 1820. It is the largest fortress in the Western Hemisphere and completely dominates the terrain of northern Haiti. It was conceived for 142 cannons of the heaviest caliber of the period and a 2,000-soldier garrison (or up to 5,000 men in case of an emergency). It has long since been largely abandoned to nature, and few tourists climb the winding cobblestone track to visit the crumbling fortress.

So impressive is the fortress, stretched across the mountain peak with sheer cliffs on three sides and the only point of access subject to cannon fire, that the United Nations included the Citadelle in its list of cultural treasures, along with such marvels as the ancient metropolis of Tikal in northern Guatemala, the pyramids of Egypt, and the temple of Borobudur in Indonesia. The bastion is Haiti's most revered national symbol of what the Haitians can do when they put their minds to it, even though the imposing structure was constructed by forced labor, with 20,000 men perishing during the construction.

The people who occupied the barren foothills around the Citadelle were typical of the rural Haitians of the country's outlands—hard-working, earthy people who toil in the fields that cling to the sides of the rugged hills. They have few pleasures other than an occasional drink of a fiery alcoholic concoction called *clairin,* a sugar-based moonshine that is Haiti's national drink. While the outer provinces were relatively serene, the cities presented the bigger challenge to the multinational force.

In Port-au-Prince, as Berdy's light infantrymen and Sullivan's MPs uncovered more and more weapons caches, the number of false reports about weapons also increased. Neighbors were settling old scores and turning each other in, leading to raids that usually harvested one or two weapons, mostly relics of the past. At the same time, a weapons buy-back program funded by the U.S. government was initiated.

The program, executed by the multinational force, netted mixed results. Weapons were being turned in for cash, but without a reliable estimate of how many weapons were in Haiti it was impossible to measure progress. The combined total of weapons seized or bought during the entire period we were in Haiti was near 15,000. Of that total, 9,915 weapons were exchanged for cash in the amount of $1,814,550. In the early stages of the buy-back program an automatic weapon would go for $200. Four months later the same automatic weapon would fetch $800.[1]

The multinational force headquarters was located just west of the international airport in an old industrial complex consisting of large open-bay warehouses. The headquarters was humming with activity as the staff led by COL Jim Campbell focused on preparing the city and the nation for President Aristide's return on 15 October. It was during this early period that the ROE underwent a major revision.

Our troops were working alongside the Haitian police to maintain order, but the Haitian manner of enforcing the law is a far cry from

10th Aviation Brigade Task Force Command Group: Left to right: MAJ Chester Egert, MAJ Stan Oliver, CPT David Bruner, LTC Russ Forshag, CPT David Tohn, CSM Dwight Brown, MAJ Steve Semmons, the author, MAJ Richard Everson, LTC Raoul Archambault, CW4 Franz Carbonneau, unidentified officer, LTC William Driver, CW5 Gerald Cartier, CPT Scott Conners, and CPT Richard Peterson how our MPs conducted business. Haitian-style brutality was tough on our soldiers, and our ROE did not address how to deal with the behavior of bad cops. The soldiers' mission was to work with the policemen, not against them, but each day it was becoming more apparent that the local police knew no other way to conduct their job than to thrash and intimidate the people.

Bloody scenes of thugs beating marchers prompted a review of the U.S. mission. After a couple of incidents where U.S. troops were near Haitian police when the law officers beat citizens, the ROE was adjusted to allow the soldiers to step in and restore order. The revised ROE allowed the trooper to make a judgment to stop the loss of life, and this essential adjustment led to a number of real American heroes with the grade of sergeant who intervened and made a difference. It was a disconcerting and perilous time for our soldiers on the streets.

But U.S. troops were making a difference. At the port, a truckload of attachés pulled up where a crowd had gathered to talk to some 10th Mountain Lightfighters. PFC Richard Ostrander stood up with his

10th Mountain soldiers in downtown Port-au-Prince

machine gun on a tripod at his feet, gestured at the thugs, and said, "Thank you for coming. Now have a good day and move on." A hush fell over the crowd as the attachés momentarily hesitated. Two more infantrymen joined Ostrander with their M16s at the ready, and the attachés hurriedly drove off to the jeers of the crowd.[2]

With the demise of the Haitian military, the existing police force disintegrated. This presented a void in public safety that had not been anticipated. Although Aristide had made it clear from the outset that he wanted the FAd'H dissolved and replaced by a revamped police force, it was those left over from the FAd'H who were initially recruited as the new force.

Building a Haitian police force, which was to be established under a UN program, fell on the shoulders of Raymond Kelly, chief of the international police monitors and a former commissioner of police for New York City. He had the job of leading the 821 police monitors from twenty nations as they organized, taught, mentored, and became confidence builders to the new Haitian police force. The early recruits comprised vetted FAd'H members who received training from the U.S. Justice Department International Criminal Investigation Training Assistance Program.

However, my problems did not encompass the Haitians or our security as we began to settle into a routine with the preponderance of our flight missions involving general support. The AWACS aircraft that provided aircraft flight-following during the early stages of our occupation had departed, and this hampered our ability to flight-follow our own aircraft and left a void in our ability to directly communicate with the crew members as they traversed the mountainous country. Our fix for this lack during the times we had aircraft airborne outside the immediate Port-au-Prince area was to launch a helicopter to fly a race-track pattern at 10,000 feet to performed radio relay, that altitude being sufficient for communicating anywhere in Haiti. (It was a monotonous mission for the crew, but a necessary one.) Later, remote radio relay transmitters were positioned throughout the mountain peaks, solving this problem.

But I had bigger problems brewing at the airfield. I was under pressure from the multinational force headquarters staff to move the aviation task force. I couldn't understand why anyone would want the helos deployed to a field site, because there were no suitable fixed facilities to go to. As an army unit, we were certainly equipped to operate from an unimproved environment, but the cost to our aircraft availability would suffer, without even counting the time lost to pack up and move. I estimated that such a move would take a week (if we were lucky) to regain our current operational tempo. We were averaging over 100 flight hours a day while sustaining in excess of 90 percent of availability for the entire fleet of eighty aircraft. Additionally, I was concerned about turning any field site into a dust bowl or, worse, a lake—this being the season of hurricanes and tropical storms.

Dust was my primary concern. There is a direct correlation between high concentrations of dust and aircraft maintenance and operation. Visibility impairment is a major problem for a helicopter pilot, whether hovering or landing. After a couple of days, a helicopter sucks the very essence of life out of vegetation, moisture. Any living thing that might act as a dust retardant, like grass, quickly expires from the constant turbulent winds, resulting in a desert-like terrain. The CH-47 Chinooks were especially good at this with their 100-mile-an-hour rotor wash. The sheer might of this medium-lift helicopters rotor blast was known to knock over small structures. (Once, when landing in a confined area in the city of Gonaïves, the wind from a Chinook blew a block wall down and an infant from its mother's arms.)

Putting aside any practical reasons for our not relocating, it took a little longer to find out who wanted us off the airport. Soon, however, it was clear that, for one, pressure for our relocation came from air force–supplied air traffic controllers who, along with the army, provided much needed direction of the congested airspace. The airmen were having difficulty with the high density of helicopter traffic. When it came to ten to fifteen helicopters moving about the airfield at any one time to rapidly refuel, drop off personnel, sling-load supplies, or just land and park, the controllers were overwhelmed. Bad instructions from the tower became commonplace, and a rift between pilots and controllers began. The airmen probably weren't accustomed to so many hovering helicopters in such a restricted space.

Eventually a portion of the airfield was placed under the control of army ATC, restricting the helicopters' movement. We erected a tower on top of a sea-land container so that army controllers could manage the movement of the helos on the airfield. We had a day-only helicopter approach that afforded the aircraft direct landing and departure from our assembly area. At night, all activity was controlled by the air force and movement outside the area required coordination and passage to either an air force or Haitian controller in training. The arrangement between the two services worked well except for one night shortly after we started flying NVG training missions. An air force master sergeant inadvertently broadcast a comment to a fellow controller that "he wasn't sure if he was going to let the army fly tonight." He went on to say "he'd think about it." He then went on to make one of our aircraft wait with its engine running at full operation for nearly 20 minutes for no apparent reason, until he was prompted several times by the pilot. What the controller didn't know was that his arrogant comment had been transmitted for everyone to hear. So the tower tapes were confiscated, and the on-site air force commander sent the errant sergeant home. Fortunately this was an isolated incident, and the cooperation between the two services was never again in question.

The second entity that wanted us gone from Port-au-Prince International Airport consisted of American Airlines and the Federal Aviation Administration (FAA), with ideas of their own.

President Clinton had stated that he wanted the port and the airfield opened for commercial operations as soon as possible. Opening the points of embarkation was an essential ingredient in getting Haiti's commerce jump-started, and the FAA, with the urging of American Airlines, was eager to get on with it. The FAA manager for Airspace and Procedures for the Southern Region, Mike Powderly, was in Port-au-Prince to recertify the airfield for U.S. commercial flights.

I was approached by Powderly, who provided me a list of compliances the brigade had to meet to remain collocated with the commercial facility. We had many discussions, as each day the pressure intensified from my higher headquarters. I quickly held meetings with the aviators to heighten their awareness and ensure that they were doing everything according to regulations and published procedures and in a courteous, professional manner. At one point, I physically walked the ground with Mr. Powderly to ensure that I understood what was expected and to assure him that we would comply. This was followed by personally escorting Lieutenant General Shelton and Major General Meade through our area to underline the need for us to stay put. Both agreed.

One day, after we had demonstrated our good faith, Powderly indicated that a briefing to a couple of executives from American Airlines, who were scheduled to arrive in a few days, might be appropriate. He suggested I discuss our plans to ease congestion and guarantee positive control over the military helicopters. I wasn't sure there was any utility in a briefing, but Powderly assured me it would pay dividends. He was right. Little did I know that the highest levels of American Airlines' management were involved in the brigade's destiny.

American Airlines' Caribbean routes are some of the most profitable, and, with American the only certified U.S. air carrier into Haiti, the Port-au-Prince service was worth millions. The airline's senior

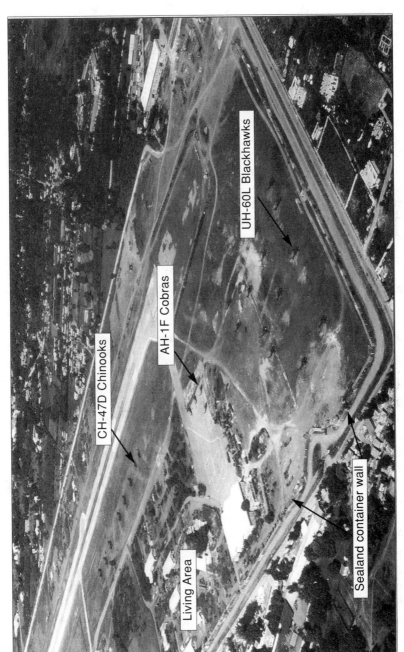

CH-47D Chinooks

AH-1F Cobras

UH-60L Blackhawks

Living Area

Sealand container wall

The east end of Port-au-Prince International Airport

executives were becoming impatient with the progress of reopening the international airport, which prompted calls to senior State Department officials in Washington. It wasn't long before the embassy was instructed to meet President Clinton's intent and get the airport open.

Steve Semmens quickly put together a desktop computer–generated presentation, and with that in hand, I went to American's offices at the passenger terminal to meet with the two executives. They had flown into the Dominican Republic, traversed the mountainous border separating the two countries in a leased Sikorsky S-76 executive helicopter and arrived at Port-au-Prince by noon.

The terminal building, by now ringed with concertina wire and vehicle obstacles, was in pretty good repair compared with most of the government and commercial structures in Haiti. Haitians were painting everything in typically bright reds, yellows, and greens in anticipation of Aristide's 15 October arrival.

I climbed the stairs to the second floor, stopping at the top to remove my helmet and wipe my brow. Mr. Powderly greeted me at the door. The cool air from the air conditioner rushed out passed him. It felt so good that I hurried toward the source of the air conditioning and caught my web gear on the door jam—shades of my canopy incident. Powderly introduced me to a Haitian woman in her mid-thirties who was identified as the Haiti station manager for American Airlines. She in turn, led me to a side office where I was introduced to American's Caribbean regional manager and the airline's chief of security. The stylish regional manager had a boyish look and could have passed for my son, but the chief of security looked like an older brother with the lines of time deeply etched in his face and steadfast eyes, and was wearing an expensive suit. Both men appeared out of place.

I unburdened myself of my web gear, protective vest, and helmet, while retaining my 9mm pistol in its shoulder holster. I was soaked with perspiration. I placed my briefing book on a small metal desk in front of the regional manager and began my briefing. I defined the problem and described the measures we were taking to ensure uninterrupted commercial service, while at the same time emphasizing the importance of retaining U.S. presence at the airport. I concluded by giving them my assurances that everything was under control, and that I was personally involved. The bottom line was that I had a firm handle on all military helicopters on or near the airfield. With that, the two airline executives looked at each other and the regional manager said, "Well, I don't see any reason why we can't start the flights on Monday."[3] They then glanced at Mr. Powderly, who nodded approval.

With Powderly, I left the office feeling a sense of victory that was to be short-lived. At that very moment, four helicopters had converged on the terminal apron and the grassy area to its front. The helos were in different stages of flight. One, an MH-47 with black radar cowling protruding from its nose, was at a high hover blowing dirt and small rocks onto the apron where the large commercial airliners would disembark passengers. Another, a U.S. Air Force HH-60 Pavehawk, taxied up in front of the terminal, vibrating the building and its occupants. The third and fourth helicopters were MH-60s hovering over the grass and tossing debris onto the taxiway.

Mr. Powderly grimaced and yelled above the deafening noise in an irritated, disappointed voice, "What's this all about?" I responded, "Those are special operations' aircraft. I'll get them under control, I assure you." He shook his head in disgust and went back inside the office. I was angry and felt betrayed, although the special operators were unaware of my problem.[4]

Although embarrassing, the incident with the special operations forces (SOF) aircraft did not cause any of the parties to renege on the deal for the use of the airfield. I did periodically take heat from my chain of command for low-flying SOF helos rattling windows and disturbing the local residences. The attitude of the multinational force command was that if it was military and it flew, it belonged to me.

Before the day with the airline executives was through, procedures were in place for all helicopters, and our stay at the international airport was never again in jeopardy. But the same could not be said for the operations in the city.

Things were beginning to heat up on the streets of Port-au-Prince. On 6 October, 10th Mountain Lightfighters waded into a riot along the road to the port that broke out after a hand grenade had been tossed into a group of demonstrators celebrating the reinstatement of Port-au-Prince Mayor Evans Paul, who had spent 3 years in hiding before the liberation. The blast had injured several people, and five victims were fatally wounded.

The next day Lightfighters, supported by Sheridan light tanks from the 82d Airborne Division, took up positions behind concertina wire along a parade route for pro-Aristide marchers commemorating the third anniversary of the coup that had driven President Aristide from power. We provided attack helicopter teams overhead, and Andy Berdy and I once again found ourselves sharing hours in the back of a Black Hawk.

As we circled a thousand feet over the city, we flew near a hundred or so palatial homes clinging to the steep hills overlooking Port-au-

Prince. These were mansions reflecting the latest architecture that were accented by unique swimming pools, imaginative Jacuzzis, and multiple tennis courts. This was where the rich and powerful lived, these dwellings rivaling anything found in the exclusive neighborhoods of the United States. The inhabitants were above the pollution and odor of the impoverished urban neighborhoods and were representatives of a Haiti seen only by the privileged. In the cramped spaces of the city, Aristide followers prepared to demonstrate.

As we flew overhead, about 5,000 pro-Aristide demonstrators began walking apprehensively through the city toward the presidential palace. Suddenly, and indiscriminately, attachés armed with rifles, pistols, machetes, and clubs viciously attacked the demonstrators. One man was shot point-blank in the head, spattering fragments of bone and tissue on a television crew the victim had crouched behind for protection. The marchers fought their attackers off with rocks, iron bars, and sheer numbers. This was when I came to realize the lethality of the machete and the average Haitian's skillful use of this third-world tool.

Downtown Port-au-Prince (Note the humvees surrounded by Haitians)

This incident created concern in General Meade's headquarters. With President Aristide due to arrive in 15 days, increased street violence was the last thing the Clinton administration needed, and the entire multinational force headquarters shifted its energy to Aristide's return.

Notes

1. "Operations in Haiti—Planning/Preparation/Execution," 10th Mountain Division, Fort Drum, N.Y., June 1995, p. 10-D-2.

2. "Can Haiti Be Saved?" *Newsweek,* 3 October 1994, p. 33.

3. The arrival of scheduled airline service to Port-au-Prince direct from the United States brought a new challenge—the threat of lonely husbands and wives suddenly appearing outside our perimeter looking for their soldier-spouses.

4. A couple of days later I was visited by COL Doug Brown, regimental commander of the army's SOF aviation, TF 160. I didn't know Brown personally, but he had a good reputation. We exchanged pleasantries and discussed operations in and around the airfield. We ended with an invitation to his change of command with COL Del Daily on board the USS *America.* Del and I had endured the army's air assault course together some years earlier en route to our respective battalion commands, and like Brown, Del was a solid citizen and a credit to the corps.

24

ARISTIDE'S RETURN

Peace and reconciliation. . . . Do not be afraid. We say no to vengeance, we say no to retaliation.
—*President-in-waiting Jean-Bertrand Aristide,*
remarks directed to Haitian armed forces, 23 September 1994

The Clinton Administration had established eight elements that were critical to Aristide's return to Haiti:

- The U.S. military had to arrive and the U.S. government had to support his return.
- Raoul Cedras, Phillipe Biamby, and Joseph-Michel François had to depart.[1]
- The residual FAd'H had to become cooperative or be dismantled.
- FRAPH and the attachés had to stop their violence.
- Aristide supporters had to be convinced to not be violent and to not seek retribution.
- The Jonaissant government had to leave office.
- The Aristide government in Washington had to prepare for return to Haiti and stay informed.
- The Aristide government in Haiti had to develop a plan and execute it. It also had to stay informed by the multinational force.[2]

In late September, the framework for the new government began to take shape with the Haitian legislature returning to the government buildings. This was followed in early October 1994 with Jonaissant's leaving the presidential palace and the ministers appointed by Cedras being replaced by those selected by Aristide. To complete the expulsion of the Jonaissant regime, Cedras, his former chief of staff, Philippe Biamby, and Cedras family members were ushered to the

Port-au-Prince airport late on 12 October for their departure from Haiti.

Raoul Cedras did not leave Haiti empty-handed. The United States agreed to unfreeze the millions of dollars he had secured in U.S. banks, and there was the tidy sum of $5,000 a month of U.S. taxpayers' money to cover the rent of his three luxury estates. This deal had little benefit for the United States, and it required U.S. soldiers to stand 24-hour guard to prevent the local populace from looting the properties. Additionally, the United States provided a jetliner to Miami for twenty-three relatives and associates of Cedras and Biamby, who, after routine U.S. government checks, were allowed into the United States.

With Cedras and his entourage out of the way the multinational force headquarters focused on Aristide's return, developing an elaborate security plan that involved much of the brigade's aviation. We would not only provide Black Hawks to shuttle dignitaries and guests from the Port-au-Prince airport to the presidential palace, but we would have a number of attack teams airborne along with UH-60s on standby to transport Andy Berdy's strike force. General Meade worked hard to integrate Haitian police into the plan, but he was determined to maintain overall control of the operation. The entire multinational force was prepared to respond, including the SOF a few miles off shore on *America*.

On the morning of 15 October, I found myself once again sitting in the back of a command-and-control Black Hawk staring at a map of Port-au-Prince and vicinity. A U.S. government blue-and-white Boeing 707 landed at Haiti's International Airport with Jean-Bertrand Aristide and his retinue. Also on board the jetliner was U.S. Secretary of State Warren Christopher, as well as other government and civilian dignitaries. (A separate aircraft had arrived prior to the official party with a host of Aristide's guests, a who's who of African-American politics and entertainment with everyone from the Reverend Jesse Jackson to Harry Belafonte.)

The triumphant Aristide emerged a little after 12 noon from the aircraft sporting a black suit and the presidential sash across his chest. He waved his hands high above his head in victory. After he descended the stairs of the airplane, Ambassador Swing and Generals Shelton and Meade greeted him. A partisan crowd had formed outside the airport entrance, and after the ambassador and the generals had a quick exchange with him, Aristide briefly addressed the gathering. He was an eloquent speaker who captivated the crowd, and it was easy to see why he had the support of the Haitian people.

We had eighteen UH-60s in single file on the apron next to the passenger terminal to transport dignitaries and guest to the presidential palace. There was a small grassy area on the palace grounds large enough for a single Black Hawk to land. The distance between the airport and the palace was less than 10 miles, and traveling by air all but eliminated the chance of a hostile act against President Aristide. Because of the short distance, the helicopters were given 45-second separation, which produced a long wait for those toward the end of the procession. Aristide and his security occupied the lead helicopter, with everyone else, including Warren Christopher and a number of U.S. senators and congressmen, either following in the remaining seventeen helicopters or being transported by bus to the palace.

This aviation support went off as planned, and the ground security operation was conducted without a hitch. The palace grounds and surrounding buildings were lined with U.S. infantry and military police. We employed snipers, and Meade wanted to be sure they were able to distinguish between U.S. soldiers and uniformed belligerents, so he required the palace soldiers to wear a fluorescent yellow safety strap.

It was a balmy Caribbean day and Aristide's arrival at the chalk-white palace was a gala event with worldwide media coverage. The international attention was appropriate, for he was Haiti's first democratically elected leader returning from exile. The Haitian people were ecstatic because they were viewing someone who brought hope and a chance for opportunity and prosperity; they saw one of their own who was going to lead them from the despair and misery of daily life. From the palace, Aristide addressed the crowd from behind a bulletproof shield as the streets and open areas near the stately structure were filled with thousands of Haitians singing and dancing.

For the United States and the multinational force it was the culmination of the entire operation. Aristide's arrival meant the return of democracy to Haiti and a foreign policy success for the Clinton administration. There was still much to be done, but from this point on the multinational force would focus on maintaining a secure environment while the new Haitian security police force was trained and Aristide's government began to take roots.

Notes

1. Phillipe Biamby was chief of the general staff, FAd'H, and a key political strategist for the military regime and a determined opponent of change.

2. "Operations in Haiti—Planning/Preparation/Execution," 10th Mountain Division, Fort Drum, N.Y., June 1995, p. 10-D-2.

25

WINDING DOWN

You cannot create experience. You must undergo it.
—*Albert Camus*

On 24 October, Major General Meade assumed command of all forces in the Haiti joint operations area (see Figure 25.1). Lieutenant General Shelton and his XVIII Airborne Corps staff packed up and returned to Fort Bragg. With their departure came new challenges.

Many of the soldiers were getting bored with the mission and with Haiti. There were few pleasures, but one occasion was most eagerly awaited—the use of the multinational forces' video teleconference (VTC) facility at force headquarters. When the VTC was not in use for official business, Meade directed that it be placed at the disposal of the troops. For the first time these soldiers could view their spouses, children, and friends and see with their own eyes their loved ones. This was an overwhelming success.

In Somalia, soldiers had been provided with a dedicated telephone line to the United States to speak with their families, and at some locations there was even access to e-mail. Here in Haiti expectations were raised a notch as visual contact took center stage. The troops quickly took to their newfound perk, and I can only conclude that our soldiers will expect nothing less in any future operation.

We were busy performing general support aviation not only for the multinational force, but also for a number of U.S. government agencies. The Chinooks were transporting many vetted FAd'H members who had completed the police training by the International Criminal Investigation and Assistance Program to towns throughout Haiti. Additionally, the large helicopters were busy transporting Special Forces troops and equipment to a number of villages and remote sites.

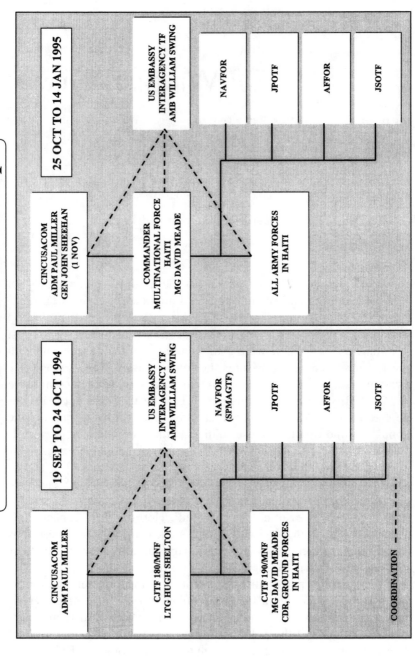

Figure 25.1 U.S. Command Relationships in Haiti

The 3-25th Black Hawks were also resupplying the Special Forces daily, as well as performing a variety of missions. One such mission involved transporting the remains of a Catholic nun from the southwestern tip of the country back to Port-au-Prince. The elderly nun escorting the deceased was so grateful for the aircrew's support that upon arrival in the capital city, she offered money to pay for the help. But the majority of the Knighthawks' missions were not so gratifying, as the Black Hawks increasingly functioned as an aerial taxi service. At times I felt that the brigade's tactical operations center was an extension of the multinational force protocol office. A day did not go by that we didn't have a visitor who needed to be chauffeured somewhere. Unlike Somalia, where visitors were presented with a couple of days to reach the isolated area, a chance of being killed, and a stay in austere accommodations, Haiti was just a couple of hours' flight from Washington, the environment was calm, and the hotels and villas were inviting. But I never begrudged the many visitors their stay: these were important people who would go back home and tell your story.

Our number one priority became VIP transport, and the importance of the passenger determined the resources committed. Flying a visiting major general from home required a single aircraft, but transporting then U.S. Ambassador to the United Nations Madeleine Albright involved several aircraft, a lot of security (including Cobra gunships), and a great deal of preparation. At times, it felt as if these visitors would awaken on a Saturday morning and say to their spouse, "Honey, How about a day trip to Haiti?"

Shortly after President Aristide's arrival, we were directed to commit three Black Hawk helicopters for his personal use. Russ Forshag placed one of his company commanders, CPT Phil Mitchell, in charge of the small detachment. This became Mitchell's sole mission and he was authorized to communicate directly with the multinational force J3 operations for his taskings. We developed a package that either traveled with Aristide if he flew outside of Port-au-Prince or remained on standby at the airfield if he was traveling close in. The support aircraft consisted of a UH-60V Medevac, a UH-60L with a Special Forces team, an OH-58C Scout helicopter, and a couple of Cobras. Aristide's Black Hawks were distinguishable from the rest of the fleet by a placard in the troop window depicting the Haitian flag. To transport his staff and security all three Black Hawks were committed when he traveled. Additionally, we rigged one of the aircraft with an elaborate configuration of cord and straps to support an M24 sniper rifle and its operator.

A sniper in a UH-60 Black Hawk
(Note the Haitian flag on the window in the right of photo
designating the aircraft as one that supports President Aristide)

Al Page and half of his Chinooks returned to their home base at Fort Bragg, as did the fire-fighting aircraft from Fort Campbell. We developed several force proposals for General Meade and his staff in anticipation that our numbers were going to be further reduced, although in looking at our daily mission requirements, it was hard to imagine an aviation fleet any smaller than the one we currently operated. We ultimately arrived at a battalion task force formed around the 3-25th Knighthawk headquarters. Despite our reduction in ranks, we continued to focus on force protection and the health of our soldiers.

The multinational force experienced an unusually high number of suicides. The first was a 21-year-old marine aboard the USS *Nashville*. This was followed a month later by a 20-year-old 10th Mountain specialist in an infantry battalion. The suicides became an epidemic when a second 10th Mountain soldier died during the third week of October on a hot, humid night in Port-au-Prince, when he put his M16 on automatic, placed the muzzle in his mouth, and fired a burst of three rounds. This was an alarmingly high suicide rate for 16,000 solders deployed in theater. During the 15 months in Somalia, when 96,000 troops passed through the East African country, there had been only one suicide, and while 650,000 troops were deployed during Desert Shield/Desert Storm there were only eight suicides.

The theories about the suicides ranged from stress caused by multiple deployments and soldiers being "primed" to fight who weren't ready, to young soldiers coming face to face with the harsh realities of the impoverished third world. The media were calling it the "Haitian stress syndrome," which I thought was poppycock! We all travel on these journeys with baggage from home, and certainly the environment can make it weigh more than it should. The killer is a combination of how we are made, and just how heavy our burden is. The killer is not the land, its people, or the environment. The tragedy here was that all three of these deaths could have been prevented had only someone known how troubled these young people were. It is a sad sidebar to an otherwise flawless mission. The troopers' deaths heightened our awareness and sensitivity, and preventing suicide became everyone's business. Our champion leading the effort was MAJ Chester Egert.

As brigade chaplain, Egert had served the soldiers throughout the Somalia deployment. An impressive officer with a boyish face and muscular build, the guitar-playing chaplain not only provided inspiration to the soldiers in Somalia, but had been responsible for five battalion chaplains and their assistants. Egert had done extensive research before our deployment to Haiti, traveling to churches and communities in the United States that sponsored schools and training programs in the poverty-stricken country.

Major Egert approached me one day to solicit aid for a middle-class school in the suburbs of Port-au-Prince that was supported by one of the U.S. communities he had visited. I told him I understood the need to volunteer time outside our compound, especially for the sake of education. As the former chief of staff of the army, GEN Edward C. Meyer said, "The chaplain, like the artillery, is never held in reserve." But I took Egert's involvement in the community a step further and told him that I viewed his work outside our brigade area as an element of force protection.

I believe he was somewhat taken aback by this. I explained that he needed to concentrate his energy on the religious and educational institutions nearby, for I was sure there were plenty of schools in our neighborhood that could use the help. I went on to explain that it was important to focus on the surrounding community, thereby ensuring its support. Assisting the local children would benefit both the local community and us: the children would reap the benefits of our labor while we gained a neighborhood that would look out for our welfare. Co-opting our neighbors was another aspect of our overall security plan—a sort of neighborhood watch program in which the locals would inform us of any undesirables in the community, and in some cases physically expel shady characters. Chester agreed, and soon located a small school directly across from our perimeter gate. Our force protection measures were the best of all the camps, thanks to the abundance of sea-land containers, miles of concertina wire, a dedicated ground cavalry troop, and the likes of Chaplain Egert. The aviation brigade's assembly area was never violated.

Complacency was a challenge for some, but everyone supporting the aviation fleet had little free time. By early November multinational force headquarters had approved our redeployment plan. November also marked the end of Russ Forshag's 2 years in command. The incoming commander was LTC James Barclay, a youthful fellow from Alabama who would soon be heading all the aviation in Haiti.

During Forshag and Barclay's change-of-command ceremony, we experienced a foul-up in a multinational force strike force reaction exercise. The strike force was similar to the QRF of Somalia—a task force positioned to react to a crisis on a moment's notice. The change of command was conducted on a confined apron in front of the hangar complex we had occupied since our first day in Haiti. Two of the four sides of the paved apron were bordered by a 5-foot-high earth berm layered with sandbags (the berm having been built in the early days of our occupation). Four strip-alert Cobras were parked diagonally nose first to the protective berm to prevent an accidental round from one of the gunships going astray.

The bright morning sun reflected off the brass instruments of the 10th Mountain Division band. The speeches were finished and the band was playing marches as the 3-25th commenced its pass in review. I stood at attention between Forshag and Barclay on a foot-high reviewing stand as the troops made turns in the cramped space for their pass in front of the reviewing party. Out of the corner of my eye I picked up hurried movement. As I stood at attention, I shifted my eyes to the left to see soldiers skirting the formation and running to the parked Cobras. They began disconnecting the rotor blade tie-downs and turning the blades 90 degrees to the aircraft's fuselage. The Cobra pilots weren't far behind, as they clambered up the sides of the aircraft and quickly strapped themselves into their cockpits.

I whispered to Russ, "Say, what's going on?" Forshag responded humorously, "Hell, sir, I don't know, it's not my outfit!" I frowned, than glanced at Barclay, who peered at me with his eyes locked as far to the left as his sockets would permit while pointing his head directly to the front. "Don't look at me, sir, I just got here!" I was standing between two comedians.

All of this activity was occurring in a space maybe three-quarters the size of a football field. The guests to our rear—every senior leader in the multinational force—were stirring as I heard their voices becoming louder and more inquisitive. The last company passed the reviewing stand at about the same time as the blades on one of the Cobras began to turn, along with a billow of black smoke and the accompanying low muffled sound of the turbine spinning up.

Brigadier General Close yelled, "What's going on?" I responded that I didn't know. At that very time the brigade tactical operation center officer, CPT John Poppie, approached and said that he was directed by multinational force operations to launch the aircraft: a Special Forces team had been ambushed. Close was angry, and it showed on his face. Little did anyone know that he had earlier ordered a test of the alert procedures based on a simulated ambush of SOF troops. He thought that initiating an alert while the leadership was away from headquarters would be a good evaluation of the units' alert procedures. General Close's intent was not to physically involve any of the soldiers on alert. Our question was whether this was a practice alert or a real one? A quick radio call to force headquarters confirmed that it was a test exercise that somehow had been miscommunicated. By this time, all the multinational force leadership was energized and scurrying to vehicle radios to ensure that its piece of the operation was on track. Everything was quickly shut down, but it certainly made for a few exciting minutes and a memorable change of command.

I experienced an equally memorable moment early one morning as I was driving in my Humvee to the multinational force headquarters. It was a typical Caribbean day: before the sun would top the mountains, the early morning glow was casting a soft blanket of light across the city. I was traveling on the main street next to the terminal, which was covered by the graffiti that turned just about every wall in Port-au-Prince into a billboard of political expression. In a few hours, driving this quarter-mile stretch of roadway would take nearly 30 minutes because of traffic and young beggars obstructing vehicle movement. We had passed a vehicle-loading dock used for cargo destined for air freight warehouses, when I observed movement on the concrete slab.

As I adjusted my eyes to the motion on the dock, I saw a pile of sack-like objects, brightly colored, and looking like tattered and worn clothes discarded and awaiting pickup by Goodwill Industries. Focusing my attention, I realized that the pile was a group of sleeping children. There must have been twenty of them. They were huddled like a pack of animals, legs and arms overlaid in an attempt to seek warmth as they lay on the cold concrete.

These were the beggars, the young boys—the age of my own children—who begged on the streets. Unlike the child at the pool of stagnant water in Somalia, these children did have a future, even though it wasn't much. The boys epitomized the poverty and desperation of the Haitian people—and we were not going to change much of anything for them. Change would be up to their leaders. We were going home.

The brigade had been redeploying soldiers throughout the month of November. Bill Driver and his 2-25th Dragons relocated from Cap-Haïtien to Port-au-Prince for their trip back to Fort Drum. A small aviation contingent remained to support the 2d Brigade. The aviation brigade headquarters passed responsibility for aviation operations to the 3-25th Knighthawks, and the brigade headquarters staff departed on the first of December; but General Meade directed that I remain in Haiti until he was comfortable with Barclay. Jim Barclay certainly didn't need my oversight, so I let him command his outfit while I attended the daily command updates at multinational force headquarters. These meetings, often filled with tension, provided me an opportunity to chat and, at times, lament with my fellow brigade commanders, Andy Berdy, Freddie Valenzuela, and Terry Juskowiak. I rarely saw my good friend Jim Dubik, the "mayor" of Cap-Haïtien: He had his hands full in northern Haiti.

By mid-December, General Meade was convinced that Barclay had everything well in hand, and so I went to the other end of the airfield and boarded a C-141 for the brief flight to Charleston Air Force Base, South Carolina. In my battledress uniform I traveled alone, trading the air force transport at Charleston for a USAir flight to Syracuse. I arrived without fanfare, which was just fine by me. I was met at the Syracuse airport by the brigade duty NCO and driver, who drove me the last hour and a half of my journey home.

A little more than a month later, Barclay and his task force returned along with Meade and his headquarters. The 10th Mountain transferred the mission to the Hawaii-based 25th Infantry Division commanded by MG George Fisher, who in turn transferred the mission on 31 March to the UN Mission in Haiti (UNMIH) commanded by U.S. MG Joseph W. Kinzer.

Lieutenant Colonel Barclay shipped the Cobras and OH-58 Kiowas by sea from Port-au-Prince and self-deployed his Black Hawks by island hopping to Florida and then flying up the East Coast—the reverse of an earlier course of action to get us to Haiti. The return flight took him 3 full days, and he arrived at Fort Drum on a wet and stormy mid-January day. The last day, his flight of Black Hawks experienced several weather delays and rerouting, all of which gave me an uneasy feeling until his last aircraft was on the ground and the crews were reunited with their families.

26

MISSION COMPLETE

In the final measure, nothing speaks like deeds.
—*General Edward C. Meyer,*
Chief of Staff of the Army (1979–1983)

P eace and democracy briefly returned to Haiti, but the road to prosperity was well out of reach. A May 1998 article in the *Wall Street
Journal* characterized our country's approach to Operation Uphold
Democracy as following three rules: take no casualties, spend very little cash, and get out fast.[1] Suffering and poverty continue. Haiti moves
backward to when bloodletting settled political differences. The situation there remains ambiguous as turbulence and violence persist, sending the country further into economic desperation. What is in store for
Haiti is anyone's guess, and I can only hope that the plight of that nation never again involves large numbers of U.S. soldiers..

The indiscriminate killing, intimidation, and clandestine operations
by the Cedras regime and its hooligans were eliminated only to be replaced by the actions of a new group of thugs. Meanwhile, the people
still want democracy and they need an economic boost and a revamped
infrastructure. Sustaining the success of Operation Uphold Democracy
required Haiti and the international community to embrace a plan for
economic assistance, and the elected government desperately needed to
restore the people's confidence in Haiti's means for law and order. But
the country and its leaders have failed on both counts. The much
needed external support has fallen far short of promises and expectations, while the Haitian politicians have yet to forge a relationship with
the country's business class.[2] The police and courts are in a state of
disarray and are no better than before. It was up to Aristide to demonstrate that his government was capable—something he was never quite
able to do, nor was his handpicked successor, René Préval.

Haiti's April 1997 election failed because of widespread apathy and fraud, leaving Mr. Préval to rule by decree. One of his first actions was to dissolve the parliament and permit the terms of all other elected officials to lapse.

As for the military and government privileged we ousted from power, Cedras is retired and living comfortably in Panama on his U.S. dole, Biamby, who accompanied Cedras to Panama, lives a lavish life, and François spent several months in a Honduran prison fighting extradition to the United States after being charged with trafficking in millions of dollars in illicit drugs through Haiti for Colombian cartels over a 9-year period.[3] The United States was unsuccessful in its bid for custody of François, and he now lives comfortably in Central America. Provisional president Emile Jonassaint died of natural causes in October 1995.

The 10th Aviation Brigade soldiers did, however, chalk up another success. The men and women of the brigade once again demonstrated their mettle as they secured their place in military history. We accomplished the mission without experiencing a major accident or serious injury—logging over 14,000 flight hours, all attributed to talented, safety-conscious crew members and support personnel. Our soldiers consistently carried the day by their hard work, dedication, and innovative thinking.

The Falcon Brigade soldiers did everything that was asked—and more. Most important, we brought everyone home. The operation was indeed a success, even though the dynamics of our mission demanded that we quickly regroup and move on. The brigade's focus shifted to recovering equipment, regaining the readiness for its aircraft fleet, and getting reacquainted with loved ones. I resumed my role of managing our force modernization effort, while preparing the brigade for the next mission. There is always a next mission.

Notes

1. "America Is Learning to Play World Cop, but Only Reluctantly," *Wall Street Journal*, 21 May 1998.

2. Robert Oakley and Michael Dziedzic, "Sustaining Success in Haiti," *National Defense University Strategic Forum* 77 (June 1996), p. 3.

3. The U.S. government charged François in February 1997 with transporting 33 tons of cocaine and heroin to this country during his reign in Haiti.

27

OBSERVATIONS

Don't go to war in white painted vehicles.
—*General Sir Michael Rose,*
Commander, UN Protection Force, Bosnia-Herzegovina (1994)

I am not convinced there was anything new derived from Operations Continue Hope and Uphold Democracy. Almost everything planned, conducted, or accomplished had been experienced before. Although our going to the Horn of Africa purely for humanitarian reasons was a first for this nation, and soldiers' air-assaulting from an aircraft carrier was a first for the army and navy, our lessons from both Somalia and Haiti were more a matter of what we had forgotten and had to relearn, as opposed to learning something new.

Someone once said, "Experience is a hard teacher because she gives the test first, the lesson afterwards." There is little doubt that the experience gained in Somalia was directly translated to Operation Uphold Democracy strategically, operationally, and tactically, and in large part led to the success of that operation. From the brigade perspective, the wealth of experience in Somalia accumulated by the rank and file and by the unit's leadership ensured our success in Haiti.

Involvement of Political Leaders

During Uphold Democracy the president and his men were engaged from the beginning, and they remained involved long after the multinational force was redeployed. The entire administration along with the Defense Department was immersed in the Haiti operation—it was a team effort. The same could not be said for operations in Somalia until after 3 October 1993.

Overwhelming Force

We arrived in Somalia with a robust force ready to do what was necessary. The use of overwhelming force, coupled with a clear chain of command, was a proven approach, as it had been 3 years earlier during Desert Storm. Yet when the mission was transferred to the United Nations, the fighting force was a mere fraction of what the United States had arrived with in Somalia and the chain of command was convoluted.

We tricked ourselves into thinking that humanitarian assistance meant a peaceful, orderly, and cooperative relationship with the indigenous population. This attitude lulled us into conducting the operation on the cheap, resulting in a less than desirable force mix. An example was the reluctance of the planners to initially equip the 10th Mountain Division forces with attack helicopters because of the contradictory image it might convey—U.S. imperialists armed to the hilt administering a humanitarian operation. Perception was most important. The commanders destined for Somalia made a convincing argument for the aircraft, resulting in the 10th Mountain soldiers deploying with four AH-1F Cobra attack helicopters. This attitude persisted as the attack helicopter fleet for the QRF remained at only four Cobra aircraft—a number that grew threefold by August 1993 in an attempt to provide adequate aerial fire support in what quickly went from humanitarian assistance sectors to a combat zone.

We arrived off Haiti with more than enough combat force. Some critics argued that it was overkill—that we amassed way too much force for such a two-bit foe. These critics weren't the people who would set foot uninvited on Haitian soil. The overwhelming show of force guaranteed that there would be little or no resistance from the military junta. If you have it, use it. Additionally, we maintained a credible presence throughout Uphold Democracy and the initial phases of the follow-on UN mission. We did what was planned. We passed a safe and secure environment on to the United Nations force.

Unity of Command

A combat force must be under a single field commander: unity of command is an essential ingredient for success. In Somalia, Major General Montgomery, commanding his theater assets, and Major General Garrison, his strategic assets, both reached back to the commander and chief of Central Command for guidance and approval. CENTCOM in return exercised long-distance control over the coequals in the remote theater. It was not a practical arrangement and violated a principle of war, unity of command. The command relationships permitted room for interpretation and ambiguity. It was only the personality, professionalism, and mutual respect by both men that made it work.

Command and control in Somalia was further aggravated by the refusal of too many countries, including the United States, to accept a unified UN command. UN commanders have no legal authority over their forces, therefore the on-site UN leadership's authority, including General Montgomery's, was undercut by too many orders coming from too many capitals. The result was parallel lines of authority. Additionally, the UNOSOM forces were fractured, with some contributing states cutting deals with Somali factions on their own. Lieutenant General Bir, an extremely capable leader, was never able to effectively exercise unity of command, or even unity of effort. Even consensus building proved difficult because no one wanted to accept the reality that there was a war being fought.

Establish Objectives

There must be a clear set of objectives. When working with the United Nations, this is nearly impossible. It becomes imperative to create your own set of objectives in the absence of any, or when saddled with impractical ones. In Somalia, the objectives given UNOSOM II during Operation Continue Hope were unrealistic and not properly resourced, and were therefore unattainable. This was aggravated by a lack of will on the part of the UN command and its coalition members to take the initiative against the Somalia National Alliance (SNA). During Uphold Democracy the objectives were clear, concise, and adequately backed.

Urban Operations

Demographic trends have led to sprawling urban and suburban environments in the developing world, and there is no indication that such expansion will subside. Accordingly, at the operational and tactical level we must learn to fight in cities, while at the strategic level our political leadership must have the will to commit our forces to urban combat, especially if it will bring a conflict to a close.

At the tactical level, there is a need for more research and development resources directed toward finding technological solutions for the formidable task of close combat in built-up areas. There is also a need at the operational level for an increased awareness of urban combat, but the most pressing requirement is incorporating into our national security strategy the option of committing ground forces in city centers, even if that means entering a city like Baghdad or Belgrade.[1]

Tactically our soldiers and small unit leaders know what to do, and they do it very well. We held our own in Mogadishu, but most combat was by chance and not planned. Some have suggested that had we mounted an offensive in Mogadishu after the arrival of the reinforcements in October, we would have eliminated Aideed and the influence of the SNA. Our political leadership did not have the stomach (nor did many of us who remained in theater) to commit itself to a final military solution. Instead, the administration opted to place a mark on the wall and pull out. Once that was done nothing else mattered.

In Port-au-Prince we were not confronted with the rigors of close combat, although we anticipated that possibility. Despite the environment of passivity we encountered in that sprawling city, the urban terrain still presented a number of unique challenges—limited observation and weapon trajectories, restricted maneuver, large concentrations of noncombatants, and the inability to distinguish the "good guy" from the "bad guy." These issues had been discussed during our preparation, but never in the context of an all-out assault on the port city. It is in these areas that technology can provide solutions and have the greatest impact: locating mines and booby traps; seeing through walls and roofs; looking and shooting around corners without exposure; deploying ordnance that negotiates urban terrain; maneuvering soldiers between buildings without going to street level; denying terrain without soldier presence; and distinguishing belligerents from noncombatants.

We need more work at the operational level. It has been my experience during war games and simulations that far too often we draw circles around urban centers on our maps and then selectively ignore their existence or quickly bypass them as we move the forces toward a more manageable objective. We rarely, if ever, tackle the tough issue of how we would enter and secure a city. It always seems to fall into the "too hard to do" box. It is imperative that we incorporate the urban challenge into our operational scenarios and exercises.

Finally, placing urban warfare into a strategic context is a daunting task. Despite the reality that Saddam Hussein and Slobodan Milosevic remain in power in their respective countries, the current and past U.S. administrations have been reluctant to endorse a policy that clearly articulates the intent to enter a city, if necessary, to bring a conflict to a close. It is much more palatable for our policymakers to direct our military to engage in battle from the air and from afar. This approach invariably results in a partial solution, which seems to satisfy the advocates of such an approach. Committing ground forces to any conflict, especially an urban environment, appears to be taboo—certainly so if there is the slightest hint of sustaining casualties. Consequently our current policy leaves us with military operations that remain open-ended, consuming scarce resources and diminishing our international political capital.

In any case, we were extremely lucky in both operations that we were never required to ferret out a formidable enemy and secure a city. That would have required a much larger force and a political administration with the will to commit.

Equipment Compatibility

We do a great job of equipping our troops, but when we team up with a coalition force it is crucial that equipment and capabilities are compatible. If not, we must be very selective of what we ask of the other forces. We do not want to ever again place ourselves in the position we experienced during the Ranger rescue effort in Mogadishu. The hesitation by the Pakistanis to place their tanks at the head of the rescue force as it departed the New Port was in large part due to their lack of night-vision devices. We are comfortable with our NATO allies because we have a shared standard of materiel, but we fall short when we find ourselves occupying terrain with third-world countries' armies that are unable to afford that standard of materiel. In this circumstance, we must never rely on them to do something they are not equipped or trained to do.

Presence

Physical presence reinforces a soldier's sense of purpose, while at the same time creating doubt, apprehension, and, most important, respect from the adversary. The more that troops are out patrolling, tanks are rolling, or AC-130s are flying, both the soldiers and the belligerents know you are on the ready. I saw it time and again in both Somalia and Haiti, where disciplined, well-equipped U.S. soldiers in full battle dress acted as the strongest deterrent. Leading a potential antagonist to avoid messing with them. The 2-14th Infantry Golden Dragons were good at this. When these troopers exited the compound in Mogadishu to perform a cordon-and-search operation or secure a convoy, the Somalis stayed away. By contrast, I saw fellow coalition troops get mobbed and harassed when they conducted routine missions because they didn't look or act like soldiers.

Information Compartmentalization

Intellectually, the need for secrecy and compartmentalization of information is arguably necessary and easily justifiable. But, in both Somalia and Haiti, compartmentalization hampered the brigade's ability to perform its mission. Secrecy and deception are essential elements when planning and executing a military operation, but intentionally leaving supporting forces out of the information loop in the name of security is inexcusable and has no place either as you prepare for battle or as you enter the fight.

Rules of Engagement

The rules of engagement are critical to any operation, and must be defined and distributed as early as possible. They must be simple, straightforward, and clearly understood by all—that is, almost second nature. If a soldier hesitates in his actions because he lacks understanding or has doubts, then the rules of engagement are meaningless. Lawyers need to craft them, but field commanders must ensure that they makes sense and are functional.

Zero Defects

Force protection is a primary concern for all commanders. I have always erred on the side of protecting the force, but it is important that we do not allow our mission focus and judgment to be obscured by the perception that a casualty is unacceptable and denotes failure. No commander willingly expends a soldier, but armies are fielded to fight, and fighting means there is a risk of casualties. The prudent commander will reduce the risks, exploit circumstances, and execute the mission—even if it costs lives. If the mission is to take the hill, then take the hill.

In recent years the harsh reality of combat operations seems to have become alien to many of our political leaders, perhaps because so few of them have served in uniform and even fewer have experienced combat. They have demonstrated the propensity to demand zero military casualties. Media hype surrounding a casualty reinforces this unrealistic expectation. All of this not only affects how the military executes operations, but has a direct impact on foreign policy. Somalia exemplified this syndrome when the president set a troop withdrawal date in reaction to the casualties of 3 and 4 October 1993. I have a concern that this "zero defects" attitude may be permeating the military ranks as well. I hope I am wrong, but I have observed a number of commanders who feel that any casualty, especially a fatality, diminishes the success of a mission and tarnishes the leadership.

The Media

The media are major players in the entire spectrum of warfare. If you don't anticipate their impact and take their influence into account in your planning, you are behind the power curve before you get started. I hold the media responsible for our involvement in Somalia; it's that clear and simple. But once we were in Somalia, their absence during the late summer and early fall of 1993 resulted in military operations that did not have to stand the scrutiny of the press. If they had been there, some of the operations probably would have been rethought and the U.S. administration and citizenry would have been better informed.

When you are a leader, your individual performance for the media will determine how you rate with your superiors, as I experienced in my brief brush with the electronic and print media before sailing on *Eisenhower*. With office televisions broadcasting CNN "Headline News" to every leader in the Pentagon, you can count on close scrutiny by the hierarchy. A great deal of importance is put on how you perform in front of the camera.

How the leadership views you as you publicly deliver the message and respond to questions will result in an impression of how capable a leader you are. This was reinforced on 29 September 1998 by the chief of staff of the army, GEN Dennis J. Reimer, in a communiqué to his senior leadership when he stated, "I am convinced now more than ever that . . . communications is an important senior leader responsibility. Our success . . . depends in large part on the degree to which all leaders communicate to the American people through the news media." Although

Reimer's message focused on strategic communications, it highlights the importance our leadership places on leader-media relationship. At the operational level, there may not be a correlation between leader competence and media savvy, but in today's military, performing in the media environment is a fundamental. It is part of doing business.

Leadership Training

Without question our commissioned and noncommissioned officer corps, regardless of service, is nurtured and shaped by the most comprehensive and challenging military professional development program provided by any nation in the world. Our leaders are knowledgeable, decisive, and fit, both mentally and physically. Our leadership, coupled with the finest equipment, realistic training, and a priority on readiness, makes our military the best in the world. Unlike some militaries that focus on peacekeeping, military observer, and humanitarian missions, our services are geared for warfighting.

Our military leaders bring strength and added value to any coalition operation, but we also bring weakness with our inability at times to view objectively many foreign militaries as useful team members. On many occasions I have observed U.S. leaders of various ranks disparage coalition armies because they were not up to our standards, and therefore did not meet our expectations. Instead of exploiting a coalition partner's strength, we trivialized its contribution and only tolerated its presence. It is easy to become frustrated with an army that does not meet your own professional benchmark, speak your language, or see eye to eye with your political views. Early on I was guilty of this bias, but quickly overcame it when I realized that everyone brings something to the fight. You just have to figure out how best to use it.

Our leaders need to be better prepared to handle these disparities, and must have a better understanding of the forces they are teamed with. Our leaders must be trained to overcome their biases and preconceived notions, and schooled on how to make the most of a foreign army's strengths.

Moral High Ground

We must always maintain the moral high ground. This is an ingredient many nations and armies do not bring to the battlefield. It does not take long for the people of any land we occupy to quickly determine our intentions and decide whether we are neutral, impartial, and unbiased. Equally important is that our motives and purpose be known and understood by our own soldiers. If our soldiers understand and believe in what we are doing, they will act accordingly. By maintaining the moral high ground we are able to influence not only a potential aggressor but all those around us, including allies and coalition partners.

The Soldier

Finally, it all comes down to the young American soldiers, sailors, airmen, and marines. They carry the load. They performed magnificently in both operations, serving with valor and dignity. Their fundamental service skills provided the necessary foundation for them to execute their duties in volatile, unpredictable environments. Because of the compression of the strategic, operational, and tactical level of operations like Continue Hope and Uphold Democracy, today's service members must be prepared to perform simultaneously in political, civil, and security environments while under the constant scrutiny of the press.

Our troops can and will do anything to accomplish the task at hand. If given a clearly defined mission with a sense of urgency, they will work together to solve any problem, confront any challenge, and fight any battle. From the American Revolution to war-ravaged Bosnia and Kosovo, our servicemen and women have invariably rallied to the cause, as one, to ensure success.

Note

1. LTG William R. Hawkins, "Putting Urban Warfare in a Strategic Context," *Army*, January 2000, p. 8.

Appendix

UNITED STATES SERVICE MEMBERS KILLED IN ACTION/ NONBATTLE DEATH SUMMARY

Operation Restore Hope,
9 December 1992–4 May 1993

Pfc. Domingo Arroyo, USMC, 21, Elizabeth, New Jersey, 3d Battalion, 11th Marine Regiment, Twentynine Palms, California. *12 January 1993—killed in action during a firefight near Mogadishu airport.*

L. Cpl. Anthony D. Botello, USMC, 21, Wilberton, Oklahoma, C Company, 1st Battalion, 7th Marine Regiment, Twentynine, Palms, California. *26 January 1993—killed in action near soccer stadium in Mogadishu.*

PVT David J. Conner, USA, 19, Huntington Beach, California, 57th Transportation Company, 10th Mountain Division, Fort Drum, New York. *Nonbattle death—15 February 1993 of injuries sustained in a vehicle accident on 7 February ten miles northwest of Baledogle.*

PVT Don D. Robertson, USA, 28, Tustin, California, 157th Field Service Company, Fort Hood, Texas. *Nonbattle death—2 March 1993 of injuries sustained in a vehicle accident 25 miles north of Baidoa.*

SFC Robert H. Deeks, USA, 40, Littleton, Colorado, Company A, 2d Battalion, 5th Special Forces Group, Fort Campbell, Kentucky. *3 March 1993—killed in action (vehicle landmine) 125 miles northeast of Beledweyne.*

L. Cpl. William A. Rose, USMC, 20, San Joaquin, California, Company B, 1st Battalion, 7th Marine Regiment, Twentynine Palms, California. *Nonbattle death—6 March 1993 in Mogadishu.*

PVT Daniel L. Harris, USA, 21, Newsoms, Virginia, Headquarters Company, 13th Corps Support Command, Fort Hood, Texas. *Nonbattle death—drowned 18 March 1993 in a hotel swimming pool while on rest and recreation visit in Mombasa, Kenya.*

Operation Continue Hope, 4 May 1993–25 March 1994

SP4 Mark E. Gutting, USA, 25, Grand Rapids, Michigan, 977th Military Police Company, Fort Riley, Kansas. *8 August 1993—vehicle destroyed in command-detonated explosion in Madina district of Mogadishu.*

SGT Christopher K. Hilgert, USA, 27, Bloomington, Indiana, 977th Military Police Company, Fort Riley, Kansas. *8 August 1993—vehicle destroyed in command-detonated explosion in Madina district of Mogadishu.*

SP4 Keith D. Pierson, USA, 25, Tavares, Florida, 977th Military Police Company, Fort Riley, Kansas. *8 August 1993—vehicle destroyed in command-detonated explosion in Madina district of Mogadishu.*

SGT Ronald N. Richerson, USA, 24, Portage, Indiana, 300th Military Police Company, Fort Leonard Wood, Missouri. *8 August 1993—vehicle destroyed in command-detonated explosion in Madina district of Mogadishu.*

PFC Matthew K. Anderson, USA, 21, Lucas, Iowa, Company B, 9th Battalion of the 101st Aviation Regiment, Fort Campbell, Kentucky. *25 September 1993—UH-60 Black Hawk helicopter struck by an RPG while flying over Mogadishu.*

SGT Ferdinand C. Richardson, USA, 27, Summermead, California, Headquarters and Headquarters Company, 2d Attack Helicopter Battalion, 25th Aviation Regiment, Fort Drum, New York. *25 September 1993—UH-60 Black Hawk helicopter struck by an RPG while flying over Mogadishu.*

SGT Eugene Williams, USA, 26, Chicago, Illiniois, Company B, 9th Battalion, 101st Aviation Regiment, Fort Campbell, Kentucky. *25*

September 1993—UH-60 Black Hawk helicopter struck by an RPG while flying over Mogadishu.

SP4 Edward J. Nicholson, USA, 21, Houston, Texas, Company H, 159th Aviation Regiment, Fort Campbell, Kentucky. *Nonbattle death— 6 October 1993 of injuries sustained from a shark attack 30 September near Mogadishu.*

CWO Donovan L. Briley, USA, 33, North Little Rock, Arkansas, Company D, 1st Battalion, 160th Special Operations Aviation Regiment, Fort Campbell, Kentucky. *3 October 1993—killed in action during battle in Mogadishu.*

SSG Daniel D. Busch, USA, 25, Portage, Wisconsin, U.S. Army Special Forces Command, Fort Bragg, North Carolina. *3 October 1993— killed in action during battle in Mogadishu.*

CPL James M. Cavaco, USA, 26, Forestdale, Massachusetts, Company B, 3d Battalion, 75th Ranger Regiment, Fort Benning, Georgia. *3 October 1993—killed in action during battle in Mogadishu.*

SGT Thomas J. Field, USA, 25, Lisbon, Maine, Company D, 1st Battalion, 160th Special Operations Aviation Regiment, Fort Campbell, Kentucky. *3 October 1993—killed in action during battle in Mogadishu.*

SFC Earl R. Filmore, Jr., USA, 28, Blairsville, Pennsylvania, Special Forces Command, Fort Bragg, North Carolina. *3 October 1993—killed in action during battle in Mogadishu.*

CWO Raymond A. Frank, USA, 45, Monrovia, California, Company D, 1st Battalion, 160th Special Operations Aviation Regiment, Fort Campbell, Kentucky. *3 October 1993—killed in action during battle in Mogadishu.*

MSG Gary I. Gordon, USA, 33, Lincoln, Maine, Headquarters and Headquarters Company, Special Forces Command, Fort Bragg, North Carolina. *3 October 1993—killed in action during battle in Mogadishu.*

SGT Cornell L. Houston, USA, 31, Compton, California, Company C, 41st Engineer Battalion, Fort Drum, New York. *3 October 1993—died 7 October from wounds received during battle in Mogadishu.*

SGT James C. Joyce, USA, 24, Denton, Texas, Company B, 3d Battalion, 75th Ranger Regiment, Fort Benning, Georgia. *3 October 1993— killed in action during battle in Mogadishu.*

PFC Richard W. Kowalewski, Jr., USA, 20, Crucible, Pennsylvania, Company B, 3d Battalion, 75th Ranger Regiment, Fort Benning, Georgia. *3 October 1993—killed in action during battle in Mogadishu.*

PFC James H. Martin, Jr., USA, 23, Collinsville, Illinois, Company A, 2d Battalion, 14th Infantry Regiment, Fort Drum, New York. *3 October 1993—killed in action during battle in Mogadishu.*

MSG Timothy L. Martin, USA, 38, Aurora Dearborne, Indiana, Special Forces Command, Fort Bragg, North Carolina. *3 October 1993—killed in action during battle in Mogadishu.*

SP4 Dominick M. Pilla, USA, 21, Vineland, New Jersey, Company B, 3d Battalion, 75th Ranger Regiment, Fort Benning, Georgia., *3 October 1993—killed in action during battle in Mogadishu.*

SGT Lorenzo M. Ruiz, USA, 27, El Paso, Texas, Company B, 3d Battalion, 75th Ranger Regiment, Fort Benning, Georgia. *3 October 1993—killed in action during battle in Mogadishu.*

SFC Randall D. Shughart, USA, 35, Newville, Pennsylvania, Headquarters and Headquarters Company, Special Forces Command, Fort Bragg, North Carolina. *3 October 1993—killed in action during battle in Mogadishu.*

SP4 James E. Smith, USA, 21, Long Valley, New Jersey, Company B, 3d Battalion, 75th Ranger Regiment, Fort Benning, Georgia. *3 October 1993—killed in action during battle in Mogadishu.*

CWO Clifton P. Wolcott, USA, 36, Cuba, New York, Company D, 1st Battalion, 160th Aviation Regiment, Fort Campbell, Kentucky. *3 October 1993—killed in action during battle in Mogadishu.*

SFC Matthew L. Rierson, USA, 33, Nevada, Iowa, Headquarters and Headquarters Company, Special Forces Command, Fort Bragg, North Carolina. *6 October 1993—killed in a mortar attack on Mogadishu airfield.*

L. Cpl. Jesus Perez, USMC, 20, San Antonio, Texas, 13th Marine Expeditionary Unit. *Nonbattle Death—14 December 1994 from injuries received during a training accident (mortar firing) near Mogadishu.*

S. Sgt. Brian P. Barnes, 26, USAF, Cole Camp, Missouri, 16th Special Operations Squadron, Hurlburt Field, Florida. *Nonbattle death—14 March 1994 as a result of an aircraft accident (AC-130H gunship) off the coast of Malindi, Kenya, as the plane was en route to support forces in Somalia.*

T. Sgt. Robert L. Daniel, 34, USAF, Gray, Georgia, 16th Special Operations Squadron, Hurlburt Field, Florida. *Nonbattle death—14 March 1994 as a result of an aircraft accident (AC-130H gunship) off the coast of Malindi, Kenya, as the plane was en route to support forces in Somalia.*

M. Sgt. Roy S. Duncan, USAF, 40, Miami, Florida, 16th Special Operations Squadron, Hurlburt Field, Florida. *Nonbattle death—14 March 1994 as a result of an aircraft accident (AC-130H gunship) off the coast of Malindi, Kenya, as the plane was en route to support forces in Somalia.*

S. Sgt. William C. Eyler, USAF, 32, Tulsa, Oklahoma, 16th Special Operations Squadron, Hurlburt Field, Florida. *Nonbattle death—14 March 1994 as a result of an aircraft accident (AC-130H gunship) off the coast of Malindi, Kenya, as the plane was en route to support forces in Somalia.*

Capt. David J. Mehlhop, USAF, 30, Zellwood, Florida, 16th Special Operations Squadron, Hurlburt Field, Florida. *Nonbattle death—14 March 1994 as a result of an aircraft accident (AC-130H gunship) off the coast of Malindi, Kenya, as the plane was en route to support forces in Somalia.*

S. Sgt. Mike E. Moser, USAF, 32, Mt. Ayr, Iowa, 16th Special Operations Squadron, Hurlburt Field, Florida. *Nonbattle death—14 March 1994 as a result of an aircraft accident (AC-130H gunship) off the coast of Malindi, Kenya, as the plane was en route to support forces in Somalia.*

Capt. Mark A. Quam, USAF, 27, Madison, Wisconsin, 16th Special Operations Squadron, Hurlburt Field, Florida. *Nonbattle death—14*

March 1994 as a result of an aircraft accident (AC-130H gunship) off the coast of Malindi, Kenya, as the plane was en route to support forces in Somalia.

Capt. Anthony R. Stefanik, Jr., 31, USAF, Johnstown, Pennsylvania, 16th Special Operations Squadron, Hurlburt Field, Florida. *Nonbattle death—14 March 1994 as a result of an aircraft accident (AC-130H gunship) off the coast of Malindi, Kenya, as the plane was en route to support forces in Somalia.*

Operation Uphold Democracy
19 September 1994–31 March 1995

SP4 Alejandro Robles, USA, 20, Los Angles, California, A Company, 1st Battalion 22d Infantry Regiment, Fort Drum, New York. *Nonbattle death—27 September 1994 in Port-au-Prince, Haiti.*

L. Cpl. Maurice A. Williams, USMC, 21, Oak Park, Michigan, B Battery, 1st Battalion, 10th Marine Regiment, Camp Lejeune, North Carolina. *Nonbattle death—5 October 1994 aboard USS* Nashville *at U.S. Naval Station, Roosevelt Roads, Puerto Rico.*

PVT Gerardo Luciano, USA, 22, New York City, New York, C Company, 1st Battalion, 22d Infantry Regiment, Fort Drum, New York. *Nonbattle death—16 October 1994 in Port-au-Prince, Haiti.*

SFC Gregory D. Cardott, USA, 36, San Mateo, California, A Company, 3d Battalion, 3d Special Forces Group, Fort Bragg, North Carolina. *12 January 1995—killed in action while attempting to question two nationals at a roadblock near Gonaïves, Haiti.*

Acronyms and Abbrevations

AAAA	Army Aviation Association of America
AC-	Attack cargo aircraft
ACE	Armored combat earthmover (M9)
AFB	Air force base
ALQ-144	Infrared airborne jammer
AMERICA/CVW-1	Aircraft carrier *America*/Commander Air Wing One
AN/TPQ-36	Antimortar radar
AOR	Area of operation
APC	Armored personnel carrier
ATC	Air traffic control
AWACS	Airborne warning and control system
BDU	Battle dress uniform
CAG	Commander, air group
CATF	Commander, amphibious task force
CCG	Commander, carrier group
CENTCOM	Central Command
CH-	Cargo helicopter
CIB	Combat Infantryman's Badge
CINC	Commander in chief
CJTF	Commander, joint task force
C-NITE	Cobra—Night integrated target enhancement
DOD	Department of Defense
FAA	Federal Aviation Administration
FAd'H	Force Armée d'Haïti (Armed Forces of Haiti)
FARP	Forward area rearm and refuel point
FLIR	Forward-looking infrared
FRAPH	Front pour l'Avancement et Progrès d'Haïti (Front for the Advancement of and Progress of Haiti)
G2	General staff 2—intelligence

G3	General staff 3—operations
GPS	Global positioning system
GRG	Grid reference graphic
GTMO	Guantanamo, Cuba
HEED	Helicopter emergency egress device
HUMINT	Human intelligence
HMMWV	High-mobility, multipurpose, wheeled vehicle (Humvee)
ID	Infantry division
ISB	Intermediate staging base
J3	Joint staff 3—operations
JAG	Judge Advocate General
JRC	Joint reconnaissance center
JSOTF	Joint special operations task force
JTF	Joint task force
Medevac	Medical Evacuation
MEU	Marine Expeditionary Unit
MH-	Multimission helicopter
MP	Military police
NGO	Nongovernmental organization
NIMA	National Imagery and Mapping Agency
NOD	Night observation devices
NSA	National Security Agency
NVG	Night-vision goggles
OH-	Observation helicopter
OPCON	Operational control
PIC	Pilot in command
PLAT	Pilot landing assistant television
PSYOPS	Psychological operations
Q36	AN/TPQ-36 radar
QRC	Quick reaction company
QRF	Quick reaction force
ROE	Rules of engagement
RPG	Rocket-propelled grenade
RPM	Revolution per minute
S2	Staff 2—intelligence
S3	Staff 3—operations
S4	Staff 4—logistics
S5	Staff 5—civil affairs
SAR	Search and rescue
SARP	Somalia aircraft recovery program
SIGINT	Signal Intelligence

SNA	Somalia National Alliance
SOF	Special operations forces
TACON	Tactical control
TF	Task Force
TOC	Tactical operation center
TOW	Tube-launched, optically tracked, wire-guided missile
UAE	United Arab Emirates
UH-	Utility helicopter
UNITAF	Unified Task Force
UNOSOM	UN Operations in Somalia
USACOM	U.S. Atlantic Command
USCINCCENT	U.S. Commander in Chief of Central Command
USFORSOM	U.S. Forces in Somalia
USLO	U.S. Liaison Office
USS	United States Ship
XO	Executive officer

BIBLIOGRAPHY

Adams, LTC Thomas K. "Intervention in Haiti: Lessons Relearned," *Military Review* 5 (September–October 1996).
Air Assault Operations. Department of the Army Field Manual 90-4 (Washington, D.C.: 1992).
"A Man with a Mission," *Newsweek,* 3 October 1994.
"Anatomy of a Disaster," *Time,* 18 October 1993.
Archambault, LTC Raoul, III. "Joint Operations in Haiti," *Army* (November 1995).
Atkinson, Rick. "Fire Fight in Mogadishu," (Parts I and II), *Washington Post,* January 30/31, 1994.
Bolger, LTC Daniel P. *Savage Peace: Americans at War in the 1990s* (Novato, Calif.: Predisio Press, 1995).
Bowden, Mark. *Black Hawk Down* (New York: Atlantic Monthly Press, 1999).
Brown, Stephen D. "Psyop in Operation Uphold Democracy," *Military Review* 5 (September–October 1996).
"Can Haiti Be Saved?" *Newsweek,* October 1994.
Delong, Kent, and Steve Tuckey. *Mogadishu: Heroism and Tragedy!* (Westport, Conn.: Praeger Press, 1994).
Doucette, J. H. "Army Fliers Conquer Flight Deck," *Rough Rider* 8, no. 49 (August 1994).
Ferry, CPT Charles P. "Mogadishu, October 1993: A Personal Account of a Rifle Company XO," *Infantry* (October 1994).
Gordon, John, IV. "Joint Power Projection: Operation Torch," *Joint Force Quarterly* 4 (Spring 1994).
Hackworth, COL (Ret) David H. *Hazardous Duty* (New York: Avon Books, 1997).
Haiti Information Handbook (Washington, D.C.: Department of Defense, 1994).
Hasenaurer, Heike. "Medal of Honor," *Soldier* (July 1995).
Hawkins, LTG (Ret) William R. "Putting Urban Warfare in Strategic Context," *Army* (January 2000).
Hayes, Margaret Daly, and R. Adm. Gary F. Wheatley. *Interagency and Political-Military Dimensions of Peace Operations: Haiti—A Case Study* (Washington, D.C.: National Defense University, 1996).
Heinl, Robert D., Jr., and Nancy G. Heinl. *Written in Blood* (Boston: Houghton Mifflin, 1978).
Hirsch, John L., and Robert B. Oakley. *Somalia and Operation Restore Hope: Reflections on Peacemaking and Peacekeeping* (Washington, D.C.: National Defense University Press, 1995).
Hornbarger, CPT Christopher. "TF Raven's Role on 3 October," December 1993.

Moore, LTG (Ret) Harold G., and Joseph L. Galloway. *We Were Soldiers Once . . . and Young* (New York: Harper Perennial Publishing, 1993).

Oakley, Robert, and Michael Dziedzic. "Policing the New World Disorder," *National Defense University Strategic Forum* 84 (October 1996).

Oakley, Robert, and Michael Dziedzic. "Sustaining Success in Haiti . . . ," *National Defense University Strategic Forum* 77 (June 1996).

Oakley, Robert B., Michael J. Dziedzic, and Eliot M. Goldberg. *Politics and the New World Disorder: Peace Operations and Public Security* (Washington, D.C.: National Defense University Press, 1998).

"Operations in Haiti—Planning/Preparation/Execution," 10th Mountain Division, Fort Drum, N.Y., 1995.

Perkins, Ed. "The Charge of the Light Division," *Watertown Daily Times,* 2 October 1944.

Sharp, Walter Gary, Sr. *United Nations Peace Operations: A Collection of Primary Documents and Readings Governing the Conduct of Multilateral Peace Operations* (New York: American Heritage Custom Publishing Group, 1995).

Stevenson, Jonathan. *Losing Mogadishu* (Annapolis, Md.: Naval Institute Press, 1995).

Success in Peacekeeping, United Nations Mission in Haiti: The Military Perspective (Carlisle Barracks, Pa.: U.S. Army Peacekeeping Institute, n.d.).

Tata, Robert J. *Haiti—Land of Poverty* (Washington, D.C.: University Press of America, 1982).

United Nations. *The United Nations and Somalia, 1992–1996.* UN Blue Book Series, Volume 3 (New York: United Nations Dept. of Public Information, 1996).

INDEX

Military Units Index

1st Battalion, 87th Infantry Regiment (1-87th Infantry/1-87th), 57, 165, 208

1st Battalion, 159th Aviation Regiment (1-159th Aviation/1-159th), 217

1st Infantry Brigade, 10th Mountain Division, 164

1st Marine Expeditionary Force (MEF), 10

1st Special Forces Group, 199

1st Squadron, 7th Cavalry Regiment (1-7th Cavalry/1-7th), 66

2d Battalion, 2d Marine Regiment, 199

2d Battalion, 14th Infantry Regiment (2-14th Infantry/2-14th), 21, 27–29, 53, 63, 75, 89–90, 95, 111, 254

2d Battalion, 22d Infantry Regiment (2-22d Infantry/2-22d), 99, 117, 122, 128, 130–131, 136, 165, 206

2d Battalion, 25th Aviation Regiment (2-25th Aviation/2-25th), 129, 147, 244

2d Battalion, 159th Aviation Regiment (2-159th Aviation/2-159th), 217

2d Infantry Brigade, 10th Mountain Division, 102, 220, 244

3d Battalion, 25th Aviation Regiment (3-35th Aviation/3-25th), 129, 163, 174, 239–240, 242

3d Special Forces Group, 219

3d Squadron, 17th Cavalry Regiment (3-17th Cavalry/3-17th), 21, 126, 129, 147, 167

4th Battalion, 4th Aviation Regiment (4-4th Aviation/4-4th), 128, 130, 136

4th Squadron, 2d Cavalry Regiment, 175, 217

7th Infantry Division, 191

9th Battalion, 101st Aviation Regiment, 16, 59

10th Aviation Brigade, 10th Mountain Division, 1–2, 6, 102–103, 129, 138, 248

10th Mountain Division (Lightfighters), 1, 3, 6, 10, 16, 19, 21, 72–73, 76, 81, 103, 105, 143, 145–146, 161, 164, 179, 194, 200–202, 223, 229, 231, 235, 240, 242, 250

13th Marine Expeditionary Unit (MEU), 93, 117

14th Infantry Regiment (Golden Dragons), 2, 79–80, 82, 86, 114, 127

16th Military Police Brigade, 218

XVIII Airborne Corps, 151, 176, 178, 182, 237

22d Marine Expeditionary Unit (MEU), 117, 130

24th Infantry Division, 93, 100, 152

24th Marine Expeditionary Unit (MEU), 130, 136

25th Infantry Division, 115, 176, 245

41st Combat Engineer Battalion, 76, 164

43d Combat Engineer Battalion, 100, 101, 127

46th Combat Support Hospital, 48, 87, 91

46th Forward Support Battalion, 21, 100, 130

57th Medevac Company, 185

82d Airborne Division, 199–200, 217, 229

101st Airborne Division (Air Assault), 164, 178, 217

159th Aviation Regiment, 82, 176

224th Maintenance Battalion, 130–131

Subject/Name Index

Abgal clan, 67, 96, 131
Accidental discharges, 114–115
Ahmad, Abdul Latif, 54
Aideed, Hussein Mohammed, 141, 142
Aideed, Mohammed Farah, 24, 31, 33, 35, 89, 97, 109, 125, 131, 132–133, 140, 141
Air force loadmasters, 129
AirBoss, 172
Aircraft fleet, 70, 126, 129, 146, 147–148, 152, 162, 167–168, 170, 185, 195, 239, 250
Ali Mahdi, 66–67, 109, 131, 140, 141, 142
Alliman, Perry, 26
American Airlines, 226–228
Anderson, Matthew K., 26
Apache helicopters, 70
Arap Moi, Daniel, 141
Archambault, Raoul, 126–127, 129, 145, 148, 153, 170, 175, 182, 183, 194
Aristide, Jean-Bertrand, 158–159, 160, 224, 233–235, 239
Army Aviation Association of America, 146
Army Component Headquarters (TF Mountain), 185–186
Arnold, Steve, 103
Aspin, Les, 44
Atkinson, Rick, 73, 90
Atlantic Command (ACOM) headquarters, 151
Aviation Unit of the Year Award, 146

Barclay, James, 242, 244–245
Bedard, Buck, 105
Bendyk, John, 24, 28, 51, 97, 153
Berdy, Andy, 164–165, 178, 195, 202, 208, 209, 218, 221, 229, 234
Biamby, Philippe, 233–234
Bir Cevik, 11, 13, 116, 251
Blackburn, Todd, 35
Blackburn, Tony, 59
Bogosian, Richard, 109, 128
Bolger, Infantry Lieutenant Colonel, 103
Bordner, Ronald, 211
Boynton, Andrew, 75
Breen, John, 66, 72

Brennan, Frank M., 174
Breton, Ronald R., 174
Brigadier General Carl I. Hutton Memorial Award, 146
Briley, Donovan, 38
Brodrick, Matt, 130, 136
Brown, Dwight, 21, 91
Brown, Hank, 125
"Bullet Car Wash," 68
Bush, George, 10, 159
Byrd, Robert,92

Campbell, Jim, 151, 221
Carter, Jimmy, 199, 200
Cavazos, Dick, 5
Cedras, Raoul, 124, 158–160, 200, 208, 233–234
Central Command (CENTCOM), 251
Christenson, Ronald L., 171–172
Christopher, Warren, 234, 235
Citadelle, The, 220–221
Civic action, 131–132
Clark, Robert, 100, 117, 122, 130
Clinton, Bill, 3, 13, 41, 93, 97, 102, 109, 123, 140, 159, 182, 199, 200, 226, 228
Close, George, 151, 185, 194, 201, 243
CNN, 96, 123, 187, 191, 205, 255
Coalition soldiers (Somalia), 89–90
Coates, Dave, 29–30, 71, 174
Cobra helicopters, 70, 146, 147
Collins, J. Lawton, 21
Columbus, Christopher, 155
Combat Infantryman's Badge (CIB), 90–91
Command relationships, 251
Commander Task Force 158, 93
Commander Task Group (CTG) 156.1, 93
Congressional Black Caucus, 9–10, 159
Counts, Gerry, 69

Daedalians, 146
Dallas, Mike, 17
David, Bill, 21, 24, 28–29, 44, 46, 48, 51–53, 56, 59, 65–81, 85–87, 90–91, 112, 113–114, 117
Davis, Larry, 100, 127
Davis, Scott, 46, 69, 72

Desert Storm/Desert Shield, 32, 90
Diamond, Richard, 189
Dole, Bob, 179–180
Driver, Bill, 147, 163, 170, 194, 202,
    205, 206, 209, 217, 220, 244
Dubik, Jim, 165, 220
Durant, Michael, 39–41
Duvalier, François, 157–158
Duvalier, Jean-Claude, 158

Eastwood, Clint, 126
Egert, Chester, 241–242
Ellerbe, Mike, 53, 72, 79
Elmi, Omar Salad, 32
Enwright, Leo, Jr., 183
Ernst, Carl F., 103–105, 106, 111,
    115–120, 122–123, 125, 127, 146
Everson, Richard, 179, 185
Eyes over Mogadishu mission,
    112–113, 115, 123

Falcon Brigade. See 10th Aviation
    Brigade, 10th Mountain Division
Federal Aviation Administration (FAA),
    226
Feir, Philip R., 189
Finnegan, Robert, 167
Fisher, George, 245
Flaherty, Michael, 80
Force Armée d'Haíti (Fad'H), 159,
    224, 237
Force modernization, 147
Force protection, 219, 254–255
Forshag, Russ, 163–164, 170, 205, 206,
    210, 215, 217, 239, 242–243
Fort Drum, future of, 180
Fraher, Jeff, 85, 86
François, Joseph-Michel, 158
Front for the Advancement of and
    Progress of Haiti (FRAPH), 159

Gaddis, Evan, 146
Garrison, William, 28, 31–32, 33,
    35–36, 39–40, 44–45, 46, 51–52, 79,
    92, 102
Gemmill, Alan M., 183–185, 186–187,
    193, 196–197, 201, 210
Gile, Greg, 28, 46, 52, 85–86, 106–107
Goffena, Michael, 40
Golden Dragons (14th Infantry
    Regiment) Task Force, 21, 53, 57,

67, 75–76, 77, 91, 114, 127
Golson, Ellis, 22–24, 126, 147
Gordon, Gary, 40–41
Gore, Lee, 21, 29, 51, 53, 54, 56,
    59–62, 65, 67, 70, 73, 74, 80, 81, 83,
    85, 112, 128, 129, 147
Gosende, Robert, 109
Governors' Island Accord, 159
Grid reference graphic (GRG), 24
Griggs, Otis, 128

Habr Gidr clan, 18, 24, 45, 73, 96, 131
Haiti: historical overview, 155–159;
    and U.S. relations, 155–160
Haiti operations, 1, 2, 3–4, 143–144,
    161–248, 249; aftermath, 247–248;
    assault, 205–215; occupation,
    217–231; operation plan, 161–165;
    preparations, 167–191
Haskell, Tom, 85
Haynes, James K., 76–77
Hayslett, Kevin, 120
Hempstone, Smith, 10
Hirsch, John, 142
Hoar, Joseph P., 13, 16, 32, 35, 43,
    105, 123
Hollis, Mark, 68, 76
Houston, Cornell L., 76
Howe, Jonathan, 11, 31, 35
Humanitarian assistance, 131, 250

Incidental damage compensation,
    134–135
Intelligence, 135–136
International Criminal Investigation
    and Assistance Program, 237
International Medical Corps, 133

Jacobsen, Eric, 69, 71
Johnston, Robert B., 10, 13
Joint special operations task force
    (JTF-Somalia), 93
Joint Task Force-180, 151, 199–200
Joint Task Force-190, 152, 164,
    199–200
Jonaissant, Emile, 159, 200, 233
Judge Advocate General (JAG) officer,
    135

Kelley, Jim, 15, 147
Kellogg, Bill, 59, 73

Kelly, Raymond, 224
Kinzer, Joseph W., 245
Kiowa Warrior helicopter, 126, 147–148
Knight, Richard, 89
Kokorda, Bob, 87

Labin, Dan, 218–219
LaBlonde, George, 24
LaCoste, Gene, 176
Laye, Jesse, 194, 203
Levin, Carl, 107–108
Logistic support, 130
Lust, Larry, 130
Lynch, Chris, 85

MacDonald, Scott, 29–30, 69, 71, 74–75
Marine Humvee removal operation, 119–123
Marino, Chris, 80
Marsh, John O., 95
Martin, James H., 75–76
Matthews, Thomas, 40, 53, 67, 73, 79, 85
Mazur, Andy, 107
McCredy, Bob, 108
McKnight, Danny, 32, 39, 45
McPherson, John, 44, 51, 53–54
Meade, David C., 16, 106–107, 163–165, 176–179, 191, 193, 194, 199, 202–203, 205, 208, 226, 231, 234, 237, 240, 244
Media coverage, 96–97, 123, 134, 170–171, 182, 187–191, 205, 241, 255–256
Metheny, Bill, 29, 66, 69, 80
Meyer, Edward C., 241
Meyerowich, Drew, 53, 57, 68, 72, 80, 81, 85
Miller, Admiral, 164, 169, 191, 193–194, 200
Miller, Tom, 16, 164, 182
Mita, Dave, 79
Mitchell, Phil, 239
"Mogadishu Mile," 85–86
Monroe Doctrine, 155
Montgomery, Thomas M., 11, 13, 16, 28, 33, 35, 43, 44, 46–48, 52, 54, 56, 83, 100, 103, 106, 107, 113,

116–117, 119–120, 123, 127, 128, 130, 137, 146, 251
Moore, Hal, 66
Mubarak, Hosni, 142

Namphy, Henri, 158
Neely, Chief Warrant Officer, 71–72, 74
New Port operation, 46–49, 51–57, 59–82
Nicholas, Edward J., 81
Nixon, Craig, 85

Oakley, Robert, 11, 97, 109, 125, 142
Operation Provide Relief (Somalia), 10
Operation Restore Democracy, 151
Operation Show Care, 119
Operation Torch, 2, 173
Operation Uphold Democracy. See Haiti operation
Organization of American States (OAS), 159
Osman Atto, 37, 141
Osterholzer, Steve, 210
Ostrander, Richard, 223–224
Outlaw, Larry, 117

Pace, Pete, 105
Page, Al, 176, 217, 240
Paul, Evans, 229
Pede, Charles, 71
Perry, William, 191, 193–194
Planchak, Joe, 196
Poppie, John, 243
Port-au-Prince International Airport, 226
Potter, Dick, 219
Powell, Colin, 44, 193, 199
Preval, René, 247
Purdom, Theodore, 151

Quick Reaction Company (QRC), 28–29 44, 46, 62
Quick Reaction Force (QRF) (Somalia), 31–32, 43, 53, 93; casualties, 89; as milestone, 1–2, 102; planning and tactical control, 11–13

Ramaglia, Randy, 38–39

Ranger Task Force, 24, 31–42, 48; three-phase plan, 35; end of, 102
Raven Task Force, 21, 59–62, 128
Reid, Christopher, 127
Reimer, Dennis J., 255
Richardson, Ferdinan C., 26
Riedel, Jeffrey, 25
Rierson, Matthew L., 95
Roberts, Richard, 75
Robinson, Randall, 159–160
Rodriguez, Carlos, 37–38
Rogney, Mike, 90–91
Rosa, Paul, 16–17
Royal Moroccan Task Force, 119
Rules of Engagement, 134, 200–201, 221–223, 254

Sardo, Chuck, 16
Savage Peace (Bolger), 103
Scott, Harry, 115–116, 122–123
Semmens, Steve, 153, 168, 175, 179, 228
Shaheen, Imtiaz, 9
Shalikashvili, John M., 107, 200
Shantali, Umar, 41
Sharif Hassan Giumale, 73
Shelton, Hugh, 151, 199, 200, 208, 209, 226, 234, 237
Shelton, Jeffrey, 176
Shrader, Dale, 25–26
Shughart, Randall, 40–41
Siad Barre, Mohammed, 18, 62–65, 117
Signal intelligence (SIGINT), 136
Smith, Eric, 99, 117, 122, 130, 136
Smith, Zannie O., 105
Sniper flights, 133–134
Soldier suicides, 241
Somalia Aircraft Recovery Program (SARP), 146
Somalia National Alliance (SNA) militia, 18, 24–25, 31, 35, 37, 45, 67, 73, 78, 108, 113, 133, 251; casualty figures, 90
Somalia operation, 1, 2, 3, 5–6, 10, 15–124; casualties, 89, 139; command and control, 251; peace agreement, 131; post-withdrawal cease-fire agreements, 141–142; withdrawal and outcome, 125–142.

See also Quick Reaction Force; Ranger Task Force; specific unit
Somalia and Operation Restore Hope, 142
Soviet Union, 17, 18
Special operations forces (SOF), 31
Stafford, Keith, 128
Steele, Mike, 79
Suggs, Ralph R., 175
Suich, Mark, 80
Sullivan, Ed, 208
Sullivan, Gordon R., 99, 127, 193
Sullivan, Mike, 218, 221
Support troops, 120–122, before
Swing, William L., 208, 234

Task Force-1-64, (1st Battalion, 64th Armored Regiment, 24th Infantry Division), 100, 102, 110, 117, 120, 130
Task Force-160, 32, 37, 42, 53, 81, 199, 231
Task Force Mountain, 185
Task Force Ranger, 2, 24, 28, 32–33, 35–37, 39, 41–42, 44–46, 48, 51–52, 62, 64, 80, 86, 89, 95, 102
Task Force Raven, 21, 48–49, 64, 82, 87, 128
Terry, James, 206
Tippin, Terry L., 172
TOP SCENE (Tactical Operational Scene), 195
TOW missiles, 6, 70
TransAfrica, 160
21 October Road operation, 117–119

United Arab Emirates (UAE) troops, 120–122
United Nations, 159; chapter VII operations, 139–140; 814, 142; Security Council resolutions, 10, 11, 31, 160; World Food Program, 133
United Nations Operations in Somalia (UNOSOM) missions, 9, 11, 13, 29, 32, 109, 112, 127, 139, 140, 251; medical community, 83
Unified Task Force (UNITAF), 10–11, 13, 97, 139
UN Quick Reaction Force (QRF), 1–3, 6, 11, 13, 17, 25, 37, 41–43, 46, 48,

54, 70, 89, 93, 100, 102–103, 250
UNOSOM II, 11–13,
Urban combat, 251–253
U.S. Army Rangers, 32
U.S. Atlantic Command
    (CINCACOM), 152
U.S. Central Command (CENTCOM),
    29, 105, 117, 250
U.S. Commander of Chief of Central
    Command (USCINCCENT), 3, 13
U.S. Department of Defense, 3
U.S. Forces in Somalia (USFORSOM),
    11, 13
U.S. Foreign Claims Act, 134
U.S. Office of Foreign Disaster
    Assistance, 9
USS *America*, 93, 175, 186, 199, 234
USS *Chenango*, 173
USS *Comfort*, 199
USS *Dwight D. Eisenhower*, 143–144,
    182–191, 195–197, 199, 201, 207,
    208, 209, 212, 214–215
USS *Harlan County* incident, 123, 151,
    159
USS *Kitty Hawk*, 11
USS *Mount Whitney*, 199, 209
USS *New Orleans*, 93
USS *Ranger*, 11
USS *Theodore Roosevelt*, 170–174

Van Arsdale, Lee, 57
Vincent, Jean-Marie, 160

Wall Street Journal, 247
Ward, Ed, 28, 29
Warner, John, 107–108
Washington Post, 73
Watkins, Tom, 96–97
Watson, Douglas K., 203
Weapons and weapons systems
    (Somalia), 22, 69–71, 74, 94, 95–96,
    99, 111, 113, 120, 128, 130,
    133–134, 167, 169
Webb, Jeff, 85
Weiss, Jack, 21, 100, 130
West, Togo, 193
Whetstone, Michael, 28, 77
"Wide-body Escort" mission, 112–113
Williams, Eugene, 26
Wills, Tom, 189
Wilson, Woodrow, 155
Wolcott, Clifton, 38, 40, 79, 81

Xiong Ly, 76

Yeltsin, Boris, 92

Zegler, Scott, 210
Zenawi, Meles, 142

ABOUT THE BOOK

C ol. Lawrence E. Casper (U.S. Army, Ret.) narrates the first documented account by a military officer of the harrowing U.S. operations in Somalia and Haiti.

As commander of the Falcon Brigade, 10th Mountain Division, and the UN Quick Reaction Force (QRF), Casper experienced Operation Continue Hope firsthand. Falcon Brigade and Special Operations aviators shared the skies over Mogadishu on 3 October 1993, providing cover as the ground QRF fought block by block to reach the stranded troops and remove them to safety. Casper's candid account of Operation Continue Hope, and the brigade's continuing involvement in Somalia until the U.S. withdrawal from the war-torn region some 5 months later, showcases the leadership skills and courage necessary for troop survival under beleaguered circumstances.

Just 6 months after their return from Somalia, Casper and Falcon Brigade were on the flight deck of the nuclear aircraft carrier USS *Dwight D. Eisenhower,* preparing to air-assault 10th Mountain Division Lightfighters onto the shores of Haiti during Operation Uphold Democracy. Casper brings to life the frustrations and challenges the brigade soldiers experienced as they worked around the clock for 30 days, and he captures the untiring cooperation between soldiers and sailors as they joined together to ensure the success of the operation. His account concludes with the brigade's subsequent 4-month involvement in Haiti.

Not only a telling and vivid history, *Falcon Brigade* is an insightful—and rare—discussion of what did and did not work, and what went on behind the scenes at the operational level.

Lawrence E. Casper has served in the U.S. Army as infantry and aviation company commander, attack helicopter battalion commander, and aviation brigade commander, among other command and staff assignments. He has served in the 2d, 7th, 9th, 10th, and 25th Infantry Divisions and commanded the unit that conducted the operational test on the AH-64 Apache helicopter. Additionally, he served in the Pentagon and was a member of the Secretary of Defense Strategic Studies Group. Casper's last assignment in the Army was as a joint commander of all U.S. military observers assigned to the UN and multinational peace-keeping missions worldwide. His awards and decorations include the Defense Superior Service Medal, the Legion of Merit, the Bronze Star, and the Air Medal.

DATE DUE

DEC 19 2001			

Demco, Inc. 38-293